W9-DED-006

GENDER, WORK AND LABOUR MARKETS

Gender, Work and Labour Markets

Sue Hatt
Senior Lecturer in Economics
University of the West of England
Bristol

Consultant Editor: Jo Campling

First published in Great Britain 1997 by
MACMILLAN PRESS LTD
Houndmills, Basingstoke, Hampshire RG21 6XS and London
Companies and representatives throughout the world

A catalogue record for this book is available from the British Library.

ISBN 0–333–65778–0 hardcover
ISBN 0–333–65779–9 paperback

First published in the United States of America 1997 by
ST. MARTIN'S PRESS, INC.,
Scholarly and Reference Division,
175 Fifth Avenue, New York, N.Y. 10010

ISBN 0–312–17246–X

Library of Congress Cataloging-in-Publication Data
Hatt, Sue, 1946–
Gender, work and labour markets / Sue Hatt.
p.   cm.
Includes bibliographical references and index.
ISBN 0-312-17246-X (cloth)
1. Women—Employment—Great Britain.   2. Men—Employment—Great
Britain.   3. Work and family—Great Britain.   4. Unemployed—Great
Britain.   I. Title.
HD6135.H377   1997
331.4'0941—dc20   96–43973
                                                            CIP

This book is printed on paper suitable for recycling and made from fully managed and
sustained forest sources.

 8   7   6   5   4   3
05   04   03   02   01   00

Printed and bound in Great Britain by
Antony Rowe Ltd, Chippenham, Wiltshire

Contents

List of Tables

List of Figures

Acknowledgements

Although the authorship of a book is attributed to an individual it inevitably involves a far wider group of people. I would like to express my gratitude to all those who have contributed to this project. Without the encouragement and support of family, friends and colleagues this book would never have been completed. Shirley Dex deserves a special thank you for painstakingly reading and commenting upon the first draft. Jo Campling, as consultant editor, has provided much needed help and advice. My colleagues and friends at UWE have provided continual support, especially Alan Greer who provided constructive criticism in the early stages and Gerry Crawley who read the initial draft and without whom this book would never have been written.

I owe a debt of gratitude to my own family who have had to live with me whilst I was writing the book and put up with the constant attention which it has demanded. John, especially, has been an invaluable source of support and encouragement. He has provided a very useful source of advice and has always been ready to discuss my ideas with me. All those students and friends who have listened to me and discussed the central themes with me have helped to clarify my thoughts and the final text has been significantly improved by their contributions. Any errors which remain are, of course, my own.

1 Labour Resources
Men and Women in the Economy

What is Economics about? Men and women in the working population. The use of productive resources. Unemployment and underemployment. An increase in the production possibility frontier. Changes in the working population. Men and women in production. The participation rate of men and women. Women's participation and production. Summary.

What is Economics About?

Many people find the prospect of studying economics rather daunting. They might have heard that the subject is all about making money; they may have only a very imprecise idea about the scope of the discipline. News items about economic issues are a very familiar part of our everyday world and anyone living in Britain in the 1990s cannot help but be aware of some economic issues and problems which our society faces. We hear every day of proposed tax changes, of mergers, of the privatization of certain industries, or of job losses and redundancies. All of these are economic issues since they concern the production and consumption decisions of men and women. But for neo-classical economists none of these issues would be fundamental; they regard the scarcity of resources as the basic economic problem facing society.

Women and men find that they can rarely achieve as much as they would like; they come up against an economic constraint since their resources are limited. For example, there are only 24 hours in every day and that never seems sufficient for me to do the countless jobs which face me – teaching economics, cooking the meals, helping with children's homework, tidying the garden and so on. My resources are limited. Similarly a household might want to have a bigger car, to buy new furniture for the living room, and to travel abroad for a summer holiday, yet its budget will not run to all these things at once. Its resources are limited.

The same problem faces a company. It would like to install a new computer system, employ more sales staff, and move into larger office premises, but once again it is constrained since it too has limited resources at its disposal. Even for the economy as a whole the scarcity of resources restricts production. There is a limit to economic growth imposed by the availability of land, labour and capital. The efficient use of scarce resources is one of the most fundamental issues which economics seeks to address. Since resources are scarce they

1

should not be wasted. Resources which are unemployed or underemployed are not being used to their full potential, reducing the output of the economy and the standard of living. Resources used to produce goods and services which are not in demand are also wasted. They could have contributed to raising living standards by producing goods and services which men and women wanted to buy. Since resources are scarce they need to be used efficiently to produce the highest possible level of output in accordance with consumer preferences.

The productive resources of a society are the land, labour and capital with which it produces goods and services. Natural resources, like the climate and the fertility of the soil, represent a considerable productive opportunity for an economy. Capital is represented by the buildings and machines which have been produced to assist the productive process; capital assets are the fruits of investment from previous periods. The labour resources of the economy are the men and women of working age who are capable of producing goods and services for consumption. In recent decades women in developed countries have increased their participation in the paid workforce. In the United Kingdom equal numbers of men and women were in employment in 1995. Women work within the household too. Cooking meals, washing clothes and caring for the elderly and young children also contribute to the standard of living. Productive activity takes place in both the workplace and the household.

Men and Women in the Working Population

The labour resources of an economy include men and women engaging in productive activity in either the labour market or the household but when economists refer to the working population they are including only the men and women who participate, on either a full- or part-time basis, in the market sector of the economy. The working population includes all those men and women who are either in paid employment, self employed, in H.M. Forces, on a work related government training scheme or registered as unemployed. In 1995 there were 28 million people in the working population in the United Kingdom, nearly 26 million of these were in employment whilst the remaining two million were unemployed. The working population includes all those who are considered to be participating in the labour force whether or not they actually have a job. Women or men who are working in the unpaid sector are not included; full-time homemakers are considered to be non-participant in the working population.

The size of the working population will depend on demographic and sociological factors. The more people of working age there are within an economy, the higher one would expect the working population to be.

Substantial immigration into a country will increase its working population. In West Germany during the 1950s and 1960s the working population rose when fugitives from Eastern Europe were admitted and migrant labourers (*Gastarbeiter*) were recruited to fill vacancies in the job market. Similarly a rise in the birth rate will lead to an increase in the working population when these children leave education; the increase in the working population in Britain in the early 1980s was partly due to a high birth rate in the 1960s.

Social factors are also significant. If children spend longer in full-time education then this will delay their entry into the working population. As it has become more acceptable for mothers to work outside the home, the working population has risen in industrialised countries. Similarly if affordable child care is widely available, this will increase the workforce participation of women with pre-school children. In France 34 per cent of two year olds, 95 per cent of three year olds and 100 per cent of four year olds are in pre-school institutions (Lane 1993). This facilitates the participation of their mothers in paid employment and increases the size of the working population.

The Use of Productive Resources

As labour and other resources are employed, goods and services will be produced for consumption. The more efficiently an economy uses its productive inputs, the greater the level of output will be, enabling its citizens to enjoy a higher standard of living. The maximum level of output which an economy is capable of producing can be depicted on a graph by a production possibility frontier. This illustrates the range of productive possibilities facing an economy with limited resources and a given state of technology.

In Figure 1.1, productive resources can be allocated between the production of goods, like loaves of bread, tonnes of coal and thousands of motor vehicles, and the production of services, such as insurance cover, bus rides and hair cuts. Any combination of goods and services within the frontier or on the frontier can be produced. For example, points A and B are possible production combinations if the land, labour and capital resources are fully employed.

At point A resources are being used to produce 50 million units of services and 50 million units of goods whilst at point B some resources have been shifted out of service industries and redeployed in the production of goods. The production of the extra goods crowds out, or prevents, the production of some services since there are only limited resources which can be employed in either one sector or the other. The combinations of goods and services are different at the two points on the frontier, but in both cases all resources are being productively employed.

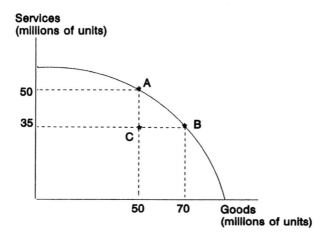

Figure 1.1: Production Possibility Curve

The British economy has experienced considerable changes in its pattern of production over the last 30 years with the growth of the service sector of the economy and the relative decline of manufacturing industry. The contraction of manufacturing employment which began in the late 1960s in Britain was linked to the poor competitive performance of British manufacturing goods and to the increase in productivity due to changes in technology. In the mid 1960s one employee in every three worked in the manufacturing sector in Britain but by the mid 1990s manufacturing employment accounted for only one job in every five. The contraction of the manufacturing sector has sometimes been attributed to the rapid rise in government spending which occurred in Britain in the mid 1970s (Bacon and Eltis 1976). The increase in government spending, it was argued, drew resources out of the manufacturing sector and into the provision of public services; it was equivalent to a move around the production frontier from point B to point A on Figure 1.1. Had the British economy been enjoying full employment in the 1970s such an explanation might indeed have been plausible. In fact, though, de-industrialization – that is the decline in manufacturing employment – was accompanied by a rise in unemployment, innovations in production methods and a change in the size and composition of the labour force. Since more resources were becoming available crowding out therefore provides an unlikely explanation for the fall in manufacturing employment.

In order for production to take place at either point A or B on the production possibility frontier, then production must be organized as efficiently as possible – that is by making the lowest possible demands upon scarce resources. If the economy is producing at either point A or at point B, it is then said to be achieving productive efficiency. The efficient use of scarce resources raises at least one other issue. Since resources are limited, it is important to ensure that they are used to produce those goods and services which men and women, both individually and collectively, want to consume. To use resources efficiently, an economy must not only be producing out on its production frontier but it must also be at that particular point on its frontier which gives it the most highly valued combination of goods and services. Resources must be carefully allocated between alternative uses. If resources are used to produce goods upon which consumers place a low value and diverted from producing goods which consumers value more highly, then this represents an inefficient allocation of resources. When the economy produces that combination of goods and services which gives consumers the highest level of satisfaction, then allocative efficiency is achieved.

If land, labour and capital are used to produce a particular combination of goods, then those same resources are not available in the current time period for the production of services. A decision to produce several thousand cars per month has implications for production in other industries. More cars produced might, for example, involve a reduction in health care services. Economists refer to this lost, or sacrificed, production as the opportunity cost of a certain activity. So the opportunity cost of the production of five thousand more motor vehicles would be measured in terms of the next best use to which those productive resources could have been put – perhaps keeping one hospital ward open.

With full employment the production of any good or service involves an opportunity cost. For this reason the particular combination of goods and services which are produced needs to be carefully evaluated. If resources are reallocated in order to produce more goods, then the opportunity to produce some services is lost. In Figure 1.1 moving from point A to point B involves the production of an extra 20 million units of goods, but the loss of 15 million units of services. The opportunity cost of one extra unit of goods can be measured as three-quarters of a unit of services. Every time resources are reallocated out of the service sector into goods production, one additional good involves the loss of three-quarters of a unit of service provision. It will be wasteful and inefficient to produce at point B if services are valued more highly by consumers. The actual combination of goods and services produced will depend upon the allocation of productive resources between goods and services. Both point A and point B are productively efficient; which one of them is allocatively efficient depends upon consumer preferences.

Unemployment and Underemployment

If an economy makes full use of its land, labour and capital assets, production can take place out on the production frontier. But in practice production often takes place inside the production frontier. Point C in Figure 1.1 depicts this situation. Since it has sufficient land, labour and capital to produce 35 million units of services and 50 million units of goods point C is a possible production point for this economy. This level of production implies that the economy is wasting some of its scarce resources by not employing them at all or by employing them inefficiently. Unemployment implies that scarce resources, either land, labour or capital, are left standing idle rather than being used productively. This waste of resources reduces the total output of the economy, resulting in a lower level of production of both goods and services. In Great Britain in September 1994 for example, there were 2.5 million workers – 1.9 million men and 0.6 million women – registered as unemployed (Department of Employment 1994). The country lost the output these workers could have produced had they been productively employed and this is equivalent to an economy operating at point C.

Married women often return to paid employment, after a break for childcare, on a part-time basis doing jobs for which they are overqualified (Elias 1988). This occupational downgrading implies that productive resources are not being put to their best possible use. Once again production is taking place within rather than on the production possibility curve. In both of these cases the production of goods and services is lower than it might be; the inefficient use of scarce resources constrains the standard of living.

Resources, which are not employed to their full capacity, are resources which could be employed more productively; resources used to produce goods and services, which are surplus to demand, are resources which are inefficiently employed; resources which are unemployed, or underemployed, are wasted since their productive output is foregone. In each of these situations the economy's scarce resources are not used efficiently.

These decisions about the use of scarce resources are affected by social and political factors as well as by economic variables. The political framework and social custom will both have an important influence upon the production and consumption of goods and services. In Britain, for example, agriculture is subsidized for political reasons whilst coal mines are allowed to close. Economic choices are also constrained by social custom. The terms upon which women participate in paid employment, for example, are affected by their domestic responsibilities. In 1995, 86 per cent of part-time workers in Britain were women. Economic decisions are not taken in a void; they are influenced by the political and social environment which often affects women and men in different ways.

An Increase in the Production Possibility Frontier

Whilst an economy's resources and its technical knowledge remains fixed, its level of output is constrained. If resources increase or technology advances, economic growth becomes possible and the production possibility curve moves outwards enabling the economy to produce more goods and more services. The discovery of a new natural resource, a change in technology or an increase in the size of the working population provide examples of factors which raise the economy's productive potential. When the United Kingdom discovered oilfields under the North Sea in the 1960s just such an outward shift of its production frontier occurred. Innovations in technology, such as the introduction of computers, have made production more capital intensive raising the potential output of the economy through increases in the productivity of labour. Between 1960 and 1990 the United Kingdom's working population rose from 25 to 28.5 million people and such a change usually indicates a rise in the ability to produce goods and services for consumption. This increase in the production possibilities available to the economy is illustrated as a shift of the production possibility curve from PP1 to PP2 in Figure 1.2. With the shift in the productive possibility curve it becomes possible for the economy to produce more goods without sacrificing its service provision. If production had been occurring at point B on PP1 then as technology advances and available resources increase it would be possible to move to point D on PP2. Comparing production at points B and D, the output of goods is identical at 70 million units but the provision of services is significantly higher at point D by 15 million units. More services can be produced with no opportunity cost in terms of goods sacrificed since the production possibility curve has shifted outwards.

A country though does not always make full use of its productive potential. Whilst the production possibility curve has shifted outwards to PP2 production might still take place upon the original curve, PP1. The extra resources could be wasted as unemployment rises. The growth of public sector services in the 1970s has sometimes been held responsible for crowding out manufacturing employment and causing the economy to move around its original production frontier from point B to point A on PP1. Yet during these three decades the production frontier had shifted outwards as technology changed increasing labour productivity and as women moved into the working population. If PP1 represents the potential output of the British

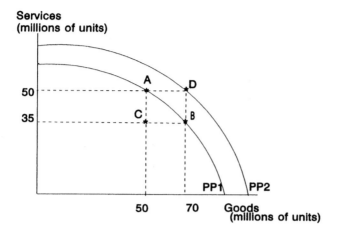

Figure 1.2: Increase in the Production Possibility Curve

economy in the mid 1960s, then by 1990 this frontier had moved outwards to PP2. It would have been possible to increase output in the service sector as well as maintaining, or even increasing, manufacturing production.

As technology has advanced production techniques have changed, increasing labour productivity in both the manufacturing and service sectors of the economy. Since the demand for services has expanded, employment in this sector has increased whilst in manufacturing industry the position has proved to be less favourable. With the new production methods the same volume of manufactured goods could be produced with a significantly reduced workforce. The rise in labour productivity has shifted the production possibility curve outwards but the demand for British manufactured goods has not risen proportionately. Consequently employment in manufacturing has declined. De-industrialization has been accompanied by rising unemployment, especially amongst men. Britain has not made full and efficient use of its productive resources and has been operating within its production possibility frontier. In Figure 1.2 this can be depicted as producing at point A when there is the capacity to produce at point D.

Changes in the Working Population

Over the last three decades, the working population in the United Kingdom has risen by 3.5 million people as Table 1.1 shows. The number of men in the working population declined very slightly from 16.6 million in 1960 to 16.3 million by 1990. The whole of the increase in the working population therefore is due to more women entering the paid labour force; the number of women in the working population has risen from 8.4 million to 12.2 million over these 30 years representing a 45 per cent increase in the female labour force.

The slight fall in the male working population can be explained by the restructuring of the British economy, the recessions of the mid 1970s, the early 1980s and 1990s and the increasing importance of skills in the labour market. The decline of British manufacturing industry in the early years of the 1980s resulted in the loss of 1.5 million manufacturing jobs. Male unemployment rose by one million and there was little prospect of these workers finding re-employment in the same sector. Some older workers became discouraged and left the labour force. The new jobs which were created in the growing service sector in the boom of the late 1980s demanded new skills. Education and qualifications became increasingly important in the search for a job. This has increased the likelihood that men below the age of 25 will remain in full-time education and one reason for the reduction in the male working population has been a fall in the participation rate in these younger age groups.

The women's working population exhibits a very different pattern. It has shown a continuous increase. The recessions of the last two decades, the rise in the rate of unemployment and the introduction of new technology have not prevented the rising trend of the female working population. More women have entered the working population in almost every year throughout this period. These changes are illustrated in Table 1.1.

Table 1.1: The Working Population
United Kingdom (millions)

Year	Total	Men	Women
1960	25.0	16.6	8.4
1970	25.6	16.4	9.2
1980	26.4	16.1	10.3
1990	28.5	16.3	12.2

Source: *Annual Abstract of Statistics*, various issues

An increase in the working population provides more labour resources with which to produce goods and services in the marketed and government sectors of the economy. It is usually depicted as shifting the production possibility curve outwards increasing the economy's productive potential and facilitating economic growth. If this increase in the working population occurs as new workers enter the labour force on a full-time basis, then, without dispute, extra output can be generated and living standards can rise. In the United Kingdom, though, the change in the working population has occurred as women have moved into the paid labour force. This additional source of labour has become available to the British economy as fertility rates have fallen, changes in technology have made housework less labour intensive and the creation of part-time jobs has made it possible for women to combine domestic responsibilities with paid employment. If the working population rises due to an increase in part-time female employees, then the impact upon the production possibility curve, the level of potential and actual output might be of a smaller magnitude than the change consequent upon an increase in the full-time male labour force. During the 1970s in Britain the total number of workers employed in the service sector rose. However the increase in part-time employment meant that the number of employee hours actually decreased (Beechey and Perkins 1987). Since these two changes were occurring coincidentally the extent of the change in the labour resources is debatable.

Men and Women in Production

Women's position in economic activity is distinct and different from that of men. Women are far more likely than men to work on a part-time basis since their labour market activity is constrained by the extent of their domestic commitments. Both of these features of women's economic activity affect the extent to which the production possibility curve shifts outwards as more women move into the paid labour force.

The working population statistics simply refer to a headcount of the paid workforce and the unemployed taking no account of whether participation is on a full- or part-time basis. Between 1960 and 1990, 3.8 million women have entered the working population but many of these have occupied part-time positions. The increase in women's full-time employment over this period has been very slight. In 1961 there were 5.7 million women in full-time employment and this had risen by only half a million workers by 1991. The increase in part-time employment though was remarkable: 1.9 million women were in part-time employment in 1961 compared with 5.1 million by 1991 (Hakim 1993) – an increase of over 250 per cent. Since many of these female part-timers are constrained by domestic responsibilities and would not be available for full-time employment, focusing upon the headcount approach of the working population statistics might overstate the increase in the labour resources and the consequent shift in the productive potential of the economy. Women often work on a part-time basis since the extent of their domestic responsibilities is significantly greater than that of men. Productive activities take place in the workplace and in the home; baking cakes, caring for children and growing vegetables are economic activities wherever they are performed. These non-marketed activities contribute to living standards and yet are not included in the statistics on production. Cakes baked in factories are included in the nation's accounts of productive activities whilst cakes baked at home are not; time spent cleaning offices is valued in the market whilst time spent cleaning one's own home is not; the production of new motor vehicles is investigated as an economic activity whilst the care of one's own children is not.

In some ideal world, cleaning the home, baking cakes and caring for children could well be performed by men and women equally. But in the developed countries of the world today there is ample evidence that this is not what happens. A study of employed men and women in urban France showed that, in 1985, women were spending 4 hours 38 minutes per day on domestic work whilst men spent 2 hours 41 minutes on those tasks (Coré 1994). Thus women spend about twice as long as men on productive domestic activities which are not included in the statistical accounts and are often ignored in economic analysis. The focus upon market-based activity has made men's role in the economy more visible than that of women.

Before the Second World War married women used to concentrate on the provision of unpaid services for their families and their productive activities took place predominantly within the household. Nowadays married women will usually be in paid employment too – albeit on a part-time basis. If the working population rises as more women move into paid employment then the potential for increasing living standards is more debatable than if the increase were due to additional men in the workforce. Women's employment involves a greater opportunity cost than men's. Since women are more extensively involved in household production this might well be curtailed as they move into paid employment. Women are less likely to be making shepherd's pies for their families since in the 1990s they are more likely to be employed in the takeaway pizza parlour. Total output, as reflected in Gross Domestic Product, will appear to have risen although the statistics might be overstating the extent to which production has actually changed.

The Gross Domestic Product of a country tries to measure the total output of goods and services produced within a country in a given period. It attempts to show the level of actual production. The accounts are drawn up in several ways: by totalling the value of all types of expenditure within the country and making the appropriate adjustments for imports and exports; by totalling the value of the incomes earned from the country's productive activities; or by totalling the value added to goods and services at each stage of the productive process. All three of these accepted accounting procedures omit household production of goods and services for consumption within that family unit. The services provided within the household by washing the family's clothes, repairing the car, making curtains or caring for children are not included in the nation's accounts.

A production possibility frontier follows this convention and is usually drawn to include only the marketed sector and the government sector of the economy. It includes the production of frozen peas and processed bread but excludes the production of home grown vegetables or home baked bread; it includes the care of patients in hospital but excludes any care given to invalids or the elderly within the household. In the neo-classical model the production possibility curve is drawn to omit the productive activity which takes place within the household and focuses upon the marketed and government sectors of the economy. Household production remains an invisible area in conventional economic analysis.

However as women move into paid employment, this represents an increase in the economy's total output only if their production in paid employment exceeds the possible loss of household services which their employment might entail. The extent of the outward shift in the production possibility curve which the rise in the working population implies is not gender neutral. Women are more likely than men to work part time and the extent of their domestic commitments implies that their paid employment involves an opportunity cost in terms of household production. For both these reasons women's employment is different from men's. Men are employed on a full-time basis and have minimal domestic responsibilities. If the working population rises as more men move into the paid labour force then the increase in potential output is greater than that which occurs as the female working population grows.

The Participation Rate of Men and Women

Women do not participate in the working population in the same way as men. They display patterns of labour force participation which are distinct and different. Their working lives do not follow the same pattern as men's since they are subject to different social constraints. The participation rate shows the proportion of a given group which is economically active in the sense that it is participating in the working population either as part of the workforce in employment or as unemployed persons. A larger proportion of men than of women participate in the working population in every age group. Overall in 1993, 71 per cent of all men were participating in the working population either as employed workers or as unemployed whilst only 53 per cent of women were considered to be participating in the labour force.

There is a considerable difference in the extent to which men and women participate in the working population at different stages of their life cycle. The participation pattern for men indicates that once they leave full-time education, by about 24 years of age, they participate very fully in the working population; for prime age male workers between the ages of 24 and 49, participation rates were over 90 per cent in 1993 (OPCS 1995). During their fifties the participation rate for men declines. Older men find it harder to acquire new skills should they be made redundant; they tend to become discouraged and to leave the workforce if they experience unemployment. The participation pattern for men over their working life tends to be bell-shaped; high levels of participation are displayed during the middle years but these dwindle during their fifties and early sixties as retirement approaches.

For women the pattern of workforce participation is different. Their participation rate is high immediately after they leave full-time education but falls in their middle years as they become mothers. Indeed motherhood is one of the most significant factors affecting women's participation in the working population. In 1993 the participation rate for women between the ages of 25 and 34 was 71 per cent but for women with a child under five years old it fell to 54 per cent (OPCS 1995). As children enter school so the participation rate increases again.

Women's participation in the working population is still disrupted as they become mothers causing a dip in their activity rates. Their caring role constrains the employment of women with pre-school children. The typical pattern of labour force participation for women in Britain today is bi-modal or M shaped.

A woman's pattern of employment varies considerably over her lifetime. But this is only one of many factors affecting the labour force participation of women. Women exhibit different rates of participation depending upon their age, the age of their children, their marital status, the employment status of their partner, their educational qualifications and their occupation. Different ethnic groups in Britain also display variations in their pattern of paid employment. West Indian women are far more likely to participate in the working population than white women whilst Indian and Pakistani women exhibit the lowest participation rates of all. Women are therefore not a homogeneous group; some women are more likely to be in paid employment than others.

Women's Participation and Production

Although women still exhibit a discontinuous pattern of employment, it has become increasingly acceptable for mothers with small children to work. Indeed the British working population has increased primarily because mothers are now more likely to participate in the labour force. Their career breaks have become shorter during the ten years between 1978 and 1988. In 1988 McRae found that 45 per cent of mothers were back at work within eight to nine months after the birth of their first child; this figure represents a considerable increase on the position ten years earlier (McRae 1991). In 1973 only 27 per cent of British mothers with a child under five years old were participating in the labour force; by 1993 this figure had risen to 54 per cent (OPCS 1995). The working population in Britain has risen because mothers with small children are increasingly likely to be in paid employment. These were the very women who were previously providing services unpaid for their families; they were playing with toddlers, cooking meals and cleaning the house.

A rise in the working population due to an increase in the participation rate of mothers does not necessarily entail an increase in living standards; it all depends upon the consequences for production within the household. As women move into employment, the output of goods and services in the visible and marketed sector of the economy is increased. Gross Domestic Product will rise as marketed output increases. The participation of women in paid employment though is distinctly different from that of men; women's employment involves a sacrifice – a loss of labour time in the unpaid household sector of the economy. The opportunity cost is particularly noticeable for mothers with young children and it is precisely this group who have been increasing their workforce participation in recent decades. Housework and childcare affect, and are affected by, women's employment with consequences for the standard of living. Women might be going out to work and producing goods and services in the visible marketed sector of the economy instead of staying at home to provide services for their families; they can be merely substituting paid work for unpaid household work. If the loss of household services is exactly equivalent to the increase in marketed output then the average standard of living will not change even as women move into the working population. Gross Domestic Product will have increased but in real terms the standard of living will not have changed. The consequences for women though are considerable since their economic status and autonomy improves as they earn an independent income.

Alternatively women might be going out to work whilst their household tasks are left undone. Children might return home to an empty house, family mealtimes might become a rare event, and standards of cleanliness might fall. In this case there is an opportunity cost to women's employment and in some cases this might outweigh the benefits from that employment. If the reduction in household services is greater than the increase in marketed output then an overall loss will have occurred and standards of living will fall. The final possibility is that housewives have become more productive so that they can now produce household services and work in paid employment too. In the most extreme case the value of household services might remain constant whilst women also work in the labour market. In this case real output will increase as more marketable goods and services are being produced with no sacrifice of household services. As technology has been applied to housework, vacuum cleaners, washing machines and microwave ovens have made one hour's household labour far more productive now than ever it was before. Housework is no longer a full-time job and living standards increase as technology makes it possible for the economy to produce more with a given level of resources.

Summary

An economy has at its disposal limited resources of land, labour and capital with which to produce goods and services. The living standards of men and women in society depend upon the level of output which the economy actually produces within the marketed and the domestic sector of the economy. Living standards can be improved by either an increase in marketed output or by an improvement in household production. Meals cooked at home, television sets produced in factories, and 'do-it-yourself' home improvements all contribute to the total output of the economy – even though some of these activities are excluded from Gross Domestic Product.

The labour resources of the economy include both men and women but the roles they play in economic activity are distinct and different. Women often work part time, are still responsible for childcare and for the majority of household tasks; their productive activities will include production in the unpaid sector of the economy. Men though are economically active on a full-time basis in the visible marketed sector of the economy throughout their working lives. As women – especially mothers with young children – have moved into the labour force in increasing numbers, their role in the economy has increased in visibility. Their work caring for senior citizens in a local authority day centre or working in a local hotel will contribute to Gross Domestic Product; it seems as if production has risen as the working population has increased. The production frontier appears to have shifted outwards.

In practice though women's employment is different from men's in terms of its opportunity cost and its impact upon production. Women, especially mothers, are more likely to work part time thus limiting the extent to which production increases with their employment and women's employment might adversely affect household production. The methods of providing care for children and the elderly should be carefully considered if the economy is to achieve an efficient allocation of scarce resources. The current situation might not promote this objective.

2 Changing Employment Patterns
Are Women Taking Men's Jobs?

*Changes in employment. Economic analysis of employment patterns.
Segregation in labour markets. Industrial segregation and employment
patterns. Part-time employment. Changes in the participation rate for men
and women. Conclusion.*

Changes in Employment

The working population, the level of employment and unemployment are
all closely related concepts; a change in one of these variables will have
implications for the other two. Changes in the working population have
contributed to changes in the level of employment in Britain. An increase
in the working population such as that experienced in Britain over the last
few decades implies that there is an increased supply of labour available for
employment; either the level of employment or the level of unemployment
must rise as a result. There has been scarcely any change in the total number
of people employed during recent decades but there have been significant
differences in the distribution of employment between men and women. Men's
employment has fallen by almost 20 per cent whilst that of women has
increased. The change in male employment between 1980 and 1992 is partly
the result of a decline in the proportion of older men holding jobs whilst the
proportion of fathers who were employed stayed almost constant over this
period (OPCS 1994). The increase in female employment was accounted
for by a significant increase in the proportion of mothers who were entering
paid employment.

Men and women work in different ways to produce goods and services
for consumption. For men the norm is an unbroken full-time attachment to
the labour market whilst women, for part of their lives, work unpaid within
the household. The extent to which women engage in paid employment is
affected by their domestic labour. Even within the labour market, women play
a different role from men. Women are more likely than men to work on a
part-time basis, to work in different industries from men, to occupy different
positions even within mixed industries and to be under-represented in senior
positions. Since men and women display distinctive employment patterns,

17

the changes which have occurred in the British economy over the last 30 years have affected the employment of men and women in different ways.

The working population includes both the employed and the unemployed. The size of the working population is a useful measure of the productive potential of the economy but it is not so useful as an indicator of actual level of production or of living standards. The number of employees in employment will provide a better guide to the actual level of output within the economy. The working population can be rising even when employment is static or falling. Some labour resources will be wasted through unemployment reducing the actual level of both production and consumption within the economy. The labour resources of an economy are unlikely to be fully employed at any point in time. The changes in the working population thus provide an indication of the capacity of the economy to produce goods and services; it does not show the level of production which the economy is actually achieving. The level of employment shows how many men and women are engaged in paid productive activities which contribute to the nation's output of goods and services. It therefore provides a more accurate indication of living standards.

Employment can be expected to vary over the Trade Cycle since the level of expenditure will be an important influence on the level of employment. In a boom expenditure will be high, firms will be seeking to employ more labour and the level of employment is likely to rise, whilst the reverse will be the case in a recession. These cyclical patterns affect both men's and women's employment. In order to identify the general trends in the level of employment in the United Kingdom it is necessary to compare the level of employment at one particular phase of the Trade Cycle. In Table 2.1 the data for employment in the United Kingdom during the peak years of the Trade Cycle are identified and disaggregated by gender.

Table 2.1: Employees in Employment
United Kingdom (millions)

Year	Total	Men	Women
1964	23.4	14.9	8.5
1973	22.7	13.8	8.9
1979	22.8	13.3	9.5
1990	22.9	12.0	10.9

Source: *Annual Abstract of Statistics*, various issues

The total number of people in work has been more or less constant over the last 30 years; there were 23.4 million employees in employment in 1964 and 22.9 million in 1990. But there have been considerable changes in the balance between men's and women's employment. The employment of men has fallen relentlessly whilst women's employment has risen continually with every peak in the cycle. In 1964 there were 14.9 million men in employment but this had fallen to 12 million by 1990 representing a drop of 18 per cent. The employment of women has displayed a very different pattern. Despite the recessions, the lower level of economy activity, and the de-industrialization which has occurred over the last 30 years, women have been able to move into the labour market and find an increasing number of paid jobs. Women's employment has increased whilst men's has declined. By 1995 whilst the economy was still on the upswing of the Trade Cycle, there were as many women in paid employment as men. Numerical equality at least has been achieved although real equality in terms of pay, conditions and terms of employment is still a distant goal.

Economic Analysis of Employment Patterns

One way in which economists seek to explain changes in the employment patterns is by analysing supply and demand in labour markets. Firms seek to employ workers to produce goods and services for sale in product markets. The demand for labour in labour markets will thus be related to and influenced by the demand for goods and services in the product markets. The demand for labour is a derived demand.

As consumers' incomes increase, this raises the demand for those commodities whose demand is positively related to income. Other things being equal, this will then result in an increase in the demand for labour within the industries producing those commodities. The leisure industry in Britain has been expanding over the last few decades as consumers with rising incomes seek enjoyable ways to use their leisure time. The service sector too has been on a rising trend. Job opportunities and employment will increase in those expanding sectors of the economy.

Other sectors of the economy will experience different trends. As demand patterns change, certain sectors of the economy will find that their products are no longer in such high demand. British manufacturing industry has found it increasingly hard to sell its output as it has faced growing competition from overseas producers. Over the last 30 years there has been a significant fall in the demand for British manufactured goods. Britain used to be regarded as 'the workshop of the world' and its traditional trade pattern was to export manufactured goods to pay for imports of raw materials and other primary products. Industrial machinery, ships and motor vehicles would be exported tɔ earn the foreign exchange needed to pay for imports of rubber, wheat, butter and copper. This pattern has been changing rapidly over recent years. In the mid 1980s Britain experienced a deficit on manufacturing trade for the first time. At home and abroad the competitiveness of British manufactured goods has declined at the same time as increases in the productivity of labour have made manufacturing production less labour intensive. Jobs in the manufacturing sector have fallen as a consequence. The changes in the demand for labour provide part of the explanation for variations in employment patterns in Britain.

The supply side of the labour market also requires consideration. The working population is subject to changes over time and some of the relevant changes in the British working population were noted in the last chapter. The size and composition of the working population influences the total supply of labour. However this concept can be measured in at least two different ways. The total number of people prepared to accept jobs provides one measure of total labour supply whilst the total number of hours worked provides an alternative estimation. The total number of men and women in the working population provides an indication of the labour force. Not all of the labour force, though, will be in employment nor will they be in a position to accept the jobs on offer. Variations in the level of demand and rigidities in the labour market result in unemployment. A percentage of the labour resources are wasted and the extent of unemployment in the United Kingdom has risen for both men and women since the mid 1960s. The total number of men and women prepared to supply their labour, that is to accept jobs, will be slightly lower than the total labour force but will be influenced by the size of the working population. The working population includes both full- and part-time workers. Since full-time workers supply more hours of labour than part-timers an alternative measure of labour supply could be provided by the total hours of labour supplied. In this case the composition of the labour force is a significant factor. Female part-time workers will not supply as many hours of labour as the equivalent number of male full-timers. The working population in Britain has expanded in recent years due to the increasing numbers of women who wish to participate in paid employment often on a part-time basis. In terms of the total numbers, the female labour supply has risen whilst in contrast the supply of male labour has hardly changed at all during recent decades. In terms though of the number of hours of labour supplied a different picture merges.

Segregation in Labour Markets

Although there are equal numbers of employed men and women in Britain their employment is concentrated in different sectors of the economy. Men predominate in manufacturing industry whilst women outnumber men in the service sector. Horizontal segregation, by which men and women work at different jobs, is commonplace in Britain today. Women are concentrated in certain industries and occupations; clerical work, catering and cleaning are all seen as women's work. Men are found working in construction industries, or the manufacturing sector and such horizontal segregation is very marked in Britain as in all other industrialized countries in the 1990s.

Even when men and women do work in the same industry or occupation they are rarely found to be evenly distributed throughout the hierarchy. Vertical segregation is usual with men occupying the more senior positions and women in the lower ranks of the hierarchy. This occurs even in traditionally female sectors of the labour market such as primary school teaching where women constitute 81 per cent of the profession but only occupy 49 per cent of the headteachers' positions (Department of Education 1995). In higher education, a traditional male preserve, women make up only 27 per cent of academic staff in the new universities according to a National Association of Teachers in Further and Higher Education (NATFHE) analysis of the Polytechnics and Colleges Funding Council (PCFC) data. Women are concentrated in the lower grades and they account for 46 per cent of lecturers but only 18 per cent of principal lecturers and 15 per cent of heads of department (Hart 1994). Women are under-represented at senior levels throughout all occupational categories.

The extent to which men and women are concentrated in different industries in Britain in the mid 1990s can be seen from Table 2.2. One striking feature of segregation in Britain is that women are over-represented in only three industrial categories. Women represent 49 per cent of employees in all industries and services but it is only in other services, in distribution, catering and repairs and in banking, finance and insurance that their representation exceeds this percentage. In Great Britain in 1994, women constituted 68 per cent of employees in the industrial category of 'other services', 55 per cent in distribution, hotel and catering and 50 per cent in banking, finance and insurance. Men are more widely distributed throughout the industrial categories and their employment is dispersed throughout the economy exceeding 70 per cent of employees in six of the industries.

The reasons advanced to explain segregation in employment and its impact upon the gender pay gap are discussed in Chapters 5 and 8. However, segregation can also affect the efficient use of the nation's scarce resources. The impact of both vertical and horizontal segregation upon the efficient deployment of labour resources within an economy is extremely debatable and the conclusions reached depend very much upon personal viewpoints. Those who believe that men and women have much in common and that nurturing and leadership characteristics are found in both sexes, will consider that vertical and horizontal segregation impede the efficient operation of the economy resulting in men and women occupying positions for which they are not best qualified. A woman lower down the hierarchy will feel frustrated that her innate abilities and competence as a manager are not being valued, whilst a man with good caring skills will feel some doubts about deploying these in the nursing profession. In this case society is prevented from achieving a higher level of output by the practice of vertical and horizontal segregation. The unequal distribution of men and women between jobs leads, in this view, to men and women being underemployed or unsuitably employed. The efficient use of scarce resources is not achieved and the economy produces inside its production possibility frontier.

Table 2.2: Employment by Industry 1994

Great Britain

Selected Industries	% Female in total employment	% part-time in total employment
Agriculture, fishing, forestry	25	22
Energy and water supply	22	5
Other mineral and ore extraction	25	4
Metal goods, engineering and vehicles	21	1
Other manufacturing	40	11
Construction	18	9
Distribution, catering and repairs	55	44
Transport and communication	24	11
Banking, finance and insurance	50	17
Other services	68	35
All industries and services	49	28

Source: calculated from *Employment Gazette*, February 1995

Yet another view is that whilst men and women have much in common, differences in their social position make it likely that they will be attracted into separate occupations. Gender, rather than sex, is encouraging particular career paths. If women expect to have discontinuous careers then they might seek employment in areas where this will not prove too significant a disadvantage. The social constraints upon their employment imposed by their responsibility for providing care make women more likely than men to accept part-time work. Accordingly they seek employment in industries where this is most likely to be available. The constraints upon men's employment are very different. They often expect to bear the main responsibility for the financial support of the household. Accordingly they will seek lucrative and secure full-time employment if this is available. These social constraints lead men and women to seek employment in different sectors of the economy. Such choices and preferences have often been reinforced by restrictions imposed by trade unions or the government to exclude women from certain occupations (Walby 1990). Direct or indirect discrimination can play a part in establishing and maintaining segregation in employment. Owing to these constraints women and men might be unable to seek employment in the industry to which they are best suited. The efficient allocation of resources will be impaired, thus reducing living standards.

On the other hand, the alternative viewpoint contends that there are essential differences between men and women such that men are naturally suited to certain jobs and certain positions within hierarchies, then segregation will help to achieve economic efficiency. The argument runs that men are naturally stronger than women and so are better suited to heavy manual work; they are born leaders and are thus well equipped to fill management positions. Women meanwhile are viewed as being particularly strong on nurturing characteristics and so will perform better than men in the caring profession; they are good at carrying out instructions, but not so good when it comes to displaying initiative, and so they are not suited to top management positions. People with these views will argue that both vertical and horizontal segregation further the efficient use of the economy's scarce resources. Society is nearer to producing on its production possibility curve when such segregation is practised than it would be if men and women were equally distributed between occupations and industries. In this view, segregation in employment allows a higher level of production and consumption to be achieved in society.

Industrial Segregation and Employment Patterns

Industrial segregation certainly affects the changes in the employment patterns of men and women which were noted earlier. Men have traditionally looked for employment within the manufacturing sector which until recently could provide the full-time permanent jobs which a male breadwinner required. In 1977, 7.2 million workers were employed in manufacturing industry and 5.1 million of them were male. Although some manufacturing industries, like textiles and food processing, have been large employers of female labour, overall women have provided a minority of the employees for the manufacturing sector.

Since most employees in manufacturing were male, the contraction of employment in this sector resulted in a larger loss of employment opportunities for men than for women. Between 1977 and 1983 British manufacturing

Wage Rate

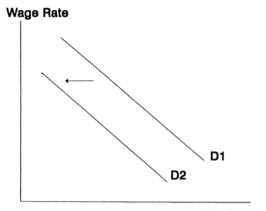

Number of Workers

(a) Male Workers

Wage Rate

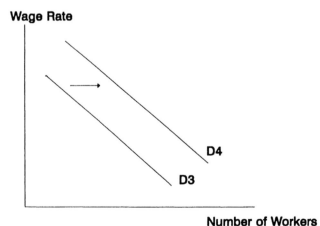

Number of Workers

(b) Female Workers

Figure 2.1: Changes in the Demand for Men's and Women's Labour

industry shed nearly two million workers and two-thirds of these were men. The changes which the British economy has undergone during the 1980s have impacted differently upon men and women. Between 1977 and 1990 manufacturing industry was shedding workers. At the same time the expanding service sector was increasing employment. For men this meant job loss; for women the situation proved more favourable. A slight loss of jobs in manufacturing industry was offset by a significant rise in employment opportunities in service industries. However, as many of the newly created service sector jobs were for part-timers the increase in the number of women in employment disguises the fact that working hours and earnings have changed far less significantly. Men and women were in contrasting positions with regard to employment.

As the British economy began to recover from the recession of the early 1980s, the service industries grew rapidly. Financial services, retailing and distribution all increased employment levels and as the service sector has traditionally been a large employer of female labour, women were more likely than men to take up employment opportunities in these industries. Women's employment in services rose from 7.1 million to 8.7 million between 1983 and 1990 representing an increase of 23 per cent whereas men's service sector employment grew at a far slower rate.

The changes in the British economy during the 1980s were affecting the demand for men's and women's labour differently. Figure 2.1a and 2.1b illustrate these positions.

The demand for men's labour fell from D1 to D2 as manufacturing industry contracted. For women the position was different. As the service sector expanded the demand for female labour rose from D3 to D4. The trends for male and female employment have been in opposite directions. Whilst women have not replaced men in the traditionally male sectors of the economy, their employment opportunities in the service sector have increased coincidentally with the contraction of male employment in manufacturing.

Part-time Employment

Another significant development in labour markets in Britain in recent years has been a considerable increase in part-time employment. Between 1981 and 1991 part-time employment increased from 4.9 million to 6.7 million workers (Hakim 1993). Part-time employment is usually defined as including anyone who works less than 30 hours per week and this type of employment accounted for one job in four in Britain by 1994 (Naylor 1994). Government policy during the 1980s has encouraged greater flexibility in labour markets. Flexible working practices can take many forms including flexible hours of work, temporary contracts, job sharing, shift working and part-time employment. The increase in these patterns of working has been in response to a variety of factors including competitive pressures to cut labour costs, employee demands and government policy measures which have facilitated the changes. More women than men have been affected by the introduction of these new working arrangements; part-time work in particular is predominantly a female phenomenon with 86 per cent of the part-time jobs in Britain occupied by women in 1995. Restructuring in some industries has meant that the opportunity has arisen to create new jobs which are often part time rather than full time. There is considerable variation in the number of hours worked in part-time employment with some workers working almost a full working week whilst others regularly provide less than five hours labour weekly. On average part-time men worked 16 hours per week whilst a part-time woman employee usually worked a weekly average of 18 hours (Naylor 1994).

As the government has moved to make labour markets more flexible, so part-time jobs have become more common. But the change in the conditions of employment has not affected all industries to the same extent as Table 2.2 shows. Some industries have been eager to respond to labour market flexibility and now have a large proportion of their workers employed on a part-time basis. Distribution, hotels, catering and repairs provide a good example of an industrial category which has responded in this way as 44 per cent of their workforce were employed on a part-time basis by 1994. At the other end of the spectrum part-time working has made very little headway in metal goods, engineering and vehicles where 99 per cent of the employees are still expected to make a commitment to work full time.

Part-time working is especially significant in those industries where women's employment predominates as Table 2.2 shows. Distribution, banking and other services all employ a majority of female labour and two out of these three industries have a higher than average proportion of part-time workers. In other services 68 per cent of the workforce is female and 44 per cent of the jobs in this industry are for part-timers. In predominantly male industries like construction or metal goods, engineering and vehicles only a minute proportion of the workforce is employed on a part-time basis. Part-time jobs have been created predominantly in the women's traditional industries.

The adoption of part-time working practices has not been neutral in its effects upon men and women at work. Women in Britain are far more likely than men to accept part-time jobs and in 1994, 46 per cent of women in the working population were working in part-time jobs whilst only 10 per cent of the male working population had accepted part-time employment (Department of Employment 1995). Firms in the service sector of the economy have responded to the changing labour market climate by creating part-time jobs at the lower end of the hierarchy, many of which are filled by women. Industrial segregation and vertical segregation combine with part-time working to affect women's overall position in employment. Whilst women have moved into the labour market in ever increasing numbers, the rise in full-time women's employment has been surprisingly small. The growth of women's employment has occurred mainly through the creation of part-time jobs which have increased significantly. By 1990 nearly five million women were working on a part-time basis whilst 6.5 million occupied full-time positions. Interestingly about six million women were in full-time employment in the early 1950s although part-time employment accounted for only 0.7 million women (Hakim 1993). Women's employment has grown through part-time work with implications for both the economy and women's status in the labour market. Part-timers frequently receive lower rates of remuneration, have less chance of obtaining training or promotion and work on worse terms and conditions than full-time employees. Since most part-time workers are women, this adversely affects their standard of living and their economic independence. Whilst female employees are as numerous as men overall, this simple headcount approach conceals the deeper reality of the very unequal terms upon which men and women participate in paid employment. For men part-time work represents a very marginal and unusual way of working. Nearly 90 per cent of employed men work on a full-time basis. For women though, part-time work accounts for nearly half of all employment. Part-time working is a common feature of women's employment but it is not unambiguously to their economic advantage.

Part-time jobs pay only part-time wages with different implications for men and women, and indeed for women in different family situations. Men still seek full-time permanent employment to pay the bills and maintain their household's economy. The notion that men should fill a breadwinner role in the household economy is still prevalent in Britain today with one third of all respondents in the British Attitudes Survey holding this view (Jowell et al. 1992/3). Women, especially those with a partner in full-time employment, are often prepared to accept part-time work. Since part-time jobs are increasingly being taken up by women with a partner in full-time employment, these households will have two income earners. Indeed dual income households in which one partner has a full-time job whilst the other works part time are increasingly common in Britain in the 1990s (Brannen et al. 1994).

Not all women are able to respond so positively to the growth of part-time employment opportunities. Single mothers or women whose partner is on benefit are deterred by the welfare payments system from accepting part-time jobs. In these cases it is not worthwhile financially for the woman to take a part-time job since any earnings will merely be deducted from their benefit entitlement. The household's income will not be augmented by part-time employment. Some households have two income earners, others are caught in the benefits trap and have no income earners at all. The resulting polarization of income levels between different types of households is a noteworthy feature of the British economy in the 1990s.

The growth in the part-time sector has increased the demand for women's labour but has had little effect upon the demand for men's labour. The increase in part-time employment has therefore reinforced the employment trends resulting from the restructuring of British industry. As the service sector has expanded there has been an increased demand for labour in this traditionally female area of employment supplemented by the shift towards part-time working. The decline in the manufacturing sector caused a reduction in the demand for men's labour which the growth of part-time service sector work did nothing to mitigate.

Changes in the Participation Rate for Men and Women

Whilst the demand for labour has been shifting the supply side of the labour market has been affected by changes in the size and composition of the working population. The male labour force has shown a slight decline but there has been an increase in the number of women in the working population. There have also been changes in the extent to which men and women have been participating in the labour force. The participation rate shows the percentage of a given group which participates in the working population. The participants include paid employees, the unemployed, the self-employed, those in the armed forces and on government training schemes. For any particular group, delineated for example by age, sex, ethnicity or marital status, the participation rate shows the workforce participants as a percentage of the total population within the group. The changes in the participation rates of men and women in Britain are summarized in Table 2.3.

The participation rate for men has fallen slightly over the last two decades as Table 2.3 shows. This pattern has emerged as men in various age ranges have responded in different ways to the changes which have occurred in the British labour market. Prime age males, those workers between the ages of 25 and 55, still exhibit a very strong attachment to the labour force. The participation rate for this group still stands at 94 per cent. The fall in the male participation rate has been particularly strong, though, for older men, that is those over 55 years of age; the participation rate has fallen from 94 per cent of those in the 55 to 59 age group in 1975 to 78 per cent by 1992. The recessions of the last two decades have caused many male workers to experience redundancy and older workers become aware that changes in technology make it increasingly unlikely that they will ever find suitable paid employment again. They become discouraged workers and drop out of the workforce. As the participation rate has fallen so too the size of the male working population has diminished.

Table 2.3: Participation Rates in Great Britain

per cent

Year	Men	Women	Married Women
1975	93	62	59
1981	90	64	61
1985	89	66	62
1990	88	72	71
1992	87	72	73

Source: *General Household Survey*, 1992

The total number of men available for employment has experienced a slight decline over the last 30 years. This situation is depicted as an inward shift of the supply curve for male labour from S_1 to S_2 in Figure 2.2.

In Britain the number of male employees in employment fell by nearly 3 million between 1964 and 1990. As the shift in the supply of male labour has been slight this in itself is insufficient to explain the reduction in male employment; demand factors too have contributed to this change. The demand for men's labour has fallen as many full-time jobs in manufacturing industry have disappeared. The demand for male labour has shifted inwards to a considerable extent from D_1 to D_2. Changes in supply and demand both help to provide an economic explanation of the changes which have taken place in men's employment patterns in Britain as Figure 2.2 shows. If the market was initially in equilibrium with N_1 men employed, then the inward shift in the supply curve to S_2 has led to a slight reduction in the number of male employees in employment as the market moves to a new equilibrium at N_2. However this is not the end of the story. The demand for male labour has also shifted from D_1 to D_2. To restore equilibrium in this new situation there must be a move down the supply curve S_2 until only N_3 workers are employed. Consequently the level of employment of male workers has been reduced from N_1 to N_3. In this case the reduction in men's employment has been due to both demand and supply factors with the fall in demand playing the more significant part.

The supply of women's labour shows a very different pattern. The participation rate for women overall has risen from 62 per cent in 1975 to

Wage Rate

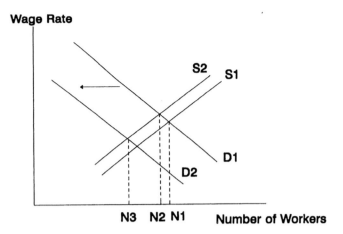

N3   N2 N1   **Number of Workers**

Figure 2.2: Changes in Men's Employment

72 per cent by 1992. In the interwar period the women who participated in paid employment would have been single women as the socially accepted pattern was for women to leave paid employment permanently once they married. Indeed before the Second World War marriage was in itself a significant obstacle to labour force participation. A marriage bar was in force throughout public and private industry for much of the interwar period and this meant that women were obliged to give up their job upon marriage. The marriage bar reflected current social attitudes that the so called 'surplus women' left unmarried after the high male mortality rate of the First World War had a prior claim upon those jobs which did exist for women. Any employment opportunities were rare and valuable at that time of the Great Depression.

The typical participation pattern for women in the interwar years was to work until marriage and then to withdraw from the labour force for good. Household duties took the place of paid work for married women; upon marriage they were expected to work full time unpaid within the household, servicing the needs of their husband and children. Paid work was for unmarried women who showed a continuous and full-time attachment to the working population.

During the Second World War women were encouraged into employment to fill the places left by men. Public nursery places were provided so that small children could receive care whilst their mothers contributed to the war effort. The birth rate had fallen during the interwar years and there was profound concern about the possibility of a falling population. In the 1940s serious consideration was given to the rebuilding of family life. The low birth rate of the 1930s needed to be reversed and government social policy sent clear signals to the women of the time that they would be expected to return to their unpaid household duties after the war and produce children. Women were expected to go back to the home and allow the returning war heroes to take their places in the labour market. Nursery schools which had provided care for pre-school children during the war were closed once hostilities ended. Even if women wanted to work, the state in Britain was doing nothing to facilitate the process.

The Welfare State was constructed upon the model of the nuclear family with a male breadwinner and a full-time female homemaker. The Beveridge Report stated that:

> the attitude of the housewife to gainful employment outside the home is not and should not be the same as that of the single woman. She has other duties ... Housewives as mothers have vital work to do in ensuring the survival of the British Race. (Beveridge 1942)

In the new Welfare State, the entitlement to benefit was on the basis of contributions paid out of wages. The division of domestic labour made this model inappropriate for married women who became entitled to state benefits as the dependents of male workers. Vital though it was, their unpaid work in the household was not to be rewarded on its own merits but only through the contributions of the male worker in the family. Although Beveridge was concerned that women should stay at home in order to increase the population, in fact women's entitlement to benefits in the new Welfare State was not as mothers but as wives.

The old pattern for women of work until marriage and then permanent withdrawal from the labour market never fully reinstated itself in postwar years. The postwar reconstruction meant that labour became a scarce commodity and it became usual for women to remain in paid employment until the birth of their first child. The high levels of aggregate demand and the commitment to full employment created labour shortages throughout the 1950s and 1960s. There were plenty of opportunities for women to work if they wanted to. By the late 1960s married women would typically remain in paid employment until the birth of their first child and then withdraw from the labour force to return only when children no longer needed full-time parental care. The typical pattern of women's participation in the labour force became bi-modal.

The participation rate of married women has shown the most significant rise. As Table 2.3 shows, married women increased their participation rate from 59 per cent in 1975 to 73 per cent in 1992. Over the last three decades mothers have been participating more and more in the working population. Women have fewer children, take shorter breaks for childbirth and even return to paid employment between births. Despite these changes in women's participation in labour markets, women's pattern of participation is distinctly different from that which men exhibit.

Wage Rate

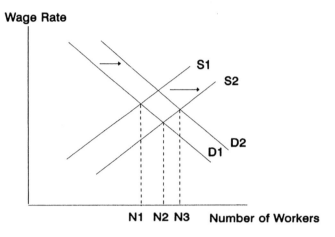

N1 N2 N3   Number of Workers

Figure 2.3: Changes in Women's Employment

Employed women now constitute a majority amongst adult women. In Britain in the 1990s it is more usual for women to undertake paid work than to stay at home. The outcome of these changes is that the number of women in the working population has increased, shifting the supply curve outwards at every available wage rate. In Figure 2.3 this increased participation is depicted as a shift of the supply curve from S_1 to S_2.

As Table 2.1 showed, women's employment in Britain has increased by 33 per cent between 1964 and 1990, from just over 8 million employees to nearly 11 million. Demand and supply factors have both contributed to this change. The demand for female labour has risen as the service sector has expanded and flexible labour markets have created more part-time jobs which are filled mainly by women. At the same time, the supply of labour has increased in terms of numbers and these two trends have resulted in a substantial rise in the level of women's employment. The demand curve for women's labour has moved outwards from D_1 to D_2 and this alone would increase the number of women employed. Simultaneously the supply of women's labour has risen from S_1 to S_2 and this reinforces the increase in employment. The overall impact is that women's employment increases from N_1 to N_3. The interaction of these supply and demand effects can be seen in Figure 2.3.

Conclusion

Whilst the overall level of employment in Britain has varied very little over the last 30 years there have been considerable changes in the distribution of employment between men and women. The British economy has undergone a period of profound change as manufacturing industry has declined, new technology has been introduced and government policy has made labour markets more flexible. The impact of these changes has not been gender neutral; men have experienced a fall in job opportunities whilst women have found their labour in high demand at a time when it is becoming increasingly acceptable for them to participate in paid employment at least on a part-time basis. The number of women in employment has risen whilst for men the pattern has been one of decline. Women however have remained within the traditionally female service sector of the economy taking the new part-time jobs which have become available. The full-time manufacturing jobs which have proved the mainstay of male employment have diminished in number. Women have not taken men's jobs as such; it is simply that the changes in the economy and in economic policy have favoured women's employment and reduced men's opportunities in the labour market.

Although women have achieved numerical equality with men in paid employment, the terms on which they participate in the workforce are far from equal. Women are still expected to care for pre-school children as well as participate in labour markets. Their dual responsibilities make them more inclined to accept part-time work and these job opportunities have increased significantly in Britain over the past 15 years. Part-time working affects a woman's long-term career prospects, their pay and conditions of employment. For women with a partner in full-time employment, the part-time wage supplements the household income. As long as the partnership remains intact their financial security is achieved. But for those women who provide for their sole support the position is less fortunate. Part-time jobs only bring in part-time wages and these often prove insufficient to maintain a reasonable standard of living. Indeed for women with an unemployed partner a part-time low wage job is not worthwhile. Accepting such a position will merely result in a loss of benefit corresponding to the income earned.

Since women work in different sectors of the economy from men, recent changes in the British economy have affected women's and men's employment in different ways. The division of domestic labour affects the terms on which women participate in paid employment. The attempt to combine these two roles proves a considerable constraint on women's employment opportunities.

3 Housework, Childcare and Employment
The Division of Labour Within the Household

Changes in households. Housework and care giving. Comparative advantage and the division of labour. The domestic division of labour. Housework, specialization and earnings. The quality of life. Waged domestic labour. Conclusion.

Changes in Households

Women's move into the workplace has not replaced their traditional role in the unpaid domestic sector of the economy; paid employment is additional to, rather than a substitute for, the provision of unpaid domestic services. Even in households where both partners work, women are likely to spend about twice as long as men on household tasks (Coré 1994). As the previous two chapters have shown women have been moving into the working population and into employment in ever increasing numbers. Economic activity also takes place within the household as well as in labour markets. These household services are of two main types – housework and care giving – and the provision of these services contributes to the overall well-being of the household. Meals cooked within the household and games played with children make contributions to the household's standard of living. In Western Europe and North America women still perform the bulk of both of these activities. In a pre-industrial, subsistence economy men and women would both have worked to produce goods and services for consumption within the family unit. They might have had clearly defined roles and some tasks would have been regarded as woman's work whilst others were identified as being a man's responsibility but there was no doubt that both men and women were making a contribution to the family's well-being.

Once the Industrial Revolution began, traditional patterns of production and consumption started to disintegrate and work began to move out of the household and into the factory. Employees were no longer simply working to produce goods and services for their own consumption; they were working for wages, to bring in an income with which their household could then buy goods and services for consumption. Work in the workplace was qualitatively different from work in the household in that factory work was paid whilst housework was unpaid. It then became more difficult to combine domestic tasks with going out to work. Children had to be cared for until they were old enough to work for their own keep, meals had to be cooked, clothes had to be washed and in fact all the tasks involved in the social reproduction of the paid workforce had to be performed unpaid within the household. Since fertility rates were high and contraception facilities were poor or non-existent, women were likely to bear many children during their lives, and these continual pregnancies disrupted their employment patterns. So women in Western Europe assumed responsibility for household work often in addition to participating in labour markets as and when they were able, whilst men assumed responsibility for earning wages continually throughout their working lives.

This traditional picture of 'man in the workplace and woman in the home' has been slow to die and still persists to some extent in Britain today. In 1992 the British Social Attitudes Survey found that overall 33 per cent of their respondents agreed or strongly agreed with the view that *'a husband's job is to earn the money: a wife's job is to look after the home and family'*. But the picture is changing; younger men and women, those with a higher level of education and those in households where women are in the labour force, were more likely to reject these traditional attitudes towards gender roles (Jowell et al. 1992/3). Indeed as fertility rates are declining and the number of people in the average household is falling, it is no longer necessary for women to devote themselves completely to unpaid domestic work. In 1961 the average household in Great Britain contained 3.1 people but by 1993 the number had fallen to 2.4 (CSO 1995). Housework is no longer a full-time permanent job.

Childcare however is rather different since it does involve the full-time attention of an adult during pre-school years. The provision of care requires the presence of a care giver. The extent of this commitment reduces as children grow older and become more self-reliant. The duration of the commitment is limited but once again it is seen as the mother's role to provide the care. Whilst the time spent on childcare is falling, the elderly are growing as a proportion of the total population. Nearly 16 per cent of the population were over the age of 65 in 1993 (CSO 1995). The elderly are more likely to require care from other family members in future decades and the provision of this care too falls predominantly to women. Unlike childcare, eldercare is hard to anticipate and can be an open-ended commitment.

As time is a scarce resource, there is a connection between the responsibility for domestic work and participation in labour market activity. Workers must divide their time between these two forms of work; the opportunity cost of one hour's housework is one hour lost from labour market participation and vice versa. Indeed it is no coincidence that as women's real wages have increased in postwar years this has been accompanied by an increase in their labour force participation. It has become more costly for women, especially well-qualified women, to work unpaid within the household.

Meanwhile the composition of households in Great Britain has changed considerably. A household is considered to be a person living alone or a group of people living together sharing a joint economy. When people live together this involves co-operation concerning the performance of certain household tasks; clothes have to be washed and ironed, household equipment has to be kept in working order, dishes must be washed and shopping must be collected. These duties have to be divided between the household members. There has been a significant increase in the number of people living alone in Britain since 1961. By 1993, 11 per cent of people were living alone (CSO 1995) and so had no-one with whom to share the household tasks.

The proportion of people living in lone parent households has increased threefold since the early 1960s. This reflects both the rise in the divorce rate and the increase in births outside a stable relationship. There is a significant difference in which parent is most likely to head a lone parent household with dependent children. Only one per cent of households with dependent children are headed by a lone father as opposed to 17 per cent headed by a lone mother. Whilst half of West Indian mothers were lone parents in 1989–91, only 10 per cent of Pakistani/Bangladeshi mothers were in this category (CSO 1995). In one parent households the presence of dependent children will increase the workload since there is only one adult available to take responsibility for these household tasks.

Over the same time period there was a decline in the proportion of people living in the traditional household composed of a married, or cohabiting, couple with dependent children. Over half of all people in Britain lived in this type of household in 1961 yet despite the decline, this household type still predominates. In Britain in the mid 1990s, 41 per cent of people live in this type of household (CSO 1995). Household tasks and childcare can be shared in these households and the British Social Attitudes Survey found in 1992 that over 60 per cent of their respondents thought that household tasks like shopping, cleaning the house, washing the dishes in the evening, organizing household money and bills should be shared equally between the partners. Interestingly though this was the practice in a much smaller percentage of households (Jowell et al. 1992/3). The presence of young children in a household increases the amount of work to be done, but studies often find that this extra work is almost all undertaken by the woman. Men usually confine their domestic activities to repairing household equipment, mowing the lawn and keeping the car in running order. Their contribution to household tasks seems to remain constant regardless of the size of the household whilst a woman's workload is significantly affected by the presence and the number of children in the household (Warde and Hetherington 1993).

Housework and Care Giving

The domestic division of labour is strongly gendered. Men and women do not spend equal time working within the household and the labour market. Despite the rise in female participation rates these are still lower than those of men and studies of household work and care giving find consistently that women spend longer than men on these tasks. Both before and after 1975 women in Europe spent more time than men on housework whilst men spent more hours than women in paid work. This position is illustrated by the United Nations data on the average hours worked by men and women which is shown in Table 3.1.

Table 3.1: Average Weekly Hours of Work
Western Europe

	Year	Economic activity	Housework	Total
WOMEN	Pre 1975	15	35	50
	Post 1976	18	31	49
MEN	Pre 1975	41	8	49
	Post 1976	34	11	45
Ratio Women/men	Pre 1975	0.37	4.4	1.02
	Post 1976	0.53	2.8	1.1

Source: *The World's Women 1970–1990 Trends and Statistics* United Nations New York 1991 p. 82

With respect to paid work and housework the difference between the number of hours which men and women spend in these activities has been narrowing in recent decades. The average working week for men has declined whilst women have been moving into the labour force in larger numbers resulting in a longer average working week for women. Before 1975 men spent about three times as much time on paid work as women, but after 1976 this declined so that men were working just double the hours of the average woman. Housework though still remains a predominantly female responsibility.

European men have increased the hours they spend in housework whilst women's housework time has fallen, but the burden is still decidedly unequal. Before 1975 women did nearly four and a half times as much housework as men; after 1976 this gap narrowed so that their share was just under three times as great as that of a man. Despite the changes in recent decades, the division of labour between men and women is still fundamentally the same; women do the bulk of the housework whilst men spend longer hours in paid activities.

Over this time period, women have increased the number of hours which they devote to paid work. The 1992 British Social Attitudes Survey found that a woman in full-time paid employment will make the evening meal, do the household cleaning, the washing and the ironing in over 60 per cent of these households. The only job which men were more likely to perform than women was that of repairing household equipment (Jowell et al. 1992/3). Although changes are occurring and men are now more likely to share in household tasks than they were several decades ago, there is still a considerable way to go before these tasks are shared equally within the household as a matter of routine.

Housework involves a range of activities, the purpose of which is to maintain household members. Preparing and cooking meals provides food which enables household members to replenish their energy levels. Satisfactory nourishment is essential if men, women and children are to be able to continue with their daily productive activities. The endless battle against dirt and grime helps to guard against disease and so helps to protect the general health of the population. Cleaning rooms, washing clothes and dishes are other examples of household services which facilitate the continuance of productive and personal activities.

The number of hours which women and men together spend on housework has fallen over recent decades. The decline in fertility rates has contributed to this trend. In 1970 the total fertility rate in the United Kingdom was 2.4 births per woman and this had fallen to 1.8 by 1992 (CSO 1995). The decline in fertility rates implies that the average household nowadays contains fewer people and so the servicing of their needs can be accomplished, even with a reduction in the hours of labour input.

Advances in technology have confirmed this trend as capital assets have been substituted for labour power. The introduction of automatic washing machines, microwave ovens, vacuum cleaners and tumble dryers have all reduced the number of hours which the average household needs to spend upon domestic tasks. But these appliances still require some labour input; someone has to put the clothes into the washing machine and the food into the microwave oven and Table 3.1 confirms that this labour input is still overwhelmingly a woman's input. Women did nearly three times as much housework as men.

Childcare is in certain respects different from housework. Although the decline in fertility rates has reduced the number of annual hours which both men and women spend on childcare, these activities are labour intensive by their very nature. A child cannot be cared for unless someone is there to do the caring and overwhelmingly this role is still being filled by the female family members. In 1992/3 only 50 per cent of under fives in the United Kingdom attended schools (CSO 1995) and this low level of provision of facilities for pre-school children constrains the ability of women to enter paid employment.

As the population ages, caring for the elderly, the sick or the disabled is a growing concern. In 1991 almost 14 per cent of the adult population in Britain were providing informal care and this figure is likely to increase as the number of elderly people rises. The elderly are more likely to be disabled too and thus to need care and attention. Although identical proportions of men and women in Britain have caring responsibilities, women are likely to spend more time providing care than men. Informal care is yet another unpaid domestic responsibility but unlike housework and childcare the time which it absorbs will almost certainly increase in future years. Population projections suggest that by the year 2001 there will be a 30 per cent increase in the number of people in Britain over the age of 85 (Corti and Dex 1995). The care of these people will affect the labour force participation of their carers.

The domestic division of labour between men and women is widely documented. Men are taking more part in household tasks than they did previously but they are still not sharing these tasks equally with women even in households where the woman is in full-time paid employment. Childcare in Britain is regarded as the woman's primary responsibility and men take very little responsibility for the work involved in caring for the next generation, especially in their early years. The domestic tasks of both caring and housework still fall disproportionately on women in the 1990s.

Comparative Advantage and the Division of Labour

Whenever specialization and division of labour occur economists seek to explain this in terms of an exchange which is mutually beneficial to both parties. The principle of comparative advantage says that specialization and trade will take place if they result in a higher level of total output. Under these circumstances terms of trade can be negotiated so that both parties can end up with a higher level of consumption than in the pre-specialization and pre-trade position.

For example, one country, Marsmark, might have resources which are better suited to producing guns than butter. Perhaps it is an industrialized country, with an aggressive bent, whose skilled workers and advanced military technology enable it to produce weapons of mass destruction with considerable efficiency. The opportunity cost of producing guns is low. Their trading partner, Cloverdell, on the other hand, might have a more productive dairy industry than Marsmark. Perhaps its climate is warm and wet, encouraging the growth of lush grass upon which to graze the cows. Its opportunity costs are different from those in Marsmark since it sacrifices more butter to produce guns.

In such a situation, when the opportunity cost ratios differ between countries, then specialization and trade have the potential to make both countries better off in material terms. Even were one country able to produce more of each commodity than its trading partner, specialization could still prove worthwhile provided the opportunity cost ratios differ. If Marsmark focuses its resources upon the production of guns whilst Cloverdell specializes in butter, then specialization will increase the total output of both guns and butter.

Since the total level of production increases it becomes possible for both countries to increase their levels of consumption. Total production has increased as a result of each country specializing in the production of that commodity to which their resources are best suited. In fact both Marsmark and Cloverdell can use their scarce resources in such a way that they are able to consume at a point outside their production possibility curve, although of course the frontier still sets the limits upon the level of production. As long as the opportunity costs of production differ between countries then specialization and exchange can make both of these trading partners better off than they were before trade was opened up. Marsmark had a comparative advantage in armaments whilst Cloverdell was relatively more efficient in the dairy sector. Under these circumstances exchange can be mutually beneficial to both countries since the standard of living can improve and it becomes possible for their citizens to have more guns and butter than before trade took place.

The Domestic Division of Labour

The principle of comparative advantage can be used to analyse any situation in which specialization and exchange occurs. Thus the division of domestic labour between men and women can be analysed within this framework. Men concentrate upon paid employment to earn a money income whilst women specialize in the provision of non-marketed household services. Since there is such a widespread division of responsibilities throughout Western Europe and North America, then economists would expect to find that such a pattern of behaviour must bring benefits to both parties. Neo-classical economists seek to explain the domestic division of labour in terms of a mutually beneficial exchange.

Initially the economic analysis of the domestic division of labour was based upon supposed innate differences between men and women. Biological reasons were taken to explain why men specialized in paid work while women focused their attention upon domestic tasks. Just as Cloverdell had the necessary natural factors, the climate, the rainfall and the experienced dairy hands to produce butter efficiently, so women were simply taken to be better at childcare, washing up and cleaning the house! Men, with their superior physical strength, were considered to have an advantage in paid work – especially in those occupations requiring heavy manual labour. Specialization was supposed to be based upon the absolute advantages of each sex.

In recent years, such biological explanations have become discredited throughout the social sciences. Women certainly possess a biological advantage in bearing and nursing babies, but beyond that point there are no good biological explanations of the domestic division of labour. Men can care for children, clean the bathroom and cook meals. Some fathers do take responsibility for these tasks in western society and in other societies these functions are sometimes deemed the appropriate role for men to play. Women can go out to work as wage earners and with modern technology there are very few occupations from which they would be barred purely on the grounds of their inferior physical strength. The principle of comparative advantage had to be used rather differently to explain why men go out to work whilst women work unpaid at home.

The New Home Economics developed by Gary Becker based the analysis of the domestic division of labour upon the differences in the average rates of pay between men and women (Becker 1965). In every developed country there is a wage gap between men's and women's average earnings. In Britain a woman accountant would earn on average £423 per week whilst her male counterpart would receive £489. In 1994 women's hourly earnings were on average only 79 per cent of those of men (Department of Employment 1994). It is this variation in labour market earnings which makes the opportunity cost of housework different for women and men. This dissimilarity in opportunity costs forms the basis of the neo-classical analysis of the domestic division of labour. One hour's housework for a man involves a larger loss of earnings than one hour's housework performed by a woman.

Assuming that it is possible to value the goods and services produced by men and women within the household in terms of their equivalent market value, then estimates can be made of the monetary worth of the meals cooked, the clothes washed and the cleaning tasks performed. This would provide a total account of the goods and services which are both produced and consumed within the household. If both partners were equally skilled at household tasks then the value of the two partners' household services would be identical. But in paid employment there will be a difference; in all countries in Western Europe men's average hourly earnings exceed those of a woman. The value of his time in the labour market will on average be greater than hers.

On this basis it is possible to construct a table showing the following values for one week's work by a man and a woman.

Table 3.2: Domestic Division of Labour

Value of 1 week of	Man	Woman
Household work	£350	£350
Paid work	£500	£400

The same analysis which we used earlier for the two countries producing guns and butter can now be applied to the domestic division of labour within the household. If the man and the woman, in this hypothetical example, decide that they will both have careers and share the housework equally, one possibility might be that they will each work on alternate weeks. The man works on the first and third weeks in the month whilst his partner stays at home and keeps house. On the second and fourth weeks of each month their roles are reversed and she pursues her career whilst he engages in domestic tasks. Under such a scheme, the total value of their monthly work would be as follows

Total value of man's work	= (£350 × 2) + (£500 × 2)	= £1700
Total value of woman's work	= (£350 × 2) + (£400 × 2)	= £1500
Total value for household	= £1700 + £1500	= £3200

In this example the total resources available to the household would be the combined value of their household services and their incomes from paid employment: a total monthly income of £3200.

Since a man on average will be paid more in employment than his partner, this earnings gap is reflected in the opportunity cost of his time in household work. Although he is no more skilled than her at domestic tasks, he must forgo a higher rate of earnings in order to devote his time to such responsibilities. One week in housework for a man means that the household loses £500; whilst for a woman one week's housework involves a smaller loss of earnings – only £400. Since the opportunity cost of the man's time is greater than that of the woman, he has the comparative advantage in paid employment. The woman then possesses the comparative advantage in housework since in this sphere her contribution to the household's well-being equals that of her partner. The principle of comparative advantage suggests that the household will be able to enjoy a higher standard of living if he specializes in paid employment whilst she focuses upon domestic work. The value of their month's activities thus becomes:

Total value of man's work   = £500 × 4   = £2000
Total value of woman's work = £350 × 4   = £1400
Total value for household   = £1400 + £2000 = £3400

Since the total value of the household's income and the services they produce for themselves now becomes £3400 the household is able to enjoy an extra £200 worth of goods and services each month if specialization takes place. Once again there is the potential for both partners to be better off in material terms through such an arrangement. Their joint production will be greater if specialization takes place and as a result the household's standard of living will increase.

The analysis becomes slightly more complicated if the man's productive ability exceeds the woman's in both spheres. If he can earn a higher income from paid employment yet he is also a better cook and cleaner than she is, then the value of the household services which he provides will be greater than hers. In this case it is not immediately apparent in which direction specialization should take place. Consider the following table:

Table 3.3: Comparative Advantage and the Domestic Division of Labour

Value of 1 week of	Man	Woman
Household work	£400	£300
Paid work	£500	£450

If specialization takes place in the usual way with the man as family breadwinner and the woman as stay-at-home wife, then the total value of their weekly work will amount to £800. He will earn £500 from paid employment whilst she provides £300 worth of household services. If though they were to reverse roles and she took paid employment whilst he remained at home, their income from the labour market would fall; she only earns a wage of £450 compared with his weekly earnings of £500. But his comparative advantage in housework more than compensated for this loss of earned income. He is more efficient at housework and provides £400 of household services, that is a gain of £100 over the value of her household production. He is better at washing clothes, amusing children and cooking meals than she is so the household will enjoy a higher standard of living if he remains at home even though he has the greater earnings potential. This result sometimes seems counter-intuitive! Yet the opportunity cost ratios are different. Her paid employment is 90 per cent as lucrative as his, whilst at housework she is only 75 per cent as productive as her partner. This determines the direction of specialization. As she has the comparative advantage in waged work she will be the one to seek paid employment. The household will be better off in the current period at least if specialization takes place.

Table 3.4: Specialization and Comparative Advantage

	Man	Woman	Total
Male breadwinner and female homemaker	£500	£300	£800
Male homemaker and female breadwinner	£400	£450	£850

In these examples we have assumed that the opportunity cost of housework is constant. In such a situation the two partners in the household will gain financially from complete specialization in either housework or paid employment. Efficient production will be achieved if they specialize completely in their relatively most productive activity; this way the household's joint standard of living will be improved.

Housework, Specialization and Earnings

One of the main difficulties with this analysis is that it accepts the gender wage gap as a fixed and exogenous variable. Indeed it is the case that in every developed country of the world, men do earn more than women. Although the earnings gap has narrowed in recent years it still remains. The facts are not in dispute but the reasons for this pay differential invite further investigation. The gender pay gap is usually attributed, in part at least, to differences in the labour force participation patterns of men and women. Since women are more likely than men to interrupt their career due to domestic commitments, then men are more likely than women to acquire on-the-job experience. Since women are more likely than men to work part time whilst their children are of pre-school age, then men are more likely than women to be offered the opportunity to go on a training course. Since women are more likely than men to experience a discontinuous work history, then men are more likely than women to gain seniority in their occupation. Qualifications, training and work experience all enhance a worker's productivity; they all raise the value of the worker to the employer. Profit maximizing employers will be prepared to pay higher wage rates for more productive workers; they are producing more output and so are bringing in more revenue for the employer than the less productive worker. These job specific skills increase the worker's marginal revenue product.

When the primary responsibility for the care of pre-school children lies with women, then men as a group are more likely to be in a position to acquire such skills and experience. Their ability to focus upon paid employment, due to their comparative freedom from domestic tasks, enables them to accumulate qualifications and thus to earn higher wages. They earn more because they specialize in paid work: the gender wage gap is a consequence of the domestic division of labour rather than a cause. The argument has come full circle!

In the example in the preceding section, the domestic division of labour was examined within the context of the traditional family household. In the situation specified complete specialization by each of the partners was the rational choice. In Britain in the 1990s very few households conform to this model of a full-time homemaker and a full-time worker in paid employment. Other household patterns have become far more common. In 1992, 67 per cent of married women with dependent children were economically active; the full-time homemaker was in the minority even amongst women with caring responsibilities (OPCS 1994). The decline in average family size and the introduction of labour-saving devices into the household have made it unnecessary for women to devote themselves full time and permanently to unpaid domestic work.

Many women though still interrupt their paid employment during the period of family formation. Childcare by its very nature is labour intensive and does require the full-time presence of a responsible adult for younger children. Women have traditionally taken a break from paid employment to perform this caring role but the duration of these career breaks is becoming shorter and shorter with each decade that passes. In 1973 only 27 per cent of women with a child under the age of five were economically active; by 1981 the proportion had increased to 30 per cent and by 1992 nearly half of these women combined the care of pre-school children with paid employment (OPCS 1994).

Complete specialization in housework and childcare is becoming an increasingly unattractive option for women. Rising real wages are increasing the opportunity cost of staying at home whilst the increase in the divorce rate is making it more likely that a woman might have to support herself at some stage in the life cycle. In 1991 there was one divorce in the United Kingdom for every two marriages (CSO 1994). This rising divorce rate makes women acutely aware of the dangers to which they expose themselves by relying on the continuing support of a male breadwinner. As the risk of becoming divorced increases so women want to try to maintain their long-run earnings potential through continuing in paid employment.

If a man continues with his job, he is progressing with his career, acquiring marketable skills, and earning an income which provides him with a fair degree of independence. If his partner follows economic logic by concentrating on household work, her position is very different from his. Housework is unpaid whilst employment in the labour market brings in an income. Although housework and childcare requires the exercise of a considerable number of skills – such as time management, negotiation, interpersonal communication and forward planning – skills gained within the household have no recognized market value. Experience gained within the household is rarely recognized in the labour market. Full-time homemakers sacrifice years of seniority and experience in employment in order to provide household services and become heavily dependent upon their partner for their material well-being thus reducing their economic independence.

Indeed the disadvantages of specialization to the partners in the household invokes a strong analogy with the earlier discussion of international trade in the original example of guns and butter. In a world of free trade and open economies, the principle of comparative advantage suggests that some countries should totally abandon the production of guns in favour of specializing in dairy products. However one might question whether it is really in Cloverdell's best interests to abandon its defence industry entirely. Such a strategy might appear to make economic sense in the short term, but it would hardly be wise for any nation to leave its security so vulnerable through complete dependence upon others. Just as a nation might decide against abandoning its defence industry in order to preserve its political autonomy in an uncertain world, so too in the household. Women often decide to continue with their career even when it runs counter to the logic of comparative advantage, since their future too is uncertain.

The Quality of Life

Moreover monetary rewards are not the only determinant of the standard of living. We also need to consider the quality of life within the household. Children represent the future generation and their care within the home will affect their economic, social and emotional well-being later in life. Their ability to take their place in the world of the twenty-first century will depend in part on the quality of their experiences in their early years. The skills, which workers bring to the labour force, are not acquired in formal education alone; the domestic environment plays an important part in producing the citizens of the future. The care of children is an important economic activity and the future generation might well benefit from experiencing both men and women in the parenting role. The quality of future citizens might be enhanced if both parents contribute to childcare in the early years. A simple application of the principle of comparative advantage often ignores this point. Parents too need to consider more than just their potential level of consumption in the current period. A household might be able to enjoy a higher level of goods and services if specialization takes place between the partners on the basis of comparative advantage but this does not mean that both the partners will necessarily be 'better off' as a result. The division of the extra output might be very unequal. Men, as wage earners, do not always share their increased earnings with their dependents; some might decide to appropriate all the gains should an increase in money wages occur. Other members of the household will then not be benefiting from the specialization which has occurred. In the short run they could be no better off even though the household joint income has risen. It might even be beneficial for the non-material side of the relationship if both partners were to pursue a more varied work pattern since complete specialization can prove boring – even if productive! They might both enjoy cooking sometimes, playing with the children and pursuing their career path. Current working practices in Britain make it difficult for fathers to spend time with their children and a more equal division of labour between the partners in a household becomes fraught with difficulty.

Waged Domestic Labour

In the New Home Economics the focus is upon specialization and exchange within the household. The two partners are depicted as choosing between unpaid domestic work and paid employment. The household is seen as a self-contained unit seeking to allocate its resources in such a way as to maximize the value of the goods and services it produces and consumes. This is increasingly unrealistic in contemporary society. The growth of convenience foods and the availability of takeaway meals represent one way in which households can now buy in the services which were previously provided in the households. In modern Britain, many two career households are seeking to employ waged domestic labour to perform house cleaning and childcare activities. Between 1981 and 1991, 40 per cent of two career households with pre-school age children employed a nanny whilst 75 per cent employed a cleaner (Gregson and Lowe 1994).

Waged domestic labour is not a new development. At the turn of the century domestic service was the most common occupational category for employed women. In the 1990s too, waged domestic labour is strongly gendered; it is women who fill these positions. There are however marked differences in age and marital status between nannies and cleaners. Nannies tend to be young and unmarried whilst cleaners are more likely to be older married women, seeking to combine this form of waged labour with their own domestic commitments (Gregson and Lowe 1994). Households never have been, and are not today, dependent entirely upon household members for the provision of services. These services can be bought in and many households are taking this option.

This represents an extension of the principle of comparative advantage and is perhaps equivalent to a country acquiring more trading partners and so extending the scope of specialization and division of labour. It might well be the case that a trained nanny is better qualified to care for pre-school children on a day-to-day basis than either partner in the household. If employing waged domestic labour enables both partners to pursue their careers, then this strategy would represent a material gain for the household. Since the nanny's or the cleaner's wages are likely to be less than those of professional workers, then, if we are looking purely at monetary rewards, this might be the most rational economic solution for the household. It is debatable though whether the quality of the care provided by the mother is identical to that provided by a paid helper (Himmelweit 1995).

Conclusion

Throughout the western world the division of domestic labour is strongly gendered. Since the Industrial Revolution there has been a distinction between paid work outside the household and unpaid domestic labour within the household. The division of labour in the Western world has been such that paid work has come to be the focus of men's economic activity whilst women divide their working lives between the unpaid domestic sphere and labour market activity. The economic justification for this division of domestic labour is based upon the principle of comparative advantage. Specialization and exchange are presented as mutually beneficial to both partners in the household. Whilst specialization and exchange might bring both partners some limited short-term material gains it is debatable whether complete specialization works to the long-term advantage of any member of the household – man, woman or child.

In industrialized societies the roles which women and men play in economic activity are different and distinctive. Household responsibilities and paid employment are both valid productive activities but they are not equally rewarded by society. The present pattern, by which men remain continually attached to the labour market throughout their working lives whilst women's participation in paid employment is interrupted by domestic responsibilities, serves to disadvantage women. Housework is an unpaid economic activity which has for too long passed unnoticed; the skills, which the successful homemaker acquires, go unrecognized in wage and promotion schemes. Women, who follow a typical work pattern, find that their economic status has suffered as a result. The economic independence of women is undermined by their focus upon unpaid domestic tasks which constrain their participation in paid work. The domestic division of labour would certainly seem to lead to social injustice and it is debatable whether it furthers the efficient operation of the economy.

4 Work or Leisure?
The Labour Supply Decision of Men and Women

Households and labour supply. The individual worker's supply curve for labour. Income and substitution effects. Women's employment, income and substitution effects. Women and part-time employment. Men's employment, income and substitution effects. Part-time employment for men. Summary.

Households and Labour Supply

The unequal division of household labour affects opportunities in the labour market. If women are responsible for cleaning the house, providing the meals, caring for pre-school children and the elderly, then their labour supply decision will be constrained by these responsibilities. Men, on the other hand, are far freer from these domestic responsibilities; they do on average about half as much unpaid work in the household as women and they benefit from the household services which women provide. As a result, they are able to specialize in paid work and to give their careers wholehearted attention.

Domestic labour affects the decision about the hours worked in labour markets. In the spring of 1987 the *Labour Force Survey* estimated that on average men's usual hours of work amounted to 44 hours per week whilst for married women the weekly average totalled 28 hours (Department of Employment 1988). As family size has decreased and technology has reduced the labour input into housework, domestic labour has become less onerous; women have found it possible to increase their labour market activity. Since the Second World War women's participation in employment has increased continually but the terms upon which they are able to engage in paid work are still constrained by their continuing responsibility for the majority of household tasks. Indeed the results from the British Household Panel Survey show that very few men reported that household or family responsibilities affected their labour market behaviour whilst over 80 per cent of the women surveyed felt that family responsibilities had adversely affected their labour market participation (Dex et al. 1995).

The decision to supply labour to factor markets takes many forms. It encompasses decisions concerning whether to participate in the working population or to remain non-participant, the number of hours allocated to

51

paid employment, which occupation to pursue and whether to work on a full-time or part-time basis. Each one of these choices will affect the labour supply. Female participation and employment have both grown but women remain segregated in service industries often working part time. Male participation and employment have both fallen but men typically work full time and predominate in construction and metal manufacturing. The duration of the working week has also changed over the last 20 years. In Britain the working week is longer than in any other European Union country but the average working week has fallen for a man whilst for women there has been little change. In 1972 men's weekly working hours amounted to 43.3 hours and this had fallen to 41.6 hours by 1994; for women an average working week amounted to 37.8 hours in 1972 falling to 37.6 hours by 1994 (Department of Employment). These changes have been influenced by labour supply decisions, but also by employers' preferences, changes in legislation and macroeconomic constraints.

Since the labour supply decision is taken within the household one member's choice will affect, and be affected by, the decisions of other household members. The number of hours one partner chooses to work will be influenced by the household's total income, the presence – or absence – of dependent children, the availability of childcare and other factors. For example, a woman with small children whose partner earns an adequate income might forgo paid employment until her children are of school age whilst a woman whose partner is a low income earner faces different constraints. In households where there are two dependent children of pre-school age only 52 total hours of work will be supplied compared with 65 hours for the couple of similar ages but with no children under school age (Dex et al. 1995). The decision about hours of paid employment will be affected by the employment status, income level and general availability of other household members. In households where one member is unemployed, it is often not financially advantageous for their partner to accept part-time work. The benefits system acts as a deterrent to part-time employment by subtracting earnings from the family's entitlement to benefit. In 1987 it was estimated that a woman earning £2.50 per hour could work for 50 hours per week and add only £7.00 to the household's total weekly income if her partner was on supplementary benefit (Dilnot 1992). In this case the man's employment status adversely affects the woman's hours of paid work; in other instances the employment of one partner on a full-time basis might restrict the other partner to part-time hours adjusted in order to provide continuous care for pre-school children. The divide between work-rich and work-poor households is deepening. In 1991, 13 per cent of British couple households of working age contained no income earners at all whilst 49 per cent of households included two earners (Dex et al. 1995). The decision which one member of the household takes about his or her hours of work will be influenced and constrained by the decisions of other household members. The labour supply decision is interdependent, rather than independent.

The Individual Worker's Supply Curve for Labour

The individual's supply curve of labour illustrates how a worker divides time between paid work and other activities. An individual's supply curve of labour shows how many hours' work will be supplied at various alternative wage rates within a specified period of time. It relates the number of hours worked to the wage rate. The labour supply curve is expected to be upward sloping, implying that more hours of labour are supplied as the wage rate rises and fewer hours are offered as the wage rate falls. The upward sloping labour supply curve is the outcome of a simple choice which workers make about the allocation of their time. Time is a limited resource since there are only 24 hours in each day. Women and men must decide how many hours to devote to paid work and how much to spend on 'leisure activities', which are assumed to encompass all the other uses of time.

The basic assumption of neo-classical analysis is that workers attempt to maximize their total utility, or satisfaction. Work is assumed to be unpleasant and carries with it disutility, implying that, on the whole, men and women would prefer not to work. However, work must be undertaken; it is an essential function since it brings in a wage, the spending of which brings satisfaction and increases total utility. The rational actor must therefore weigh up the disutility of each extra hour worked against the extra utility, or satisfaction, to be gained from spending the additional money which that work will generate. The worker must evaluate the marginal costs and marginal benefits of each additional hour worked. Whether men and women act like the neo-classical 'rational economic man' carefully calculating the marginal costs and benefits of their actions is debatable. Nancy Folbre, a feminist economist, has suggested that the very concept of self-interest might be gendered and more applicable to men than to women, constrained as they are by family responsibilities and social pressures (Folbre 1994). For a man 'self' applies to him alone whilst for a women the concept often encompasses other family members as well. The neo-classical model, however, is based upon marginal analysis and, even on this basis, differences in the labour market behaviour of men and women can be identified.

Work has a cost which can be measured in terms of the disutility it brings to the worker. Each extra hour worked leaves less time for leisure since there are only a limited number of hours in the day to be divided between work

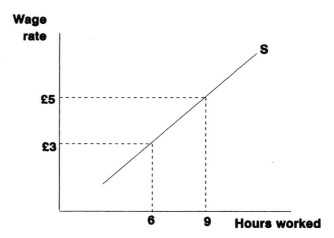

Figure 4.1: An Individual's Supply Curve of Labour

and leisure. As people work more hours, so their leisure time decreases; it becomes a scarcer commodity and they place a greater value on each remaining hour of leisure time. Thus higher wages are required in order to persuade people to work longer hours and to give up additional amounts of that increasingly valuable leisure time. There is an increasing marginal disutility of work.

It is this reasoning which justifies the payment of higher rates for overtime; if employers are to persuade workers to spend longer hours on the job then they must offer an incentive. As working hours increase, each hour of leisure becomes more valuable to the worker as it becomes harder to pursue his or her hobbies and leisure pursuits. The opportunity cost of leisure is increasing. Under these circumstances extra pay must be offered as an incentive to persuade men and women to overcome their reluctance to work longer hours. The only compensation sufficient to persuade rational workers to forgo some of their more expensive leisure time is to offer them higher wage rates for working longer hours. The marginal benefit then equals the marginal cost.

The supply curve for labour will thus be upward sloping and higher wages persuade workers to supply more hours of labour. In Figure 4.1 if the wage rate offered is £3.00 per hour, then this worker will be prepared to work for six hours per day, leaving ten hours for 'leisure activities' and eight hours for sleeping. Should the wage rate rise to £5.00 per hour, then this will provide sufficient incentive to overcome the worker's natural reluctance to labour market work and will persuade him or her to offer an extra three hours work per day.

Income and Substitution Effects

A change in wage rates affects the worker's behaviour in two ways: through the substitution effect and through the income effect. These factors work in different and conflicting ways to influence a worker's behaviour. The substitution effect will encourage a person to work longer hours as wage rates rise whilst the income effect has a negative impact upon the hours worked.

The substitution effect sees work and leisure as competing for the worker's limited time. A change in wage rates will alter the relative value of one hour's work as opposed to one hour's leisure. If wage rates rise, then the value gained from one extra hour of paid work increases and the value lost through one extra hour of leisure time becomes greater. It is simply more expensive now to spend an hour gardening, for example, since the lost earnings have increased. Thus a worker will respond to a wage increase by substituting work for leisure. The substitution effect causes more hours of work to be supplied as wage rates rise.

In recent decades higher wage rates have acted as an incentive to encourage women to engage in paid employment. Over the postwar years real wage rates for women have risen and it has become too expensive to remain 'economically inactive'. Between 1970 and 1994 women's hourly earnings doubled in real terms (Department of Employment). As wage rates have risen, one hour spent cleaning the house or caring for children involves a higher opportunity cost; this form of 'leisure activity' becomes increasingly expensive. Once a woman's earnings potential increases, she must reassess her labour supply decision. Higher wages are encouraging women to spend more hours in paid work and to reduce the time spent in housework or childcare. The substitution effect has been one factor affecting the increased participation of women in paid employment.

The income effect on the other hand looks to the benefits people gain from paid employment, namely the income they earn. Men and women have certain basic requirements with respect to their expenditure. They need to pay the rent or mortgage, they need to cover their day-to-day living expenses, they want to take an annual holiday and so on. Paid employment is therefore necessary in order to maintain this lifestyle. Men and women can calculate the income they need to enable them to attain this standard of living. This income level becomes their target and paid employment is undertaken in order to achieve the income necessary to maintain their desired lifestyle. If wage rates rise, then workers are able to achieve the same standard of living as before whilst working shorter hours. A wage rise of 20 per cent leaves them with the same income as before even if they reduce their working time by 20 per cent. In this case a wage rise results in a reduction in the hours worked. This negative relationship between wages and hours worked is known as the income effect.

If wages increase, the substitution effect encourages workers to work longer hours whilst the income effect is persuading them to spend less time at work. These two factors are operating in contradictory ways. The worker's labour supply will be affected by both of these influences and the change in the hours worked results from the interaction of both the income and substitution effects. A numerical example will help to illustrate this point. If a person is initially working six hours per day at a wage rate of £3.50 per hour, this leaves 18 hours in the day for other activities, approximately eight hours of which need to be spent in sleeping. At a wage rate of £3.50 per hour, this allocation of time is acceptable to the rational agent. If wage rates rise to £4.00 per hour, then the situation changes. Work has now become a relatively more valuable activity and the marginal benefit to be gained from each extra hour worked has increased by 50p; the rational actor responds by working longer hours. The man or woman might want to undertake nine hours of paid work at a wage rate of £4.00 per hour. The increase in the wage rate has persuaded the worker to substitute three hours of paid work for three hours of leisure time. The extra wage encourages a worker to spend more time in paid employment since the opportunity cost of unpaid activities has risen. A man or woman substitutes work for leisure as wage rates increase; in the example given above the substitution effect encourages an extra three hours' paid work to be undertaken as hourly wage rates rise from £3.50 to £4.00.

At the same time though the income effect is encouraging individuals to reduce their working hours. If the worker initially is working six hours per day at a wage rate of £3.50 per hour and earning a total income of £21 per day, then a rise in wage rates to £4.00 per hour enables this person to gain the same total income whilst reducing the hours worked; a daily income of £21 can be achieved by working 5.25 hours per day. This man or woman can now enjoy an additional three-quarters of an hour in leisure pursuits whilst maintaining his or her expected standard of living. The income effect persuades the worker to work shorter hours as wage rates rise. The income effect and the substitution effect of this increase in wage rates are both illustrated in Table 4.1.

Table 4.1: The Substitution Effect is Stronger than Income Effect

Rise in hourly wage rate from £3.50 to £4.00	Change in hours worked
Substitution effect	+3.00
Income effect	−0.75
Total effect	+2.25

Wage rate

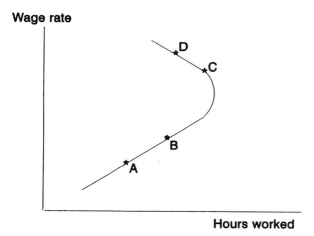

Hours worked

Figure 4.2: The Supply Curve for Labour

The combined outcome of this contradictory process will incorporate both the income and substitution effects. This person will want to spend an extra three hours in paid employment due to the substitution effect whilst also desiring an extra three-quarters of an hour for leisure time as a result of the income effect. The net result, in this case, will be that an additional two and a quarter hours will be worked at the higher wage rate of £4.00 an hour. As wage rates change both the income and substitution effects influence the supply of labour and the relative strength of these two factors will determine whether working hours are increased or reduced. If, as in the example in Table 4.1, the substitution effect is stronger than the income effect, then the supply curve will be upward sloping. The rise in wage rates makes employment a relatively more valuable activity.

In Figure 4.2, an increase in the hourly wage rate from £3.50 to £4.00 would be represented by a movement along the supply curve from point A to point B. Over this wage range the supply curve is upward sloping indicating a positive relationship between the hours worked and wage rates. The response to a rise in wage rates is an increase in working hours as the substitution effect outweighs the income effect. The supply curve is upward sloping at lower rates of pay since a worker is still seeking to increase his or her standard of living.

Women's Employment, Income and Substitution Effects

The relative strength of the income and substitution effects depends partly upon the current rate of pay. Women on average earn lower rates of pay than men. In 1994 women's average hourly earnings in Britain were £6.88 whilst those for men were £8.65 (Department of Employment 1995). As a result a woman might find herself on the upward sloping part of the supply curve and will respond to higher real wages by working longer hours. One way of examining whether the income effect or the substitution effect is the stronger is by estimating the value of the price elasticity of supply of labour. Price elasticity of supply measures the responsiveness of the supply of a commodity to a change in the price of that commodity. The elasticity co-efficient is calculated by the following formula:

PES = percentage change in quantity supplied
        ───
           percentage change in price

If the own-wage elasticity co-efficient for labour is found to be positive then this implies that the supply curve is upward sloping, as it is in Figure 4.2 between points A and B. Empirical studies have found considerable variation in the estimates of wage elasticity for the supply of labour. For women the elasticity values have been estimated to lie between –4.46 and +4.46 (Fallon and Verry 1988). In other words, at one end of the range, a wage rise of 10 per cent, for a woman, is likely to persuade her to increase her working hours by nearly 45 per cent whilst at the other end of the scale she will reduce her working time by 45 per cent. Despite this wide variation in findings it is possible to draw some conclusions; for women positive elasticity values are far more commonly observed. The supply curve for labour is therefore upward sloping and, for a woman, the substitution effect is stronger than the income effect. These results imply that the income tax reductions of the 1980s would have encouraged women to work longer hours. Even if hourly wage rates remain constant a cut in income tax increases the worker's hourly rate of take home pay. This affects the labour supply decision. For women the substitution effect usually proves stronger than the income effect and a rise in take home wage rates increases the hours worked.

Women and Part-time Employment

Over the last 30 years part-time employment has grown rapidly, especially in Britain. Whilst only one British worker in every 20 was part time in the immediate postwar years, by 1994 more than one in four were working less than a full week. Part-time employment is defined as anything less than a full working week, but in practice the British statistics include all employees working 30 hours or less per week. By 1991 the number of part-time employees had risen to 6.7 million. The *Labour Force Survey* shows that there is considerable variation in the number of hours worked. Seven per cent of part-time employees worked less than five hours per week whilst 17 per cent worked more than 25 hours weekly (Naylor 1994). This growth of part-time employment would seem to offer an opportunity for workers to respond to changes in their working conditions and their family circumstances. The range of options available to a worker has been extended since the increased availability of part-time employment provides the opportunity for a worker to increase or reduce the hours worked by opting for part-time working.

Men and women of different ages have responded to these part-time opportunities in very different ways. Some have chosen to work part time rather than full time; they have chosen to reduce their hours of work as part-time jobs have become available, whilst others have chosen to enter paid employment, albeit on a part-time basis, rather than to remain non-participant in the working population. The decision to work part time has thus to be interpreted differently for particular groups within the labour force. It is an increase in working hours for some workers, especially for mothers, whilst it represents a reduction in working hours for others, particularly older men.

Part-time working provides an example of the choices workers are making about the allocation of their time between work and 'leisure'. Certainly many people say that they work part time as a result of a deliberate choice; in 1994, 73 per cent of part-time employees stated that they didn't want a full-time job (OPCS 1994). As Chapter 2 noted, part-time workers in Britain are predominantly women. Nearly 40 per cent of women working part time fall between the ages of 25 and 39, the years when young children are most likely to be present in the household. Of this group 88 per cent stated that they did not want a full-time job. Their labour supply decision reflects their responsibility for housework and childcare. Despite the low level of public provision for childcare in the United Kingdom the employment of women with children under 10 years of age rose by 7.5 per cent between 1985 and 1988, the second biggest increase in the European Union (Moss 1990). Many of these mothers would have sought part-time jobs earning low wage rates.

As family size has fallen and housework has become less labour intensive, the provision of services for the household has ceased to be a full-time job. This though does not imply that domestic responsibilities can simply be discounted as negligible. Childcare is still essentially labour intensive and is regarded as a woman's responsibility. Many women rely upon family and friends to care for their children whilst they are at work. A number of studies between 1980 and 1991 in Britain confirmed that husbands, other relatives or friends were providing informal care for children in over half of all such arrangements (Brannen et al. 1994). The mother's – rather than the father's – hours of work are often adjusted to accommodate the need to provide continuous care for dependent children. Mothers with dependent children are more likely to work part time than women as a whole but they are now more likely to work than to remain non-participant.

Informal childcare is often provided free of charge or in return for a nominal fee for expenses. Only 29 per cent of informal arrangements involved payment in the early 1990s (Corti and Laurie 1993). Relying on family or friends provides low cost childcare but it constrains the mother's employment opportunities. By contrast professional childcare services offer greater scope for employment but are usually provided at unsubsidized market rates in Britain. Since childcare is labour intensive the cost of these services is high, especially for pre-school children, amounting on average to 25 per cent of the mother's earnings (Brannen et al. 1994). Mothers with higher qualifications, and hence higher earnings potential, are more likely to use these services; 43 per cent of working mothers with higher education used paid nannies or childminders (Bridgwood and Savage 1993). For mothers with qualifications the cost of childcare is covered by their current income. For them the marginal benefit of employment exceeds the marginal cost. Full-time employment becomes possible, increasing their total income both through the increase in their working hours and through avoiding the low rates of pay often accorded to part-timers. For their future career development continuous full-time employment can prove even more important. By investing in childcare mothers enhance their future earnings potential as their promotion prospects improve with on-the-job experience. Paying for childcare can thus prove a worthwhile investment for women, even those with GCSE education, in terms of the enhancement of their long-term earnings (Joshi and Davies 1993). These mothers will more than recoup their investment over their working life.

For mothers without qualifications, however, the situation is far less favourable. Only 9 per cent of those with no qualification used paid nannies and childminders (Bridgwood and Savage 1993) and the need to rely on unpaid childcare restricts their employment opportunities. Part-time employment might be the only viable option as they need to adjust their working hours to ensure continuous care for their children; they need to work near home and they are unable to increase their working hours due to their caring responsibilities. These constraints will reduce their earnings potential still further in both the short and the long term. Those mothers though who have sufficient earnings potential to pay market rates for childcare have far greater opportunities. Full-time employment becomes possible, increasing the chances of promotion and enhancing both the short- and long-term earnings of these women. Women's labour supply decision is thus influenced by the wage rate. Below a certain wage rate only part-time employment will be possible. These low income earners will have to rely on unpaid informal arrangements for childcare. Low wages restrict mothers to short working hours. Beyond a certain wage level though, earnings are sufficient to cover payment for formal childcare. At higher wage rates hours of work increase and full-time employment becomes possible.

Men's Employment, Income and Substitution Effects

Men face different constraints upon their employment. Fathers, unlike mothers, rarely adjust their hours of work to accommodate childcare. When real wage rates rise women usually work longer hours but for men the evidence on wage elasticities of supply suggest a different response. Men might even reduce their total hours of work as real wage rates increase. The estimates of men's own wage elasticity of supply have been rather different from the findings for women. Whilst for women elasticity values were usually positive, for men the wage supply elasticities lay within the range −1.0 to +0.34 but this time negative values predominated (Fallon and Verry 1988). Negative wage elasticity values imply that men respond to higher real wage rates by reducing their hours of work. A supply elasticity value of −1.0 implies that if wages rise by 10 per cent rise then men reduce their working hours by 10 per cent. Where the elasticity values lie between 0 and −1.0, the supply curve is backward bending as it is in Figure 4.2 between points C and D. Negative elasticity values indicate that the income effects are stronger than the substitution effects implying that a man will respond to a wage rise by reducing his hours of work. On this basis the income tax cuts of the 1980s are likely to have led to a reduction in the number of hours which a man wished to spend in paid employment provided the tax cuts were not offset by a rise in the cost of living.

The traditional depiction of an upward sloping supply curve for labour rests upon the assumption that the substitution effect is stronger than the income effect. Once a worker's pay rises above a certain level though, any further wage increase might cause workers to start reducing their hours of paid labour. Men on average earn more than women and are thus likely to experience a strong income effect as wage rates change. If the income effect becomes stronger than the substitution effect, then a wage rise reduces the number of hours worked.

The income effect always reduces the hours worked in response to a rise in the hourly wage rate. For example, if the worker was prepared to work six hours per day for an hourly wage rate of £8, then their total daily income would be £48. If this income was sufficient to achieve the desired living standard, then once the wage rate rises to £12 per hour, the same level of income can be obtained by working for only four hours daily. In such a situation workers might well decide to reduce their hours of work. The substitution effect, though, works in the opposite direction. It encourages a move towards paid work since this activity has now become relatively more lucrative. The worker responds to the rise in the wage rate from £8 to £12 by seeking to spend one additional hour in paid employment. These two outcomes are illustrated in Table 4.2.

The overall result of this rise in the wage rate is once again the combined outcome of these two contradictory processes. This worker wants to increase working time by one hour due to the substitution effect and yet to reduce working time by two hours due to the income effect. The overall impact of the wage rise, in this example, is a reduction in working hours. The worker reduces the working day from six to five hours as the wage rate increases from £8 to £12 per hour. In this case the income effect is stronger than the substitution effect and a wage rise causes the worker to work shorter hours overall. The supply curve for labour has become backward bending. In Figure 4.2 this situation is depicted as a move along the labour supply curve from point C to point D; the response to a rise in the wage rate is a reduction in working hours. There is a negative relationship between wage rates and hours worked as the income effect is stronger in this example than the substitution effect.

Table 4.2: The Income Effect Stronger than Substitution Effect

Rise in hourly wage rate from £8.00 to £12.00	Change in hours worked
Substitution effect	+1
Income effect	−2
Total effect	−1

This backward bending supply curve might apply only once wage rates rise above a certain level; at lower rates of pay the supply curve of labour could be upward sloping with the substitution effect outweighing the income effect. Wage rates have been rising in Britain over recent decades. In 1970 men's hourly earnings were 67p whilst these had risen to £8.65 in nominal terms by 1994; this represents a 60 per cent increase in real earnings (Department of Employment). Whilst men's working hours have fallen since 1972 those for a woman have altered very little; the gap between women's and men's working hours has thus narrowed. Due to the different relative strengths of the income and substitution effects women and men respond in distinctive ways to a rise in wage rates.

Part-time Employment for Men

Men are most likely to be employed on a part-time basis at the beginning and end of their working life. Nearly 80 per cent of part-time male employees are either under the age of 25 or over the age of 50. Students accounted for four out of every five part-time male employees under the age of 25 (Naylor 1994). Students decide to supply labour on a part-time basis in order to devote the remaining time to studying and other leisure activities. They have decided that they need extra money to top up the increasingly inadequate student grant but most of their time must inevitably be spent studying for their degree. Two-thirds of those men who work less than ten hours per week are students.

This division of time between paid employment and studying can be viewed as a rational decision to work just long enough to provide the extra income needed, whilst devoting the bulk of the week's working hours to unpaid academic work. For these part-time workers, the income effect might well prove stronger than the substitution effect. If they were to be offered a rise in wage rates, this would enable them to meet their bills whilst reducing their hours of paid employment. Paid employment for students is motivated primarily by the desire to obtain an adequate income and for this group the income effect probably outweighs the substitution effect.

The picture is similar for men in the older age group. Once they have passed their fiftieth birthday then some men start to choose part-time employment; 73 per cent of men over 50 years of age, who were working part time, said that they did not want to work full time and gave this as their reason for accepting part-time work (Naylor 1994). They have chosen to reduce their hours of paid employment, perhaps reflecting the reduction in financial commitments as children cease to be dependents, the mortgage repayments near completion and pensionable age draws near.

For men between the ages of 25 and 49 the position is very different. The majority of those part-time workers in this age group were accepting part-time jobs because they could not find full-time work. These men would choose to increase their hours of work if they could find full-time employment. The *Labour Force Survey* of 1994 indicated that nearly 60 per cent of male part-timers between the ages of 25 and 49 would prefer a full-time job, were one to be available. However, these men considered that it was better to work on a part-time basis rather than not to work at all; but for them part-time work was a second best alternative. It reflected the lack of full-time employment opportunities rather than a deliberate choice to work reduced hours.

Men in this age bracket are likely to have heavy financial commitments. These are the years of family formation, which provokes a different labour market response from fathers than from mothers. Mothers will frequently reduce their hours of paid employment as children arrive, whilst fathers commonly work longer hours at this stage of their life (Brannen et al. 1994). The British Social Attitudes Survey confirms that a man is still expected to carry the responsibility for supporting the family financially (Jowell et al. 1992/3). A man tries to earn an income sufficient to support a family by working full-time if possible.

Summary

In Britain in the 1990s, the evidence seems to suggest that the labour supply decisions of men and women are dissimilar in certain respects. Decisions about the hours of work, place of work, full-time or part-time employment and the response to income tax changes are taken within the context of parameters imposed by family, society and economic opportunities. The constraints which influence labour supply differ considerably between fathers and mothers. Many women, especially those with dependent children, opt for part-time work. Due to their domestic commitments and the lack of pre-school childcare facilities in Britain, these women work for less than the full working week; but increasingly they are working rather than not working. Part-time work reduces earnings potential contributing to the gender wage gap. Women, as low income earners, usually respond to a rise in wage rates or a cut in income taxes by increasing their working hours. The substitution effect predominates.

For men, on the other hand, the evidence is mixed. Part-time work is becoming more common. Students are choosing to participate in paid work on a part-time basis in order to finance their studies, and older men are reducing their working hours below the full working week. But only a very small proportion of men work part time in their middle years. Men, with more labour market experience and continuous careers, earn more than women. For men the likely response to a wage rise or an income tax cut which increases real wages is a reduction in their working hours. The elasticity of supply of labour is negative, reflecting the strength of the income effect. Men and women will adjust their labour supply decision in different ways as real wage rates rise either as a result of an increase in wage rates paid by employers or following a reduction in the rate of income tax. The different constraints affecting men's and women's labour supply result in these distinctive labour market responses.

5 Men's Jobs, Women's Jobs
The Labour Supply to Occupations

Segregation in employment. Human capital: an explanation. Education as human capital investment. Men, women and human capital investment. Human capital investment and the deterioration of skills. Training, vocational education and experience. Alternative explanations of occupational segregation. Summary.

Segregation in Employment

Tastes and preferences, distinctive talents and aptitudes, different skills and qualifications are all factors which help to explain why men and women choose to enter different occupations. Workers are not homogeneous; they do not all have the same talents and aptitudes, do not possess identical qualifications or opportunities and are not faced with the same constraints upon their employment. The subjects studied by boys and girls at school and in higher education vary considerably so that young men and women emerge into the labour market equipped with dissimilar skills and qualifications. They will often anticipate different work patterns over their employment life cycle and this in turn will affect the areas of work which they choose to enter. Men and women bring different qualities to the labour market and this will affect their choice of occupation.

One remarkable characteristic of labour markets in Britain, and indeed in other developed countries, is that men and women are not equally distributed across the occupational categories or throughout the industries in the economy. The workplace is strongly segregated by gender. In Britain in 1995 over 80 per cent of the employees in coal extraction, metal manufacture and railways were men whilst the position was reversed in hairdressing, clothing manufacture and medical and other health services; in these sectors women outnumbered men by almost four to one (Department of Employment 1995). This segregated pattern of employment is repeated in most developed countries of the world and segregation is enduring even in countries where women display a high rate of participation in the working population and in new industries like computing. As women have come to form a larger proportion of the labour force the jobs in which they are engaged are not becoming more diverse; their employment remains confined to a few specific sectors of the economy. Men and women are employed in approximately equal numbers in the labour force as a whole; but this numerical equality is not repeated in many of the occupational groups within the economy. Whilst there has always been a distinction between 'men's jobs' and 'women's jobs' the specific allocation of occupations has varied over time and place. Clerical work was a male occupation in the nineteenth century but during the twentieth century it has become essentially a female enclave. Farming is a male dominated sector in Western Europe whilst in parts of Africa women predominate in agriculture. The division of labour between men and women is not based upon biological, or sex, differences so much as social, or gender, relationships. Whilst the content of men's and women's jobs has changed men have usually concentrated in the higher paid and higher status jobs whilst women's work is usually considered to be low skill and commands a lower wage rate. In the computing industry, a relatively new area of work, the division of labour between men and women is already strongly gendered and reflects the vertical segregation prevalent in long-established occupations. Working with computers is regarded as a 'man's job'. Computers have come to be associated, not altogether accurately, with maths and science. They are usually located within these departments in schools and colleges and the masculine image of these subjects has been transferred to computing. Consequently more boys than girls study computing subjects at school. The popular children's computer games are predominantly of the 'shoot and kill' variety appealing strongly to the macho instinct. Consequently computing has attracted more men than women, especially in the higher status jobs like systems analysis. In one computing sector only women are employed almost exclusively, namely data entry which is regarded as a low status, unskilled job (Game and Pringle 1983). Gender segregation has quickly become established in the computing industry and reflects the patterns of vertical and horizontal segregation found elsewhere in the economy.

Labour market segregation can arise from differences in either the supply of, or the demand for, labour. On the demand side, employers might prefer to employ either men or women exclusively for a particular occupation. They might believe, rightly or wrongly, that men, or women, are more productive as workers in this type of job. Alternatively firms and unions might try to restrict recruitment to workers of one particular sex believing that men and women work best when apart, thus a segregated workplace will be a more efficient and productive workplace. Although discrimination in recruitment and employment is illegal in Britain and throughout the European Union, there is little doubt that such practices do still exist. In these cases the demand for labour is influencing and contributing to segregation in employment. The impact of discrimination upon wages and employment will be investigated in Chapter 9.

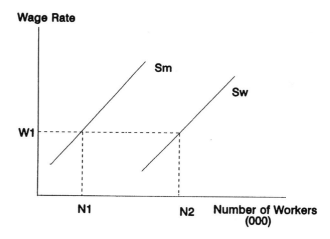

(a) Hairdressers

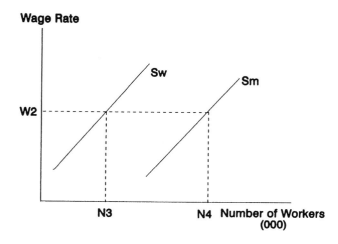

(b) Lorry Drivers

Figure 5.1: Supply of Men's and Women's Labour to two Occupations

Alternatively though, men and women might choose to supply their labour to different occupations. Girls and boys vary in the subjects they study at school and these subject choices can affect the direction of their subsequent careers. There could be inherent, or socially acquired, differences between men and women which incline them towards particular occupations. Men might prefer vehicle repair and be more prepared to become a motor mechanic whilst women tend towards service occupations. Men and women might also feel more comfortable working with those of their own gender rather than being a lone pioneer in an occupation in which those of the opposite sex predominate. In these cases men and women choose to enter occupations in which their own gender predominates. Thus women are more likely than men to become hairdressers whilst lorry driving will be an occupation which attracts more men than women. In these instances the supply of labour is strongly influencing the occupational segregation and contributing to a supply-side explanation of gender segregation in employment.

Segregation due to supply-side factors is illustrated in figure 5.1. In Figure 5.1a the market supply of hairdressers is depicted; S_m shows the number of men willing to work at various alternative wage rates whilst S_w shows the supply curve of women's labour. At every wage rate there are more women prepared to offer their labour services than men. At a wage of W_1, N_1 men would be employed and N_2 women. Hairdressing is an occupation where women predominate as workers. In Britain 91 per cent of hairdressers and beauty therapists were women in 1994 (Department of Employment 1994). The situation depicted in Figure 5.1b is very different. This diagram illustrates the labour supply position for lorry drivers; in this occupation the supply curve for men's labour, S_m, exceeds the supply of women's labour, S_w, at every wage rate. At a wage of W_2, N_3 women will be employed and N_4 men and thus lorry drivers are overwhelmingly men.

Human Capital: an Explanation

Skills and qualifications enhance a worker's productivity and can thus increase the value of that worker to the employer. Just as a new piece of machinery can increase the firm's output and reduce its unit costs, so well educated workers will usually prove more productive than those without qualifications. There is an analogy between purchasing a new piece of machinery, that is investment in capital equipment, and educating the workforce, that is investing in human capital. The skills, qualifications and expertise which contribute to people's productivity are referred to as their human capital. A course in higher education will increase the students' productive potential when they enter the labour market. Time and money spent in education can be regarded as an investment in human capital. The level of education which people receive enhances their human capital as workers. A literate worker is able to read instructions and follow safety procedures and is thus less likely to cause accidents with machinery. An employee who has completed A levels or an advanced General National Vocational Qualification (GNVQ) has demonstrated an ability to work on their own and complete academic tasks whilst a university graduate will have studied at a more abstract level and should be able to deal with complex concepts and procedures. With each level of education a student is becoming more productive as a member of the workforce. The investment in human capital will enhance the worker's productivity and will increase his or her value to an employer. For this reason better educated men and women usually receive higher salaries than those with a lower level of educational attainment. In Britain in 1992 the median weekly earnings of a graduate were approximately twice those of a worker without any qualifications (OPCS 1994).

Education enhances a person's productivity across a broad spectrum; it provides a basic intellectual grounding which should prove useful whatever occupation the student chooses to enter. Education therefore contributes to general human capital. For some occupations though, general human capital is not sufficient; workers need more specific training to equip them with the knowledge and skills to perform adequately in that particular sector. A graduate employed in a computer record centre might need particular training in the operation of certain packages used by that company; an accountancy graduate will still have to undertake several years of professional training to become familiar with all aspects of the profession. These graduates have already acquired a high level of general human capital but their efficiency and productivity can be enhanced by the acquisition of occupation-specific or firm-specific human capital. Human capital can be specific or general; the promotion of general human capital is the function of the education system whilst specific human capital is usually acquired by further training and on-the-job experience.

Education as Human Capital Investment

The possession of general human capital enhances the worker's productivity, increases the firm's output and thus justifies the payment of a higher salary. The benefits of an investment in human capital will accrue to well educated men or women through the additional earnings which they receive over their working life. Graduates are more likely to achieve management status than those without formal qualifications. They are likely to be in a job with good promotion prospects and where the salary will rise incrementally with age. The benefits of an investment in human capital are lucrative indeed.

The advantages of higher education are considerable and enduring, but at the point of decision these benefits are rather distant. For a school leaver the enhanced salary is some way off. An undergraduate programme must first be pursued, a job secured and seniority acquired before these higher earnings will be realized. Unlike the benefits though, the costs are immediate. Students embarking upon a degree programme will experience three years out of the labour market living on a student grant. They, or their parents and local education authorities, face direct costs in terms of their fees, their rent, living expenses, the cost of books and other essential study materials. Then there are indirect costs too. If young men or women take employment directly from school, they immediately start to earn a wage but by remaining in education, they forgo this opportunity. The wages sacrificed during the three years of study represent the opportunity cost of investing in human capital.

The decision to invest in human capital by remaining in higher education involves both costs and benefits. These cost and benefits can be depicted in Figure 5.2 below. A school leaver has the choice of two possible careers, clerical work or accountancy. If a clerical position can be obtained immediately upon leaving school without any further education or training, then the employee will start earning a salary at once. Clerical work will yield the higher rewards in the short term since the initial starting salary will be S_1. However the career progression is slight and by the age of retirement this salary will have risen – but only to a level of P.

Accountancy on the other hand involves three years' impoverishment on a student grant and then a further period as a trainee throughout which time the remuneration, which starts at a salary of S_2, falls below that in clerical work. Early in their career trainee accountants must accept lower earnings than clerical employees. The annual salaries of an accountant and a clerical worker are not equivalent until point R is reached. From that point onwards the accountant has the salary advantage and by retirement age is likely to have attained a salary of T.

This is substantially in excess of salary P which is the retirement salary for the clerical worker. The costs and benefits of these two occupations are distributed very differently over the worker's lifetime. Clerical employment brings immediate benefits by way of a salary and the worker is not required to make any investment in human capital after leaving secondary education. No direct costs are incurred but later in life the salary is lower than that earned in accountancy. The accountant makes an initial investment in human capital involving not only direct, but also indirect, costs since they lose the opportunity of immediate earnings. The benefits, however, accumulate as the accountant's career progresses.

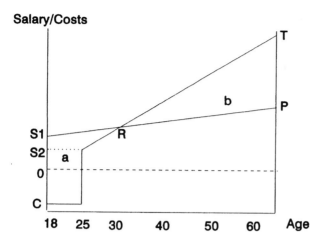

Figure 5.2: Human Capital Investment Decision

The costs of becoming an accountant are shown by the area CRS_1, or the area depicted by (a) in Figure 5.2. This area includes both the direct and the indirect costs of the extra years in education and training. If a young person decides to study at university then direct costs will be incurred. Fees must be paid, books purchased and living expenses provided for even though no income is being earned. These direct costs represent an annual outgoing from the student's budget, which is depicted by 0C in Figure 5.2. Since C lies below the zero line this represents a negative sum as the student's expenses exceed their income. 0C represents the sum of money which must be acquired annually if the student is to remain in higher education. The actual cost incurred by an individual student will vary depending upon their source of finance. In some cases generous parents agree to fund the student's living expenses in full whilst the fees are paid by the local education authority; in this situation the direct costs incurred by the student are reduced. In other cases the student is entirely dependent upon an inadequate maintenance grant and a student loan must be negotiated to cover the residual expenses. In Britain in the mid 1990s many students were taking out a loan during their three years of study. The direct costs of education must be covered either through gift, grant or loan to finance studies at university and in addition to these direct costs the student is forgoing the opportunity to earn a wage during these years in higher education. Area (a) also includes the loss of earnings to the workers during the period in further or higher education and the lower earnings during the early years of training. The lower starting salary of the trainee accountant is shown by S_2. It is not until point R that graduates find their salary equivalent to that earned by their classmates who entered employment straight from school. OS_1R represents the opportunity cost of an investment in human capital. Area (a) or CRS_1 includes the direct and the indirect costs of the human capital investment of studying at university. The benefits though are shown by area RTP, or area (b) in Figure 5.2. Both the accountant and the clerical employee earn identical salaries at point R. During later life though, the accountant's salary rises at a faster rate than that of the clerical worker. By retirement age the accountant is earning a salary of T whilst the clerical employee retires with a salary of P. In Figure 5.2 RTP, or area (b), therefore represents the salary benefit of choosing accountancy as a career.

The decision about an investment in human capital can be analysed in the usual neo-classical way of evaluating the costs against the benefits. In simple terms if area (b) is greater than area (a), then the benefits of accountancy outweigh the costs and the rational decision for this worker would be to study and train as an accountant. A more sophisticated analysis would take the interest rate into account in evaluating the gains from a human capital investment against other possible investment opportunities. However the essential point of weighing up costs against future benefits remains the same. Young people with parents prepared to finance their education and with reasonable confidence that they will secure a position in an accountancy firm after graduation will estimate that the costs of investing in human capital will be more than repaid by the benefits. The gains in later life will more than compensate for lower earnings in the training period. For some students though, the situation is rather different. Those with no parental support for their education and with little confidence in their later employment prospects will fear that the costs of their investment in human capital will outweigh the benefits. In this case area (a) is greater than area (b) and the rational agent will opt for immediate employment.

Men, Women and Human Capital Investment

These cost and benefit calculations depend crucially upon the worker's expectations about participation in paid work over the life cycle. For a school leaver who anticipates a continuous attachment to the labour market from leaving full-time education until retirement, accountancy is clearly the better option. The gains from the higher salary later in life are likely to outweigh the earnings lost in the immediate short term through the additional years spent in education and training; the investment in human capital will prove worthwhile. Men usually remain attached to the labour market throughout their working lives and for them an investment in human capital usually proves the rational choice. For women, though, the position in many countries is still rather different. Women are likely to take a career break and to find that their opportunities in paid employment are constrained by their domestic commitments, especially whilst their children are of pre-school age.

For workers who anticipate that their work history might be discontinuous, that they might move into and out of the labour market and have at least one period of non-participation in paid work, then the human capital calculations will work out rather differently. The potential gains from a higher salary look far more uncertain. Women often find that their lifetime earnings are reduced by the discontinuity in employment which usually follows childbirth. A few years might be lost from the labour market; skills, experience and seniority might be sacrificed once children are born. These factors will reduce the expected gains from human capital investment. For a woman these lost years will reduce her lifetime earnings. The future looks far less reliable and the potential benefits from an investment in human capital are far more tenuous for women than for men who usually anticipate continuous participation in the labour force.

For both men and women the costs of education and training are not only identical, but immediate and certain. A woman, considering an investment in her own human capital, faces the same costs as a man but the chances of the benefits proving to be equivalent are remote. The neo-classical calculations yield different results for men and women. Area (a) is identical for men and women, but area (b) is smaller for women than for men. The yield from a woman's investment in her own human capital is not likely to be as great as a man's and so women might refrain from making the initial outlay. Immediate employment could prove more attractive. Ironically perhaps women are deterred from investing in their own human capital since they expect to spend many years out of the workforce investing in the human capital of their children!

If the benefits for women are lower than for men, then human capital theory suggests that the rational choice for many women will be to opt for immediate employment. In this way they start earning before they become mothers. Clerical work offers higher rewards early in the life cycle, and it is at this stage that women find themselves free from domestic commitments and able to concentrate upon continuous employment. These early gains might seem very attractive since they are certain and achievable; once children are born paid work becomes much more uncertain and it is difficult to plan upon continuous employment. For some women area (a) will be larger than area (b) and so higher education will be abandoned. Women, it is argued, will tend to enter occupations where investments in human capital are not required.

Some economists have attempted to use human capital theory in this way to provide an explanation of gender segregation in employment but this approach has subsequently been challenged by feminist economists. The argument suggests that more men than women invest in human capital and so they will be found concentrated in occupations requiring degrees and other qualifications whilst women will opt for immediate employment to maximize their earnings potential before their career is disrupted by family formation. It is argued that women and men are found in different areas of employment due to the investments which they have been prepared to make in their own human capital. Indeed 20 years ago there was a considerable discrepancy between the number of men and women enrolled on full-time courses in British universities; over 60 per cent of undergraduate students were men in 1970 and this pattern was replicated all the way down the educational spectrum (CSO 1995). The graduates of the 1970s are still in the workforce in the 1990s; in 1992, 12 per cent of men of working age but only 7 per cent of women had a degree (Department of Education 1993). The investment in women's human capital was substantially less than the investment in men's human capital. This might have been due to women themselves making a rational choice concerning the costs and benefits of post-compulsory education or it might have reflected the views of their parents that it was a waste of time to spend money educating a girl.

The picture, though, has changed considerably since 1970. Women and men are now nearly numerically equal in British universities as indeed they are in the labour market. With women accounting for nearly half of British undergraduates, investments are certainly being made in their human capital. Those women with higher education qualifications are far more likely to work full time, even after children are born, than mothers with no qualifications at all (Harrop and Moss 1993). The investment in human capital increases their earnings potential and encourages these women to remain in full-time employment to reap the benefits from their qualifications. Women with no investment in human capital are more likely to withdraw from the labour force after children are born or to return only on a part-time basis.

Human capital investment is increasing the disparities between different groups of women but it no longer accounts for occupational segregation in employment. Despite the increased participation of women in the working population, gender segregation in employment remains as strong as ever. Denmark has a particularly high rate of economic activity for women yet women remain heavily concentrated in the service sector of the economy (Maruani 1992). The changing pattern of women's workforce participation has certainly increased the benefits to be derived from human capital investment. Women in the 1990s will be in the labour market for much of their lives, accruing work experience and using the skills which they have acquired through training. The salary benefits of education to a woman are higher than they used to be and consequently women are more prepared to invest in human capital. But women's willingness to invest in higher education has not resulted in a more even distribution of male and female workers throughout the economy. Horizontal segregation persists even though women now have higher educational qualifications than before.

Human Capital Investment and the Deterioration of Skills

It is not simply the acquisition of human capital which affects occupational choice; its retention might also prove influential (Polachek 1976). In the past women might have chosen occupations for which higher qualifications were not an entry requirement to avoid the direct and indirect costs of university education, but alternatively female graduates might seek out jobs which will not penalize them too heavily for discontinuous employment. This explanation of occupational segregation looks more plausible since in some occupations where an initial investment in human capital is necessary, women do form the majority of the workforce. In medical and other health services women account for 82 per cent of employees whilst they represent 72 per cent of the workforce in education. Initial training though is required for nurses, doctors, physiotherapists and teachers. In all of these occupations, prospective workers are required to make an investment in their human capital which will involve a sacrifice in terms of immediate earnings. Teacher training involves a three year degree course plus a one year postgraduate certificate; nursing requires several years as a student nurse with low earnings throughout this period. Both of these occupations have always involved a substantial initial investment in human capital.

Women have always, and still do, flock to occupations like teaching and nursing even though significant investments are required in human capital. The explanation might be that in nursing or in teaching the skills acquired through that initial training do not deteriorate significantly over the life cycle. Once a student has learnt the basic elements of educational psychology or the fundamental principles of postoperative care, then these will not alter significantly over the following 40 years. It would then be a rational choice for those anticipating intermittent participation in the workforce to opt for jobs with low penalties for discontinuous employment. The drop in earnings resulting from the career break will thus be minimized so that the benefits from a human capital investment will more than outweigh the costs. Rational actors, anticipating a discontinuous career, will not simply avoid all occupations requiring initial investment in human capital, but rather, they will be very selective in choosing those routes where the skills are perceived as less likely to deteriorate during spells of absence from paid employment. Some skills might be perceived as more likely to deteriorate than others and the penalties in those occupations might well deter women from embarking upon such a career path whilst for other occupations the skill loss from a career break might be minimal. Women then will not choose occupations where no investment in human capital is required, but instead will be selective in assessing which skills and training qualifications it is worthwhile to acquire. This assessment will, it is argued, result in women congregating in particular sectors of the economy which will thus employ a predominantly female workforce. It is argued therefore that a concern about the deterioration of human capital will help to explain occupational sex segregation in employment.

This analysis of occupational choice in terms of the expected deterioration of skills is more plausible than the original human capital theory but it still presents several problems. Women today are likely to spend a large part of their life in the labour force since a reduction in fertility rates and the opportunities for part-time employment both have reduced the length of time taken out of paid employment. Any deterioration in human capital nowadays will be far less prominent than it was in previous years. Well-qualified women are likely to spend less time out of the labour market than women without qualifications; for them the loss of skills is likely to be slight indeed. But segregation is no less prominent then it was 30 years ago. Women still enter traditionally female areas of work. Furthermore earnings in the traditionally female sectors of the economy are substantially lower than those in male dominated employment. In fact occupational segregation in employment has been found to be one of the most powerful explanations of the gender earnings gap.

Since women earn less in women's jobs it is difficult to provide a rational explanation for their occupational choice. If women become solicitors the rewards will be far higher than if they become nurses. In Britain in 1994 the weekly earnings of a female solicitor were £490.60, comparing very favourably with those of a nurse at £311.60. Even a woman who was anticipating discontinuous employment would be unlikely to find the financial benefits of nursing as a career greater than those of the legal profession. It is almost inconceivable that the skills loss from a few years' career break could be sufficient to close such a significant earnings gap. A solicitor, even with several years out of the workforce, is likely to accumulate higher total earnings in the remaining decades in employment than a nurse can ever expect. If women enter traditional female sectors of employment, then in the present circumstances, they will earn less; they will not maximize their lifetime earnings by choosing women's jobs (England 1982). Entering a predominantly female sector is unlikely to prove a rational choice for those who have invested in their own human capital and yet many women still follow this course. Human capital theory in itself does not provide an adequate explanation of occupational segregation in terms of personal preferences based upon rational choice. Social factors, trade union pressure and the role of the state have all contributed to occupational segregation by gender.

Training, Vocational Education and Experience

General education helps a woman or a man to become a more productive worker but it is not the only way to acquire human capital. Training, vocational education and experience too can help to make a worker more productive. Individuals can learn important work skills whilst they are actually on the job. This learning can be acquired through vocational education on a day release basis, through a formal training programme or by the constant repetition of a task under the guidance of a more experienced colleague. Many valuable skills can best be learnt while actually in employment and these skills will form part of the worker's occupation-specific or firm-specific human capital. The investment in these types of human capital can be made by either the employee or the employer since both will stand to gain from the process.

In many occupations young workers will be employed in apprenticeship or trainee positions. These posts have been created deliberately to provide an opportunity for new employees to learn how to become more efficient and productive. Trainees will be given the opportunity to go on courses, at their own or their employer's expense, to help them to learn about the various aspects of the business. The fees for these courses are often paid by the employer, especially if they are likely to provide the worker with firm-specific skills. The employer will capture the benefits of the training by having a more productive employee on the staff and the specific nature of the skills means there is little danger that the worker can use the training to benefit a competitor. Unlike the decision to remain in education, the trainee will not incur direct costs, which will be borne by the employer, but only indirect costs, or opportunity costs, due to the lower salary which their position commands.

It is rather different with occupation-specific or general skills. The risk here is that, once trained, the employee will prove more productive to any employer in the industry. A GNVQ in retailing is useful to any retailer, not just to one particular employer. In such circumstances the worker might be asked to bear the cost of the course whilst the employer allows them the time off for study; since both parties benefit, they must share the costs. The worker here is incurring two types of cost – the direct cost of the course fees and the indirect cost of the lower salary. The trainees' salaries though are likely to more than cover the course fees and other study expenses so, unlike full-time students, they will earn a net income whilst at the same time they are investing in their own human capital. The cost of the investment in human capital is the lower salary in the current period whilst the benefit is the higher salary which can be expected in the future. A training contract might also include provision for on-the-job training. The trainee might be required to move between departments in order to become familiar with a variety of aspects of the job. Once again a trainee will often be earning a lower salary than other workers and this will represent an opportunity cost to the trainee through loss of earnings. Both parties though stand to gain from the training. The employee is being offered an accelerated route into management positions whilst the employer will gain a more efficient worker in the long term and be receiving good value for money whilst the trainee remains on low wages. Once again there is a short-term cost to the worker in return for the prospect of benefits in the longer term.

The benefits both to the employer and the employee will depend upon the length of time the worker expects to remain in that occupation and the extent to which skills deteriorate if employment is interrupted. Both of these factors will vary by gender. Women are more likely than men to experience discontinuous employment so their training might be regarded as a more insecure investment. There are in fact gender differences in the funding of training. For male employees 75 per cent have their training funded by their employer or their prospective employer whilst such funding applies to only 65 per cent of women (Department of Employment 1995). However, well-qualified women with a high level of training and skills are those who are now least likely to interrupt their careers for family reasons (Brannen et al. 1994). The investment which they and others have made in their human capital is affecting their participation patterns. Firms too are finding ways to try and retain these valuable members of staff and to minimize the skills loss. The career break schemes introduced by two of the major clearing banks in Britain encourage women to keep in touch with developments in their profession. These firms have recognized that both they and their employees have made a substantial investment in human capital through training programmes and they are anxious to retain the services of these skilled workers. Employers are most likely to introduce family friendly policies like workplace nurseries where the replacement costs of training new staff are high (Holtermann 1995). Thus human capital investment is linked to equal opportunities policies, but the gains so far have been confined to a relatively small group of well-qualified, high-earning women.

Differences are developing between certain groups of women. Some women will be viewed as good investments by employers. They will be trained, will earn a higher salary and will be more likely to continue participating in the labour force. The benefits of the investment in their human capital will outweigh the costs for both the employer and the employee. Women with a lower level of educational attainment will be viewed as a poor investment and once in employment they will receive little opportunity for training. These women are most likely to interrupt their employment when children are born since the opportunity cost of their labour is low and upon re-entry to the labour market they will be confined to low paid, low status, part-time jobs in which the wages prove insufficient to cover the costs of childcare. For women without qualifications the market costs of childcare are rarely outweighed by their low earnings in part-time jobs. Employers will do little to promote family friendly policies for these workers. As these women lack human capital, employers do not find it worthwhile to incur the costs involved in childcare schemes in order to retain their services. Unskilled workers are cheap and easy to replace. For these women, their lack of skills is trapping them in a cycle of disadvantage.

As a final point human capital theory rests upon the assumption that full-time household responsibilities will lead to a deterioration of those skill levels acquired through training. Some types of skill might be perceived to deteriorate faster than others but the fundamental assumption is that a spell of full-time homemaking will reduce, rather than enhance, a worker's productivity. In fact this point is highly debatable. Homemakers could be adding to their human capital and acquiring skills which are valuable, but undervalued, in the labour market. Negotiation, time management and prioritization of tasks are all important skills for those occupying management positions; yet they are also essential skills for successful parenting. These skills might be enhanced by a few years of experience in a domestic role making returning workers more efficient and productive after their career break. But employers' perceptions of skills tend to be socially constructed and to reflect a belief that only labour market activity confers skills.

Alternative Explanations of Occupational Segregation

Explanations of occupational segregation such as human capital theory which focus upon free choice often overlook the strength of other considerations. Social exclusion can be a powerful influence. In a predominantly male occupation a woman might feel uncomfortable and within corporations the majority of the managers are still men. Management involves communication and decision taking and this process is facilitated between those who share a common social background. Male managers find it easier to communicate with other men. Corporate culture can thus prove exclusionary for women (Kanter 1977). Sexual harassment too can make a woman feel socially isolated in a male environment. If female Bar students face sexual harassment in chambers yet pupillages are an essential step in the training of those wishing to practise at the Bar, then some women might decide to seek employment in other occupations. It has indeed been found that women in traditionally male occupations are more likely to report sexual harassment than those in female occupations and it has been suggested that harassment can be used to maintain social closure against women (Walby 1990). The under-representation of women in some occupations presents a further barrier to the entry of other women. In such professions there are few role models for young girls to follow and the social isolation which such a choice of occupation might entail can, in itself, prove a significant barrier to entry (Kanter 1977).

The choice which a man or woman makes concerning his or her occupation is heavily constrained by social factors and expectations. In contemporary Britain the bulk of the caring for young children and the elderly falls to women. Consequently women often experience a discontinuous career path, will work part time for some of their working life and often retire from employment at an earlier age than men in order to care for an elderly relative. These constraints on labour market participation are often considered by women in their initial choice of occupation. With low levels of good quality childcare in Britain many women recognize that they will probably spend several years working part time. On this basis certain occupations look particularly attractive since part-time work is far easier to obtain in some occupations than in others. Different constraints face men who usually anticipate continuous participation in the working population, often expecting to provide financial support for dependents. Social expectations affect the occupational decisions which women and men make, reinforcing gender segregation in the labour market.

Trade unions too have in the past tried to restrict women's access to certain skilled jobs. Many nineteenth-century craft unions excluded women totally. Until the middle of the Second World War the Amalgamated Engineering Union (AEU) excluded women from membership. The first women were admitted as members in 1943 but were to be confined to certain areas of work. Gradually during the twentieth century exclusion has been replaced by segregation. The government too has co-operated with trade unions to exclude women from certain occupations. During the Second World War legislation was passed limiting women's employment in the munitions industry to the duration of the war only. Once hostilities ceased women were to be expelled from this type of work (Walby 1990). In these ways the government and the trade union movement have been reinforcing gender segregation at work.

Summary

Men and women are found doing different jobs in separate sectors of the economy. The division of labour in the labour market is marked indeed and persists even in countries where women have a high rate of participation. This segregation in employment could arise as a result of factors on either the supply or the demand side of the labour market. Employers might be discriminating against certain groups of workers or employees could simply be choosing occupations where their own sex predominates. Human capital theory evaluates the costs and benefits of a person acquiring qualifications, training and experience which will make them more efficient and productive as a worker. It offers a supply side explanation of gender segregation in employment through differences in the benefits which men and women expect to receive from a given investment in their own human capital. The simple prediction is that men will be more inclined to invest in their own education since continuous employment will make them net beneficiaries of this process over their full working life. They will therefore enter occupations for which higher education qualifications are required. Women, though, anticipating discontinuous employment will find the benefits less reliable and might be deterred from remaining in education. They will therefore seek jobs requiring a lower level of qualifications.

These straightforward predictions no longer conform to the realities of today. The picture has become more complicated. Women spend more years in the workforce than they did 30 years ago and they account for about 50 per cent of undergraduate students in British universities. They are investing in human capital but gender segregation in employment persists. Looking to evidence concerning the deterioration of skills and the occupations women enter does not seem to provide a satisfactory explanation of women's occupational distribution based upon rational choice. It is surely more lucrative to enter a well-paid occupation even if one anticipated discontinuous employment than to opt for a low paid job. Training and vocational qualifications are likely to widen disparities between well-qualified and unskilled women. Equal opportunities policies will prove a worthwhile investment for employers only for those women with specific human capital since their replacement will prove costly for the firm. The investment in family friendly policies is reinforcing the investment which has already been made in highly skilled women to give them considerable advantages in labour markets. These privileges are not enjoyed by the majority of female workers. Low skill, part-time workers are easy to replace; nothing has been invested in their firm-specific skills and so no further investment will be made to facilitate their employment. Not only are there differences between women and men but there is also considerable divergence in the position of those women who do possess human capital and those who do not.

6 Unemployment
Is it a Man's Problem?

Introduction. Does unemployment matter? What is unemployment? Measuring unemployment. Unemployment in Britain. Hidden unemployment. Women's unemployment and economic policy. Survey-based measures of unemployment. Summary.

Introduction

The two decades following the end of the Second World War now look like a remarkable interlude in economic history. Throughout these decades the British economy achieved sustained economic growth and the mass unemployment of the interwar years seemed to have disappeared for good. Recorded unemployment never rose above 700 000 workers, or 3 per cent of the working population, and indeed the 1950s and 1960s were decades characterized by labour market shortages and unfilled vacancies rather than the dole queues of the 1930s. After these two successful decades of full employment, it came as something of a shock when, in the mid 1970s, unemployment in Britain rose above one million workers for the first time since the outbreak of the Second World War. Since then it has never fallen below this level. The jobless count has risen to new heights with each recession only to fall back less markedly when the economy recovers again. Unemployment has thus been on an upward trend.

The working population includes both men and women; the terms on which they enter the labour force, their likelihood of becoming unemployed and their well-being in the face of this eventuality are different. Britain is unusual amongst the developed countries of the world in that the rate of unemployment amongst women is lower than that amongst men. In October 1994, 2.5 million workers were registered as unemployed in the United Kingdom. The 1.9 million men included in this claimant count of unemployment represented nearly 12 per cent of the male working population whilst the 0.6 million women accounted for less than 5 per cent of the female labour force. Three-quarters of the claimant unemployed were men, yet women constitute over half of the adult population, 44 per cent of the working population and 50 per cent of the employed workers. There is a discrepancy between women's representation in the adult population – and indeed in the working population – and their chance of becoming registered as unemployed. Women are under-represented in the unemployment statistics.

83

Whilst this under-representation is not in dispute, its interpretation can be decidedly ambiguous. Since the unemployed usually experience a decline in their income and their economic status, women might appear at first sight to have an advantage in this area. Men form the majority of the unemployed whilst women's employment is on the increase; women would seem to be enjoying the social and economic benefits which accompany employment. Unemployment becomes a man's problem. On the other hand if the statistics merely under-record women's unemployment, then the situation is rather different. In this case their joblessness is more invisible than men's, less likely to be covered by unemployment benefit or targeted by government policies and possibly of longer duration than male unemployment. The hidden unemployment of women then makes this issue more difficult to tackle.

Although more men than women are registered as unemployed, since the 1970s the level of unemployment has risen for both genders. Many reasons have been advanced by economists to explain the relentless rise in the unemployment figures; de-industrialization, the oil crises of the 1970s and early 1980s, and the rigidity of labour markets have featured in these analyses. These factors do not apply equally to men and women. Increased flexibility in labour markets might well have a greater impact upon women's employment than upon men's since women are more likely to accept part-time jobs; those seeking part-time jobs are not included in the unemployment statistics. The decline of manufacturing industry, on the other hand, has resulted in the loss of about 1.5 million jobs, most of which were occupied by male workers and these workers will all appear in the jobless figures. Gender-based occupational segregation is a significant feature in industrialized countries whilst the care of young children is regarded in Britain as a private responsibility falling mainly upon their mothers. Women and men show significant variations in the ways in which they engage in productive activity and these differences affect their representation in the unemployment statistics. To understand the changes which have occurred in unemployment in Britain over the last two decades, the factors which have affected men's and women's employment and unemployment must be considered. Since the causes of male and female unemployment can be different, separate policies are appropriate to get men and women back into work so that the economy can make full use of its productive labour resources.

Does Unemployment Matter?

Every economy has limited resources of land, labour and capital with which to produce goods and services for consumption. These resources are scarce in that they impose a constraint upon the living standards of the citizens and there is a maximum level of output which this economy cannot exceed. It is therefore important that an economy makes full and efficient use of all its productive resources; that factories are working, that assembly lines are in full production, that office space is utilized and that men and women are productively employed. If labour resources are not employed their output is lost for ever. The standard of living in the current period is lower than it could be, were resources to be fully employed.

The level of unemployment shows how many men and women in the working population are unemployed. It provides an indication of these wasted resources. Table 6.1 shows how many workers have been registered as unemployed in the United Kingdom since 1971. The level of unemployment in the United Kingdom has risen significantly so that by 1991 there were three people out of work for every one person unemployed in 1971. The waste of scarce productive resources has become more significant over the last three decades. Although there are always more men than women registered as unemployed, both men and women have been affected by this rising trend in unemployment. Between 1976 and 1986 the number of unemployed women showed a threefold increase whilst for men unemployment only doubled. As the recessions of the late 1970s and the early 1980s took their toll on employment opportunities the level of female unemployment was rising at a faster rate than that of male unemployment.

Table 6.1: The Level of Unemployment
United Kingdom (thousands)

Year	Total	Men	Women
1971	751	647	104
1976	1302	1006	296
1981	2520	1843	677
1986	3289	2253	1037
1991	2292	1734	552
1995 (Dec)	2228	1707	521

Source: *Employment Gazette*, various issues

It is only when resources are fully and efficiently employed that the economy is operating on its production possibility curve, producing the highest level of output of which it is capable. Unemployment therefore means that productive labour resources are not being used efficiently. As workers are laid off from motor vehicle production lines, there are not as many British cars available for purchase; as nurses find it harder to get work, waiting lists in our hospitals grow longer and as gas showrooms reduce staff, customers perceive a fall in the standard of services. Rising unemployment can reduce living standards and it is not just the unemployed who find their living standards cut; everyone suffers because the economy's output is thereby reduced.

In 1992 Gross Domestic Product in the United Kingdom was £514.6 billion at current market prices. These goods and services were produced by 90 per cent of the country's working population since nearly 10 per cent were registered as unemployed. Had all these unemployed workers been able to find suitable jobs and assuming that they were just as productive as those employees in employment, then the United Kingdom would have increased its output of goods and services by about 10 per cent. The 2.7 million workers who were without jobs in 1992 could have added an extra £50 billion worth of goods and services to our total output. The British population went without these goods and services and this reduced our average income per head by approximately £1000 in that year alone. This represents a considerable loss of output, which can never be recovered. It is of course unlikely that all the working population will be in employment; even in the best years of the 1950s and 1960s there were still 200 000 workers out of a job, representing approximately 1 per cent of the labour force. Were it possible to reduce unemployment once again to this level then the annual value of the lost output would be a mere £100 per head. In the 1990s though it might be more realistic to think in terms of reducing unemployment to 5 per cent of the working population and this would then produce an annual gain of £500 in per capita annual income. Such is the cost of the wasted resources.

The rise in unemployment affects other areas of the economy too. If there are fewer men and women in work then the government's tax revenue is reduced. The government levies taxes upon income, upon profits and upon consumption spending and in all these areas the tax receipts will be lower than they would be were resources fully employed. The average citizen thereby loses because the government has to reduce its expenditure on the provision of services. The health service or educational facilities find their budgets reduced due to the lack of public funds. The alternative is that the government has to find different sources of revenue and raise taxes in some other sectors of the economy to compensate for the loss of revenue. The tax burden is thus shifted onto others.

Unemployment also imposes significant demands upon public expenditure. Since the introduction of the Welfare State in Britain after the Second World War, the unemployed have been entitled to support from the state. The philosophy which lay behind the introduction of National Insurance was that unemployment was a risk to which some groups of workers were vulnerable through no fault of their own and the costs of that unemployment should not fall at random upon the unemployed themselves but should be borne by all employed workers. The unemployed therefore are entitled to benefits for their support during their period of unemployment and the payment of these benefits imposes a significant cost upon taxpayers. Two studies undertaken independently by the Adam Smith Institute and the Unemployment Unit estimated this cost at nearly £21 billion in 1991 (McLaughlin 1992).

In addition to these material costs of unemployment, there are also personal costs to the unemployed themselves and their families. The unemployed workers can quickly lose their skills and become discouraged from seeking work. Unemployment then becomes harder to eradicate. An unemployed worker also loses a sense of personal identity and worth; in our western society people perceive themselves to be defined by what they do. A worker who does nothing can very easily be equated with a non-person! Increased levels of mental illness, a deterioration in the health status of the unemployed, a rise in marital tension and greater social isolation have all been suggested as the consequences of job insecurity and unemployment (Gallie et al. 1993). If men and women are without work, it is a waste of our scarce resources. The economy as a whole bears the costs of this unemployment through lower living standards, cuts in the provision of government services, changes in the tax burden and the increased social costs. Unemployment is therefore a significant issue.

What is Unemployment?

Economics textbooks define unemployment as occurring when persons capable of and willing to work are not currently in paid employment. This definition appears quite straightforward; those who want a job but have not found one are the unemployed. In practice though, it is not so easy to translate this theoretical definition into figures. The unemployment statistics do not always reflect the textbook concept accurately. It is difficult to distinguish those to be included from those to be excluded from the unemployment count and both the presentation and measurement of unemployment can prove contentious. These interrelated issues arise in connection with unemployment in the workforce as a whole, but they can also affect the unemployment statistics for men and women in quite different ways. The accuracy of the statistics for men and women can thus vary.

The question of whom to include in the unemployment count is of primary concern. The standard definition refers to those capable of and willing to work and this group needs to be delineated before the unemployed can be identified. The distinction between paid and unpaid work is critical here. In the early years of the nineteenth century, the difference between paid employment and unpaid domestic work was not significant in the statistics; it was assumed that all members of the household were engaged in productive activities in one way or another. Whilst men undertook waged work, women would often take in home work for piece rates as well as caring for the household, and children too would have a productive role to play. The first census of 1841 marked a significant change in our perceptions of work and non-work. Women who were engaged in housework and childcare were to be excluded from the occupational classification. Instructions on the Census form itself reminded the householders that they should not enter returns concerning any female relative engaged entirely in domestic duties within the household (Hakim 1993).

From then onwards the housewife was not in the working population and the common perception was that she did not work! Anyone who has performed the role of homemaker for any length of time can quickly dispel this illusion; housework and childcare are in fact very demanding tasks which can occupy more hours than a full working week. Yet the housewife became 'economically inactive' as far as economists and statisticians were concerned. She was not to be included amongst those capable of and willing to work and, as she was not in the working population, she could not be unemployed either. This distinction persists today. Only job seekers within the working population are considered as unemployed.

A gender issue arises here. Men usually participate in the working population from the time they leave full-time education until they reach retirement age; if they lose their job they appear in the unemployment statistics. For women though the position is rather different. They often move into and out of the labour force several times within their working life. Spells in employment often alternate with intervals of non-participation especially whilst children are young. Their pattern of labour force participation is different from the traditional male pattern and this can affect the representation of women in the unemployment statistics. Women who are, or have been, working as full-time homemakers are non participants in the working population. Full-time domestic responsibilities constitute a brief interlude in a woman's working life in the mid 1990s. Many women combine their domestic responsibilities with paid employment and even those mothers who withdraw from the labour force completely during their children's pre-school years usually return once compulsory education begins. A common pattern for women is to move between employment and non-participation several times in their working lives as family circumstances permit. When they seek to re-enter the labour market though, any delay which they experience in finding suitable employment will not affect the unemployment figures. As re-entrants to the labour force, these women are excluded from the claimant statistics. The recording of female unemployment thus understates the number of women actually capable of and willing to work yet who have not found suitable paid employment. There is a discrepancy between the textbook definition of unemployment and the government statistics which attempt to record the phenomenon. Since women account for the majority of the re-entrants to the labour force, women's unemployment is significantly reduced by this discrepancy whilst the recording of male unemployment is scarcely affected at all.

Measuring Unemployment

The data on unemployment is usually presented in one of two ways: reference is made either to the level of unemployment or to the rate of unemployment. Both of these measures are useful as an indicator of the extent to which labour resources are being utilized and each of them proves most appropriate in certain situations. The number of men and women, who are defined as being unemployed at a particular point in time, will show the level of unemployment. Table 6.1 shows the level of unemployment in the United Kingdom between 1971 and 1995. In 1995, for example, there were 1.7 million men and 0.5 million women unemployed (Department of Employment 1995). This figure, despite its inadequacies, is useful in assessing the extent of the wasted labour resources and in providing an estimate of the jobs which would need to be created to achieve 'full employment'.

However, the actual number of people out of work can be misleading in certain situations. Using this measure makes it difficult to draw comparisons between countries and to evaluate the performance of the economy as the working population changes. For example, in 1990 Denmark had only 0.26 million people unemployed whilst the United Kingdom had 2.3 million. Simply knowing that Denmark does not have as many people unemployed as the United Kingdom does not provide sufficient information for comparing Denmark's economic performance with that of the United Kingdom. If there were 2.3 million workers unemployed in a small country like Denmark, this would be a serious problem indeed. With a working population of less than three million workers it would represent almost total unemployment! Far more appropriate for the purposes of comparison would be the rate of unemployment, that is unemployment expressed as a percentage of the working population. In 1990 Denmark had 8 per cent of its working population registered as unemployed whilst the corresponding figure for the United Kingdom was 6 per cent. Over the last 30 years the female working population has grown in size whilst there has been little change in the male labour force. Since the male working population has varied very little over the last 25 years, as men have lost their jobs the male rate of unemployment has risen accordingly. The rate of female unemployment though has not changed in line with the increase in the level of women's unemployment. Even though more women have become unemployed since 1970, the rate of female unemployment has only increased when women's unemployment has risen at a faster rate than the female working population. As more women have been moving into the working population this change has distorted the picture for women.

The statistics on unemployment can be compiled in one of two ways; either one counts those who are out of work and are claiming benefit, that is the unemployed claimants, or else one adopts a survey approach to ascertain whether those without work would accept a job offer. The first method is relatively simple to apply in that the government has these statistics readily available. The problem, however, is that it focuses upon claiming benefit rather than an individual's work status. Some people might be fully entitled to benefit and yet have no real intention of accepting a job; they will nevertheless appear in the unemployment statistics. On the other hand, some who do not qualify for benefit will be actively looking for work and they will be omitted from the figures. The claimant count can thus distort the true extent of unemployment. Since there are considerable differences between men and women regarding their benefit status the claimant count often involves a greater degree of distortion for women's than men's unemployment. Survey-based measures of unemployment provide a more accurate picture of the unemployed, reducing the gender distortions. These survey figures are on a comparable basis with those published by other countries, thus enabling international comparisons to be drawn. Although there is some difference in the figures obtained from these two approaches, both data sets tend to present a similar picture; unemployment in Britain has fluctuated with the state of the economy but the overall trend has been towards higher unemployment amongst both men and women.

Unemployment in Britain

Whilst the rate of unemployment in Britain over the postwar period has displayed significant cyclical fluctuations, it has been on an overall upward trend. In the 1950s and 1960s the rate of unemployment fluctuated between 1 per cent and 3 per cent of the working population depending on the state of the economy. As the 1970s began the overall rate of unemployment fell to 2.6 per cent during 1973 when the British economy experienced the 'Barber boom', the last attempt by a British government to adopt the Keynesian techniques of demand reflation. After the OPEC oil price rise of December 1973, the industrialized economies of Western Europe experienced a recession and the rate of unemployment climbed quite steeply. In Britain the rate of unemployment rose above 5 per cent and despite a mild recovery in the late 1970s unemployment remained high throughout the remainder of the decade. The early 1980s brought a further recession attributable to the second OPEC oil shock, the high rate of exchange for sterling and perhaps to the government's stringent monetary policy. The rate of unemployment rose yet again to a new postwar record of 12.5 per cent or three million workers out of work on recorded figures by 1982.

Table 6.2: Men's and Women's Rate of Unemployment
United Kingdom, per cent

| Year | Rate of Unemployment | |
	Men	Women
1973	3.5	1.0
1976	7.0	3.1
1979	6.5	3.7
1982	15.5	8.3
1990	7.6	3.6
1993	14.0	5.6
1995 (Dec)	10.8	4.3

Source: *Employment Gazette*, various issues

The late 1980s was a successful period for the British economy, when it enjoyed a period of sustained economic growth and the rate of unemployment fell back – but only to 5 per cent of the working population. The very low rates of unemployment experienced during the postwar reconstruction in the 1950s were not to be retrieved in the 1980s despite the widely proclaimed Thatcher economic miracle. By the early 1990s the British economy was on the downturn once again and unemployment rose, reaching 10.4 per cent by 1993. Overall two points emerge: firstly the rate of unemployment in Britain is higher in the 1990s than it was 30 years earlier and secondly the rate of unemployment has fluctuated over the Trade Cycle, falling slightly in a boom and rising again once the economy moves into recession. These general trends are illustrated by Table 6.2 which shows the rate of unemployment for men and women in the United Kingdom based upon the claimant unemployed.

The pattern is the same for both men and women; unemployment is on a rising trend and is cyclical. But here the similarity ends. Throughout booms and slumps alike, the rate of claimant unemployment for men has always been higher than that for women. The 'Barber boom' of 1973 reduced unemployment with the rate of male unemployment falling to 3.5 per cent whilst, for women, only 1 per cent were unemployed. As the British economy moved into recession in the mid 1970s following the first OPEC price shock, the rate of unemployment rose. By 1976 7 per cent of the male labour force were unemployed whilst unemployed women accounted for 3 per cent of the female working population. In the 1970s during booms and recessions, the rate of male unemployment was more than twice as high as female unemployment. This pattern is unusual; Britain is amongst a very few developed countries of the world where the rate of male unemployment exceeds female. This discrepancy has persisted through the varied fortunes of the British economy in the 1980s. The recession of the early 1980s raised the men's rate of unemployment to 15.5 per cent whilst that for women increased to 8.3 per cent. The boom of the late 1980s reduced the rate of unemployment for both men and women but still left a significant gap between the two.

Hidden Unemployment

The claimant count tends to misrepresent the rate of unemployment in the economy. It will not include people returning to the labour force, those seeking part-time work, men above the age of 60, women who pay reduced rate National Insurance contributions or those who would like full-time employment but can only find a part-time job. Since 1979 the government has made many changes to the eligibility criteria and most of these changes have served to reduce the rate of unemployment. Estimates have suggested that were all the registered and unregistered unemployed to be included in the statistics, then unemployment in the 1990s in the United Kingdom would be approaching four million workers (McLaughlin 1992).

Women in Britain have significantly increased their participation in paid employment over the last two decades such that they now account for half of all employees in employment, yet they are still under-represented amongst the unemployed. As the unemployed become dependent upon state benefit for their support, they fall amongst the low income groups in our society. If there are fewer women than men amongst the unemployed this might appear to reflect well upon their economic status. A low rate of unemployment might appear as advantageous to women. Unfortunately, though, it is the statistics which are misleading. Women in Britain are not less likely than men to be without jobs when they seek them; they are merely less likely to appear in the unemployment statistics.

The claimant count understates the overall rate of unemployment in the economy, but the degree of distortion is more serious in the case of female than male unemployment. Women are significantly less likely than men to claim benefit when they are without jobs. Their unemployment remains hidden. A typical work history for a woman differs from a man's in two significant respects: women are likely to spend time out of the labour force and they are likely to work part time. Both of these factors affect women's representation in the unemployment statistics. Women who take a period out of the paid labour force in order to care for their pre-school children or elderly dependents will form a significant proportion of the returners to the labour market. Yet as re-entrants to the workforce these job seekers are unable to claim benefit. Men seldom take career breaks and so the measurement of male unemployment is scarcely affected by this omission.

Many of the new employment opportunities which have arisen in Britain during the 1980s have been for part-time workers. The overwhelming majority of part-timers have always been women since many women find part-time work an acceptable way of combining domestic responsibilities with paid employment. Part-time work for women is a typical British compromise! If women are more willing than men to consider these vacancies, then this helps to explain both the rising employment of women and their lower rate of unemployment. Those seeking part-time positions qualify neither for benefit nor for inclusion in the claimant count. Part-time work accounted for the employment of 46 per cent of all employed women in Britain in 1994 and many of these women would not be able to accept full-time jobs. A major category of women's employment renders them invisible when unemployed. Part-time work accounts for only 7 per cent of male employment; it has an extremely marginal impact upon men's employment and unemployment. Many more women than men are thus excluded from the claimant count for this reason.

The Welfare State was established in the late 1940s based on the gendered assumptions prevalent at that time about men's and women's role in the economy. Men were seen as the family provider, engaging throughout their working lives in paid employment and so their income, upon which the household was assumed to depend, required protection against the risk of unemployment. The assumptions about a married woman's role were very different. As Chapter 1 has already shown, after the end of the Second World War women were expected to return to domestic duties to service the needs of their husbands, the current workers, and to produce and rear their children, the workers of the future. These assumptions concerning the distinctive role which men and women were expected to play in the postwar economy affected the arrangements for unemployment insurance. Under the new National Insurance scheme a woman's entitlement to benefit was through her husband's contributions and married women in paid employment were even allowed to opt for reduced rate National Insurance contributions.

These married women were then denied access to certain benefits in their own right. They were not entitled to unemployment benefit and so would not appear amongst the claimant unemployed even if they had lost their job or were actively seeking work. The right of married women to opt for reduced rate contributions was not discontinued until 1977 and so even in the 1990s there are still some married women in the labour force who are paying the reduced rate contributions. They are not entitled to benefit and so they will not appear in the unemployment statistics should they become unemployed.

Women's Unemployment and Economic Policy

Whilst the claimant count undoubtedly distorts the extent of unemployment for both women and men, the degree of misrepresentation is more serious for women. Men are more likely than women to claim benefit and thus the statistics present a more accurate picture of men's unemployment. Since economists and politicians are heavily reliant upon published data sets, the under-recording of women's unemployment presents a serious issue. Government policies have been focused upon male unemployment, upon removing the barriers which prevent men from finding paid employment. As the data for female unemployment is known to be unreliable, women have not been accorded the same attention. The assumption has been either that they too would benefit from policies which were primarily designed to get men back into employment, or that women's unemployment, at a lower rate, was a less serious problem than that of the male income earner.

If Britain is to make full use of its labour resources it is important to recognize the extent of women's unemployment and underemployment. The barriers which impede a woman's entry into the labour market can differ significantly from those which a man faces. Women work in different sectors of the economy, have heavier domestic responsibilities than men, earn lower wage rates than men and face direct and indirect discrimination in employment. Each of these factors constrains a woman's entry into paid employment. Childcare provision in Britain is extremely low compared with other European countries, limiting the ability of mothers to join the labour force. Women also spend more time than men caring for the elderly and infirm in our society. These caring responsibilities can adversely affect labour force participation. A recent study (Corti and Dex 1995) found that many women and men were prevented from working altogether or found that they had to reduce their hours of work in order to care for a dependent relative. As the population ages, this factor is going to constrain employment opportunities still further.

Women might lack financial incentives to enter paid employment. Women in Britain earn on average 79 per cent of the equivalent male rate (Department of Employment 1994); this can serve as a disincentive to work. Women with children are less likely than childless women to enter the labour market. This is especially true for women with few qualifications since their low wages barely cover the costs of childcare. For single mothers state benefits often provide a higher standard of living than could be obtained in employment – especially if the only job on offer is part time. Women with an unemployed partner are especially likely to be discouraged from working in low wage jobs. Until the mid 1990s in Britain a woman with an unemployed partner on supplementary benefit would add very little to the family's net income even if she worked a full week in a low paid job (Dilnot 1992). Employers' attitudes and practices still display some degree of discrimination towards women. The length of the working day, the expectation of a full-time commitment and promotion schemes based upon years of experience are all examples of practices which indirectly discriminate against women as workers; yet these practices are commonly found in British industry in the 1990s.

The lack of 'family friendly' policies is adversely affecting the performance of the British economy at a macroeconomic level. If women's employment is constrained through the lack of support for childcare services, then this labour resource will be underutilized. If women are employed in part-time, low paid jobs offering little scope for training or skills development, this will contribute to the vicious circle of decline in which the British economy has found itself in recent decades. Low pay leads to high turnover of staff, low levels of investment in training and low skills. This in turn constrains the opportunities for capital investment and leads to a lack of competitiveness in world markets (Bruegel and Perrons 1995). The way in which women have moved into labour markets to occupy low paid, part-time jobs has merely reinforced this vicious circle. It adversely affects the macroeconomic performance of the economy as well as trapping women in a cycle of disadvantage.

Barriers to women's employment are rarely made the target of employment policies. As the recorded rate of unemployment is lower for women than for men, the issue is regarded as less serious. In practice, however, women's productive resources are being wasted and the full extent of this underutilization of women's labour is not apparent from the statistics. The distinction between participation and non-participation serves to hide the full extent of women's unemployment. The nation's level of output and living standards are nevertheless reduced by the unemployment of women and this issue deserves the serious attention of economists and politicians alike. The emphasis upon the claimant count has contributed to the neglect of this topic. With women's employment levels rising all the time, female unemployment has been all but ignored.

Survey-based Measures of Unemployment

The alternative way of measuring the level of unemployment is through a survey. The Labour Force Survey has been run by the government since 1972 and is now conducted quarterly. It is based upon a sample of the general population living in private households and it includes about 60 000 households in its coverage. The Labour Force Survey's approach to unemployment accepts a definition which is close to that recommended by the International Labour Office and the Organization for Economic Co-operation and Development; it thus enables international comparisons about labour utilization to be made.

For inclusion in the International Labour Office unemployment figures three criteria must be met:

(i)   the person did not work for pay during the survey reference week;
(ii)   he or she is available to start work within the next fortnight;
(iii) he or she looked for work during the past four weeks or was waiting to start work.

This definition comes closer to the economist's conceptual definition of the unemployed as those capable of and willing to work yet unable to find suitable paid employment. The working population is self-defined as those who answer the last two survey questions in the affirmative. This definition of unemployment is different from the claimant count and yields different results for women and men. Some people are not really seeking work but satisfy all the criteria for receiving benefit; these will figure in the claimant count but not in the survey statistics. The Labour Force Survey for the spring of 1994 identified nearly 1 million workers who were claiming benefit but did not satisfy the survey criteria for inclusion amongst the unemployed. These would include older workers who do not intend to return to work. On the other hand there are many people, especially new entrants and re-entrants to the labour market, who would like to work but are not eligible for benefit. Many of these will be included in the survey-based measure of unemployment although they are excluded from the claimant count. In fact 60 per cent of the women identified as unemployed in the survey in the spring of 1994 did not claim benefit.

Table 6.3: Comparison of Measures of Unemployment

millions

Year	Women		Men	
	ILO	Claimant	ILO	Claimant
1984	1.3	0.9	1.8	2.1
1990	0.8	0.4	1.1	1.1
1994	0.9	0.6	1.7	2.0

Source: *Employment Gazette*, February 1995

Despite these discrepancies the two measures of unemployment nevertheless show broadly similar trends for the British economy as Table 6.3 shows. As the economy recovered from the deep recession of the early 1980s the demand for labour rose and there was a reduction in the level of both survey-based and claimant unemployment. During the past decade 1990, a peak year in the Trade Cycle, showed the lowest rate of unemployment on both these counts. When the economy moved into recession again in the early 1990s both measures showed an increase in recorded unemployment. These cyclical trends are apparent whichever measure is used.

As Table 6.3 shows the survey data agrees with the claimant count in recording a higher level of male than female unemployment at each phase of the Trade Cycle. The gap, however, is far smaller in magnitude in the survey. Many women whose unemployment is hidden in the claimant count are recorded as unemployed by the survey. The overlap between the two measures of female unemployment is far from complete. In 1990 the ILO survey estimated that 0.8 million women were unemployed whilst only 0.4 million were included in the claimant count. At all stages of the Trade Cycle the survey indicates a higher level of female unemployment than that recorded by the claimant count.

For men though the position is reversed; the level of male unemployment recorded by the claimant count is higher than the survey shows. In 1994 the claimant count showed just over two million men as unemployed whilst the survey gave a total of only 1.7 million; some men were eligible for benefit although they were not seeking work on the basis of the criteria used for the survey. The claimant count overstates men's unemployment whilst understating that of women.

The survey presents a more balanced picture of the wasted labour resources in the economy. By including a larger percentage of unemployed women the survey makes women's position amongst the unemployed more visible. Women accounted for approximately 40 per cent of survey-based unemployment whilst they only represent 25 per cent of the claimant unemployed. The survey overcomes some, but not all, of the issues concerning the recording of female unemployment. If women know that their lack of work does not entitle them to benefit and that society considers them to have a role within the household, then this will influence their response to surveys. In this case even the survey statistics might not capture the full extent of women's unemployment and underemployment. Women who are actively engaged in housework and childcare might not regard themselves as unemployed even if they would accept a job were a suitable position to become available. Their inability to perceive themselves as unemployed will affect their response to surveys.

Women are also less likely than men to consider themselves as available for work immediately. If childcare needs to be organized, women might anticipate that these arrangements could cause them to delay starting work. The responsibility which women bear for childcare will affect their response to the question in the survey concerning whether they are available to start work immediately. Women are less likely than men to answer in the affirmative (Dex 1990). Consequently even survey-based counts of women's unemployment do not represent the full picture although they are certainly more accurate than the claimant count.

Summary

Unemployment represents a waste of scarce resources and consequently its occurrence reduces the living standards of all citizens. Men and women have both experienced rising levels and rates of unemployment in the United Kingdom since the mid 1970s. If Britain is to make full use of its productive labour resources then the government needs to develop policies to help both men and women to find employment. Men's recorded unemployment is significantly higher than women's and consequently this has often formed the focus of policy. But the waste of women's labour resources is also a significant issue in Britain today and the full extent of this waste is understated in the unemployment statistics. The barriers which prevent women from working are sometimes different from those which men face and consequently appropriate labour market policies need to be developed in order to address this dimension of the problem.

7 More Jobs, Less Dole?

Employment, unemployment and the working population. Cyclical unemployment and the deflationary gap. Cyclical unemployment and gender. Real wage unemployment. The natural rate of unemployment. Conclusion.

Employment, Unemployment and the Working Population

Throughout the European Union the rate of unemployment in the 1990s stands far higher than ever it did in the 1960s. Unemployment is not just a British problem but there is one unique feature of the British experience; in 1994 Britain alone amongst the 12 member states had a higher rate of unemployment for men than for women. In all the other 11 countries women's unemployment rates were higher than those of men. In 1990 the average unemployment rates in the European Union were 6.6 per cent for men but 11.2 per cent for women; women were nearly twice as likely as men to be unemployed (Maruani 1992). In Britain, though, the position was reversed; the rate of male unemployment stood at 7.6 per cent compared with 3.6 per cent for women.

Changes in unemployment reflect the difference between the growth of the working population and the change in employment. Creating more jobs does not necessarily reduce unemployment. The new jobs might be filled by re-entrants or new entrants to the labour force. School leavers or women returning to the labour market after a break for child rearing will often seek and fill employment positions without ever appearing in the unemployment statistics. Employment can rise without unemployment falling. Some of the newly employed were previously considered to be non-participant in the working population. Women in particular often move between employment and non-participation during family formation; their joblessness never gets recorded in the unemployment statistics. Men seldom leave the working population during their working life and will usually move between employment and unemployment as their job opportunities fluctuate.

The changes in the employment pattern and in the working population in Britain have affected men's and women's unemployment in very different ways. The male working population in Britain has decreased slightly since 1960. This reduction in the size of the working population has served to mitigate the rise in male unemployment. Although the employment prospects for men

99

millions

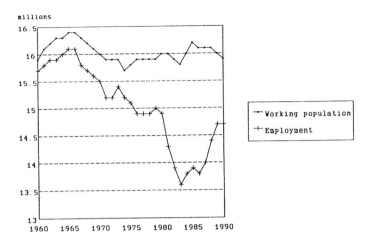

Figure 7.1: The Working Population, Employment and Unemployment for Men in the UK. Source: *Eurostat*

have deteriorated over this period, there has actually been a reduction in the number of men seeking jobs. Nevertheless male unemployment had risen from 0.6 million in 1971 to 1.7 million by 1991.

The changes in male unemployment and the working population are illustrated in Figure 7.1. In the early 1960s the fluctuations in the male working population were mirrored by changes in men's employment resulting in a low level of unemployment. It was not until the recession of the mid 1970s that male unemployment reached the million mark; a slight rise in the working population just as male employment fell ensured that this landmark was passed. The recession of the early 1980s involved a sharp fall in men's employment as high interest rates and a high exchange rate brought pressure to bear on manufacturing industry and many jobs were lost in this sector. Manufacturing industry has long been a sector where male employment predominated and so men will suffer disproportionately if jobs are lost in this sector. In the early 1980s manufacturing industry reduced its employment by nearly 1.5 million workers and men's employment fell rapidly. Male employment fell just at the same time as the male working population was increasing and unemployment spiralled upwards reaching two and a quarter million by the mid 1980s. During the late 1980s the situation improved. The male working population was falling whilst employment was rising and thus unemployment fell. The number of men in the working population depends primarily upon demographic trends and is independent from the level of activity in the economy. The working population and the level of employment can

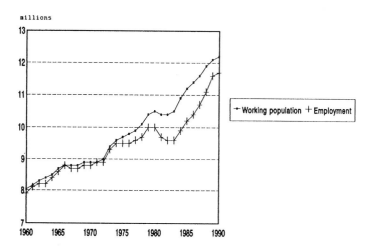

millions

Figure 7.2: The Working Population, Employment and Unemployment for Women in the UK. Source: *Eurostat*

and often do move in opposite directions causing fluctuations in male unemployment.

For women the picture is rather different. As Figure 7.2 shows, over the last 30 years the female working population has been steadily increasing as women have moved into employment – and unemployment too. Women are less likely than men to remain participant in the working population throughout their working lives. They will often enter employment if a suitable position becomes available but return to domestic duties if they lose their job. Their employment tends to be opportunistic. For many mothers employment depends upon the possibility of their finding a job with suitable hours, close to home and in a position which they find acceptable. If such a job becomes available then they will enter the labour market to take it; the female working population and women's employment both rise together. But if there are no employment possibilities then they will remain non-participant in the labour force. Many women are either in the working population as employees or out of it as the non-employed. Consequently the level of female unemployment has varied less than male unemployment.

From 1960 until 1990 the number of women participating in the working population rose in almost every year and yet in almost every year women's employment increased as well. Female unemployment remained low throughout the 1960s and early 1970s and even the recession of the mid 1970s only provoked a slight increase in the number of women out of work. The recession of the early 1980s changed the trend; female employment fell as the decline in the manufacturing sector hit women's as well as men's employment opportunities. There is one significant difference though between women and men; during this recession the number of women in the working population fell slightly. This decline helped to mitigate the rise in unemployment which occurred as the gap between the working population and the level of employment widened. Female unemployment reached the million mark by 1986, just a decade later than male unemployment had passed that milestone. The female working population has risen and fallen in the same direction as aggregate demand has fluctuated over the Trade Cycle. When there were more jobs available, women moved into the labour force but when the downturns came some women ceased to participate in the working population. Over the last 30 years in Britain female employment and the working population have often moved in the same direction as the size of the working population and the level of employment have both increased significantly.

Changes in the employment pattern and in the working population will influence unemployment and these factors have changed in different ways for men and women in Britain. Since women and men are employed in different sectors of the economy and on different terms, the causes of their unemployment, and the barriers inhibiting their employment, vary considerably. Economic analysis tries to identify the causes of unemployment so that appropriate policy measures can be adopted. The separate factors affecting male and female unemployment need to be identified to ensure that policy measures address both dimensions of this issue.

Cyclical Unemployment and the Deflationary Gap

As the British economy has moved from boom to slump and back again over the past two decades, the level of unemployment has fluctuated considerably. Cyclical trends have been apparent in both male and female unemployment. The overall demand for labour in the economy will be related to the demand for goods and services. Firms will only want to employ men and women if they feel that they will be able to profit by selling the output which will result from their employment. A buoyant economy, with increasing total expenditure will be experiencing a rising demand for labour, whilst in a recession the demand for labour will be falling as firms accumulate stocks of unsold goods. The high rate of growth achieved in the United Kingdom in the early 1970s was followed by falling output and rising unemployment in 1974 and 1975. The late 1970s brought a modest recovery whilst the early years of the 1980s witnessed the most severe recession for 50 years. The recovery

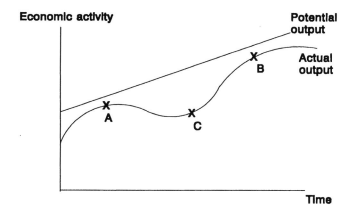

Figure 7.3: The Trade Cycle

in the late 1980s was halted when output fell in the early 1990s. Boom has been followed by slump in a regular pattern known as the Trade Cycle.

As the level of activity fluctuates cyclically, actual output will at times fall well below potential output. Potential output indicates the level of output which the economy is capable of producing if it is right out on its production possibility frontier with all its resources fully employed. The years 1973, 1979 and 1990 represent the peaks of the trade cycle for the British economy, demand was high and the level of actual output was close to the economy's potential output. In Figure 7.3 these boom years are depicted by points A and B. On the other hand 1974, 1981 and 1991 can all be identified as years when output was falling and the economy was not making full use of its productive resources. Point C in Figure 7.3 depicts the economy in recession.

The level of potential output depends upon the productive resources which the economy has at its disposal. Land, labour, capital and enterprise are all needed to produce goods and services for consumption. A change in the size of the working population will therefore affect the level of output which the economy is capable of producing. Should the working population increase over time the level of potential output will rise as it does in Figure 7.3. A change in technology causing an increase in labour productivity will have a similar impact upon potential output. Provided firms feel confident that they can profitably sell more goods and services, the level of employment will increase and actual output too will rise. On the other hand if there were no accompanying rise in the level of expenditure and hence employment, the rise in the working population and productivity will cause an increase in unemployment. The working population and productivity affects potential output whilst total expenditure, or aggregate demand, influences actual output and the level of employment. To the extent that actual output is falling below potential output, the economy is not making full use of its productive labour resources. One indication of this shortfall will be the level of unemployment. If consumers are not willing to buy the total level of output which would be produced were every worker to be employed then demand deficient, or cyclical, unemployment will result. Some men and women will experience unemployment due to this deficiency of demand.

Demand deficient unemployment is usually tackled by demand management policies. Keynes argued for the government to play an active part in macroeconomic stabilization by managing the level of aggregate demand. In a recession total expenditure is too low for firms to want to employ all those in the labour force. The level of consumption and investment expenditure which households and firms are generating is simply insufficient to lead to full employment. Actual demand is deficient in relation to the full employment level of aggregate demand.

In such situations Keynesians suggest it is appropriate for governments to adopt policy measures to stimulate aggregate demand. Taxes could be cut to stimulate consumption or investment spending whilst public expenditure projects would add government demand to that originating in the private sector. Keynesians believe that, despite crowding out, such policies should ensure an increase in total expenditure and national income through the multiplier process. The essential prerequisite for successful policy measures is for governments to estimate the size of the deflationary gap. Armed with this information they can engineer the stimulus necessary to create the desired number of jobs. Creating jobs is seen as the key to reducing unemployment.

For men this may indeed be true since men who seek jobs are usually in the working population. Creating jobs for men does usually reduce male unemployment as men move between employment and unemployment. An accurate estimation of the deflationary gap followed by the appropriate policy measures could well ensure a fuller utilization of the male labour force.

But for women unemployment can often be hidden by non-participation; there is no simple correlation between creating jobs and reducing recorded female unemployment. The new jobs generated through Keynesian reflationary measures might simply attract more women into the working population. The female working population does not provide an accurate estimation of the number of women who would enter employment if the level of expenditure in the economy increased and the full employment level of aggregate demand can prove very difficult to estimate with respect to women. The deflationary gap might thus prove a poor indicator of the extra spending needed to ensure that the economy makes full use of its female labour resources.

Cyclical Unemployment and Gender

When the economy moves into recession, demand deficient unemployment will increase affecting both men and women. There was a higher rate of unemployment for both women and men in 1986 than in 1990 as Figure 7.4 shows. The peak years of the Trade Cycle like 1973, 1979 and 1990 brought a fall in the rate of male and female unemployment whilst the recessions of the mid 1970s, the early 1980s and 1990s saw unemployment rising for both women and men. The cyclical fluctuations in the level of aggregate demand in Britain have caused both male and female unemployment to rise and fall. The overall upward trend in unemployment has been similar for both genders. There were more men and more women unemployed in the 1990s than in the mid 1970s regardless of the cyclical fluctuations.

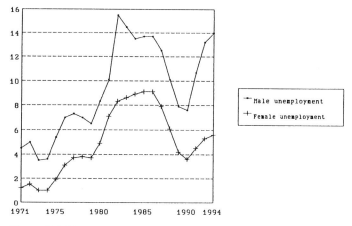

Figure 7.4: The Rate of Unemployment of Men and Women in the UK.
Source: *Employment Gazette*, various issues

Although cyclical, or demand deficient, unemployment is experienced by both men and women, the extent to which they suffer from this type of unemployment varies. In some recessions women have been more severely affected by the downturn than men as their unemployment rose rapidly. The British recession in the mid 1970s illustrates this point as female unemployment rose more rapidly than male unemployment. The pattern though is not consistent; in the recessions of the early 1980s and the early 1990s men's unemployment rose faster than women's. Women's representation amongst the unemployed in the Labour Force Survey is shown in Table 7.1. Since 1979 the percentage of women amongst the unemployed has displayed a consistent pattern over the Trade Cycle. As the recessions of the early 1980s and 1990s set in, men's unemployment rose faster than women's and women came to account for a smaller proportion of the unemployed. They represented 46 per cent in the boom year of 1979 and 42 per cent of the unemployed at the next peak in 1990. As the downturn came women formed a smaller proportion of the unemployed – 40 per cent in 1986 and 33 per cent in 1992. In both these cyclical downturns unemployment affected men to a greater extent than women.

Table 7.1: Women's Unemployment as a Percentage of Total Unemployment
United Kingdom

Year	Women's unemployment as % of total
1979	46
1986	40
1990	42
1992	33

Source: calculated from *Labour Force Survey*, various issues

Two contrasting theories attempt to explain how recessions affect men and women. Women either represent a reserve army of labour or else they are regarded as cheap substitutes for male labour. If women constitute a reserve army of labour then female unemployment will rise faster than male unemployment in a recession whereas if women are used as substitutes for male labour recessions will hit male employment particularly hard.

During both the wars in the early twentieth century men have gone away to fight whilst women have replaced men in the factories. Men joined the armed forces whilst women constituted a reserve army of labour. Women entered the paid workforce in large numbers during the Second World War but returned to domestic life once hostilities ceased and the men returned to the civilian labour market. In peacetime too women can be used as a reserve army to be drawn into employment when aggregate demand is high but they will be the first to lose their jobs with the onset of recession. In this view women are the marginal workers who are hired and fired as the economy moves through boom and slump. Their position in the labour market mirrors their social position. Their employment is insecure and their income is regarded as secondary in that the household can survive on the wage brought in by the male breadwinner. According to this view, female employment would be particularly sensitive to fluctuations in the level of expenditure and cyclical unemployment will be more pronounced for women than for men. One study suggested that in the 1970s women did suffer disproportionately to men from the declines in employment in the manufacturing sector (Bruegel 1979). This would be consistent with the use of women as a reserve army of secondary workers which can be laid off in recessions. Women's unemployment did indeed rise at a faster rate than men's between 1973 and 1979. However, as women's participation in paid employment continued to increase throughout this period it is hardly surprising that a rising proportion of women in the working population experienced difficulty in finding employment in the recessions. Women were accounting for a larger percentage of the unemployed simply because women were more numerous in the working population as a whole.

However the 1980s and 1990s present a different picture. Men's unemployment was rising at a faster rate than women's as the recessions set in. This evidence hardly suggests that women have been used as a reserve army of labour in recent recessions. There are though rational economic arguments which imply that a recession might favour women's employment. Employers, faced with a downturn in business activity, might try to reduce costs by employing a higher proportion of cheap female labour. Women might be employed instead of men in an attempt to reduce unit costs. In this case men's unemployment will rise. One study of the British economy in the 1970s suggested that evidence supported this conclusion during the more severe recessions (Rubery and Tarling 1983). A recession would thus be characterized by rising male unemployment in particular and this seems to have been the case in the United Kingdom since 1980.

Perhaps the changing gender balance in unemployment is attributable to the growth of part-time jobs. One study (Dex and Perry 1984) of the 1970s found the employment of part-timers was particularly sensitive to cyclical swings. The substitution of cheaper labour has indeed taken place in British industry as employers replaced full-time employees with part-timers. Part-time employment has displayed the greatest increase whilst full-time employment has declined proportionately. Employers were using part-time workers as a buffer against the upswings and downturns in business activity. As business activity increased more part-time workers would be employed to cope with expanding demand. Since employment in manufacturing industry has been on the decline, part-time workers were in effect being substituted for full-timers. The gender segregation in manufacturing employment, however, remained intact. The textile industry substituted female part-time workers for female full-timers whilst in the motor industry the same trend applied to male part-timers and full-timers. Women were not replacing men as such; industries remained strongly segregated even as cheaper part-timers replaced more costly full-timers.

A similar trend away from full-time and towards part-time employment was apparent in the service sector but this took place against a very different background. Service sector employment grew by nearly 20 per cent between 1977 and 1990 (Department of Employment) and service industries rely predominantly upon a female workforce. As the new part-time jobs were created in the service sector these were usually filled by women. Those women made redundant from the manufacturing sector and those entering, or re-entering, the labour force could find jobs in the expanding service sector. This expansion in employment in service industries helped to protect women from unemployment whilst the decline in manufacturing jobs aggravated the rise in male unemployment. Although for both men and women part-time employment showed particular sensitivity to cyclical swings, the number of full-time employees was declining throughout this period. Both men and women were affected by these changes but, because manufacturing industry employs a predominantly male workforce, the fall in male employment and consequent rise in male unemployment was of greater magnitude.

Real Wage Unemployment

Real wage, or classical, unemployment occurs when the wage rate has settled at a level which is too high for the employers to want to employ all those workers who would be prepared to accept jobs at the going wage rate. There will be a disequilibrium in the labour market resulting in an excess supply of labour on the market.

The labour demand curve will reflect the level of activity in the economy and will vary over the Trade Cycle whilst the aggregate supply curve for labour will indicate the total number of people willing and able to work at various alternative wage rates. Labour supply will be influenced by wage rates and any other factor which affects men's and women's willingness to participate in paid employment. Any factor which causes more or fewer workers to accept jobs whatever the rate of pay might be will cause a shift of the whole supply curve.

The labour market depicted in figure 7.5 would be in equilibrium at a wage of W_e when N_e workers would be supplied and demanded. Everyone who wants a job is able to find one. At a wage of W_e firms will seek to employ N_e workers and this exactly matches the number of workers who will be prepared to accept jobs at this wage rate. However, if real wages are set too high the labour market will be in disequilibrium. At a wage of W_1 employers will want to employ N_2 workers but N_1 workers will be prepared to accept jobs. There is a surplus of labour on the market. Unemployment occurs as a direct consequence of the disequilibrium level of wages. Wage flexibility is seen as the solution to this type of unemployment. If wages were to fall to W_e then employers will find that lower wages reduce their costs enabling them to sell more goods and also it becomes cheaper to substitute labour for capital. Under these circumstances, employers will be willing to demand more labour and a move along the demand curve from N_2 to N_e will result. The fall in wages also has an effect on the supply of labour. Some workers will be unwilling to work for lower wages and will withdraw from actively seeking work and so there is a move along the supply curve from N_1 to N_e. The market will thus return to equilibrium and unemployment will be eliminated.

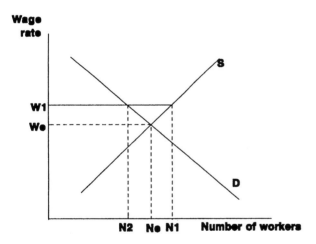

Figure 7.5: Real Wage Unemployment

Real wage unemployment applies to those workers who find themselves unable to find suitable paid employment because, either collectively or individually, they are pricing themselves out of the market. But is this situation likely to be equally applicable to both women and men? Women on average earn less than men. In April 1994 full-time male manual workers earned an average weekly wage of £280.70 whilst for women the equivalent figure was £181.90 (Department of Employment 1994). It seems possible that real wage unemployment might be more of a problem for men than for women. Since women's wages are lower than men's, this could imply that they are not pricing themselves out of the market to the same extent as men. On this analysis then, one of the reasons why there are fewer unemployed women than men is because their wages are lower.

The reasons why wages settle above their equilibrium rate are often debated. Some will suggest that it is the result of strong trade unions, which drive a hard bargain in times of labour shortage. Throughout the 1950s and 1960s in Britain there was a high level of total expenditure and with it a buoyant labour market. In fact immigration was encouraged as a way of filling vacancies in the labour markets of north-west Europe. Under these circumstances, it has been suggested that trade union power increased and so wage rates were driven above their equilibrium level. Unemployment is the result.

Despite the increase in female employment women are still less likely than men to be members of a trade union. This is related particularly to their predominance in part-time jobs. Women are also less likely to hold influential positions within the union hierarchy due to the extent of their domestic commitments. The very same factors which inhibit women's promotion in organizations also impede their progression to positions of influence within the trade union movement (Rees 1992). Women's wages therefore are less likely to include a union differential. Union bargaining is less likely to have been a significant factor in the determination of women's wages and women might thus be less likely to experience real wage unemployment than men.

The Natural Rate of Unemployment

The natural rate of unemployment refers to the level of unemployment which persists even when the labour market is in equilibrium. Some workers will not be able to take advantage of job opportunities due to a mismatch between the type of labour employers are seeking and the type of workers who are looking for jobs. However flexible wage rates might be, this imbalance will still remain. The labour market is in equilibrium but there are still some men or women unemployed. The natural rate of unemployment includes all those workers who are included in the working population but are not able or willing to accept jobs.

The working population, or the labour force, is depicted in Figure 7.6 by the line LF. This shows the total number of people participating in the working population. Its position will depend upon demographic and sociological factors such as the number of people of working age, the duration of compulsory education, the availability of childcare facilities and the skill requirements. It is usually assumed to be fairly constant. This assumption proves fairly realistic for the male working population which has changed very little in Britain over the last 30 years. The female working population however has been far from constant. The number of women in the working population has shown a continual increase over the same period. The supply curve for labour, S=AJ, shows the number of people prepared to accept jobs at the going wage rate. This will depend upon variables like the level of wages relative to benefits, the skills of the workers, the length of time they are prepared to spend searching for a job, and the area of the country in which they seek employment.

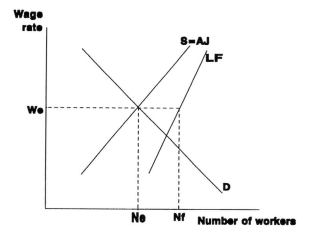

Figure 7.6: The Natural Rate of Unemployment

At a wage of W_e, the labour market is in equilibrium since Q_e workers are prepared to work and employers also demand Q_e workers. But the working population also includes some workers who are not prepared to accept jobs at the going wage rate. They are either caught in the poverty trap so that they are better off on benefit than in work, or they are waiting for a job which provides a more suitable opportunity for their particular skills or they are not prepared to travel to the available job openings. They are unemployed even though the labour market is in equilibrium. In Figure 7.6, Q_f-Q_e workers are unemployed representing the natural rate of unemployment. The natural rate of unemployment will include frictional unemployment, regional unemployment, structural unemployment, technological unemployment and seasonal unemployment. These types of unemployment will persist even when the labour market is in equilibrium and they cannot be overcome by demand management policies.

Frictional unemployment occurs because at any one point in time there will always be some people without jobs. Some people will be in the process of changing jobs and this rarely happens smoothly and easily. These job seekers spend time on the dole whilst looking for a suitable employment opportunity. They are frictionally unemployed. Women, unlike men, often look for work whilst they are non-participant in the working population. They then do not appear in the unemployment statistics. There will also be some people within the labour force who are either physically or mentally incapable of holding a job and these too will be considered as frictionally unemployed.

Structural unemployment occurs when changes take place in the pattern of demand in the economy such that workers made unemployed from one sector find difficulty in obtaining new employment elsewhere in the economy. It results from the changing structure of industry. As demand patterns change, so some industries fall into decline. There might well be job opportunities in other industries which are expanding but it is often difficult for workers to fill these posts. Their skills may not be easily transferred to another job and the expanding industries might well be in a different area. Retraining or relocation will be necessary if these workers are to find employment in other sectors of the economy. The loss of jobs in British manufacturing industry affected more men than women. Furthermore the changes which occurred in the pattern of demand in Britain in the 1980s favoured the employment of women rather than men. As the economy recovered from the recession, the new jobs which were created in the service sector were increasingly occupied by women and their unemployment fell accordingly. Male unemployment proved harder to reduce and so structural unemployment in Britain has been predominantly a man's problem!

Regional unemployment refers to the fact that the unemployed are not spread evenly throughout the country. Some parts of the country experience above the average rate of unemployment whilst other regions have fewer workers unemployed than the national average. In the United Kingdom, the North of England, the West Midlands and Scotland are some of the regions that have suffered particularly badly from regional unemployment in recent years. Manufacturing industries like textiles and shipbuilding tended to be concentrated in these areas. The decline of these industries, in the face of foreign competition, has been associated with heavy unemployment in these regions. Industrial segregation by gender means that redundancies at the textile mills will cause female unemployment to increase in some regions whilst the closure of shipbuilding yards results in the loss of men's jobs. Consequently the regional pattern of unemployment is not identical for men and women.

Technological unemployment occurs due to the introduction of new technology. The new machines can do the work of the workers and so redundancies will arise following the introduction of such technology. This type of unemployment can occur in expanding industries as they seek to maintain competitiveness in world markets. In such a situation, unemployment may well be short-lived as lower costs will stimulate demand and so lead to more job opportunities. In industries which are already on the decline the problem may well be more serious. New technology may enable the industry to survive but expansion is highly unlikely. In this case the jobs lost are rarely regained.

Seasonal unemployment arises because there is more demand for some types of workers at certain times of the year. The tourist trade is far more busy in July and August than in February and March, whilst builders usually start their operations in the spring or summer and building labourers might well be unemployed during the winter months. The unemployment figures published by the government will include a 'seasonally adjusted' rate of unemployment to take account of such trends.

The analysis of the natural rate of unemployment as the gap between those who are prepared to accept jobs and those in the labour force is readily applicable to men's working patterns; it represents an appropriate model of their employment experience. A man will remain participant in the working population from leaving full-time education until retirement age but a woman's working life usually follows a different pattern. Many women, especially mothers, will work if the right opportunity arrives; but they will rarely be considered as part of the working population at this stage of their lives except at those times when they are actually in paid employment. They are either participant and employed or else they are non-participant. Many women seeking jobs would not be included in the LF curve in Figure 7.6. But should the right job opportunity come up they will move straight into paid employment. In terms of Figure 7.6 both the AJ curve and the LF curve have moved to the right together!

Demand management policies are inappropriate for reducing the natural rate of unemployment. However much total expenditure increases, those who face barriers to their employment will still be unable to move into jobs; if they lack the appropriate skills, or live in depressed regions these factors will keep them unemployed regardless of increases in the level of aggregate demand. Supply-side measures to tackle these barriers to employment are appropriate for reducing the natural rate of unemployment. Such policies are designed to increase the number of workers who are willing and able to accept jobs at the going wage rate. Retraining will enable those workers without jobs to acquire the skills necessary for them to find work in the expanding sectors of the economy; regional measures can help to take work to the workers or to make workers more mobile geographically so that they are able to fill the vacancies in prosperous regions of the country. These supply-side measures will shift the AJ curve to the right and thus nearer to the LF curve in Figure 7.6. In other words the working population has not changed but there are now more people willing and able to accept jobs at the going wage rate thus reducing the natural rate of unemployment.

Supply-side policies have focused upon removing the barriers which make it difficult for men who are already in the working population to accept jobs at the going wage rate. Government sponsored training schemes, for example, are available for those registered as unemployed – not the non-participant job seekers. Supply-side policies are not designed to deal with the barriers which impede participation in the working population itself. These policies therefore do not address some of the significant barriers which constrain women's employment. Lack of appropriate childcare facilities often leads women to work on a part-time rather than a full-time basis or prevents them from working at all. This obstacle preventing the economy from making full and efficient use of women's labour resources is only rarely and half-heartedly the focus of government policies.

Conclusion

Over the whole of the postwar period women have come to participate increasingly in paid work. Women account for about half of all employees in employment in Britain today. Meanwhile there has been a slight fall in the number of men in the working population. Yet women and men participate in labour markets in different ways. Women are more likely than men to work part time; they are more likely to work in service industries; and women in Britain earn only about 70 per cent of the average wage of a male worker. These factors affect women's and men's representation amongst the unemployed.

There are more unemployed men than women and the rate of male unemployment is higher than that for women. The changes in the working population and in employment have affected men and women differently. Cyclical unemployment, real wage unemployment and structural unemployment are likely to represent more of a problem for men than for women. As the British economy recovered from the recession of the early 1980s government policy emphasized the importance of market forces. With regard to labour markets, this implied that all restrictions and controls were to be lifted and the markets should be free to respond to the pressures of supply and demand for labour. Accordingly Wages Councils were abolished, the power of trade unions was curtailed and the economic climate encouraged the introduction of flexible working practices.

These policy changes impacted upon men and women in the labour market in different ways. The traditional family structure of a male breadwinner and a woman whose primary role was domestic had been reinforced with the introduction of the Welfare State in Britain in the late 1940s. This family pattern has become increasingly uncommon in Britain as more and more women have entered paid employment. The terms upon which women are prepared to accept jobs are very different from those which men are willing to tolerate. Over four out of five part-time jobs are filled by women and many of the new employment opportunities which have arisen since the mid 1980s have been for part-timers. If women are more willing than men to consider these vacancies, then this helps to explain the lower rate of unemployment amongst women. It is however debatable as to whether this trend has benefited women as a group. Part-time jobs bring in part-time wages; part-time workers have not until recently received the same entitlement to pensions and other fringe benefits as are available to full-time workers; and part-time workers are likely to experience a cut in their working hours if business moves into recession. All of these factors make women especially vulnerable in this new world of flexible and deregulated labour markets. The changes in the British economy have indeed favoured the employment of women rather than men but the terms on which they are employed leave women in a very vulnerable position in labour markets.

8 Wage Rates and the Demand for Labour

The gender wage gap. Wages and prices in a market economy. The demand for labour: the market and the firm. Marginal product and diminishing returns. The firm's demand for labour. Shifts in the demand curve. The skills and qualifications of men and women. Trade unions and skill. Women's employment, skill and experience. Summary.

The Gender Wage Gap

By the end of 1995 there were nearly 11 million men and 11 million women employed in the United Kingdom; numerically at least women had achieved equality with men at work. But equal status implies more than a mere headcount. The terms and conditions of employment, promotion prospects, the types of occupation pursued, the extent of domestic responsibilities and the rates of remuneration also need to be considered. On these grounds women's position in labour markets is still very different from men's. Each one of these factors makes women's earnings inferior to men's.

Women's workforce participation affects and is affected by their rates of pay. Wages in a market economy serve two purposes: they reward workers for the productivity of their labour and they allocate labour between competing uses. A woman in Europe will be paid less than a man. In the United Kingdom in 1994 a woman's full time average pay was £255.80 per week whilst the equivalent figure for a man was £355.60. Throughout the European Union there is a considerable difference between women's and men's wages and this disparity has remained remarkably persistent throughout recent decades despite the enactment of egalitarian legislation and the increased participation of women in the workforce.

Table 8.1: Women's Hourly Earnings as a Percentage of Men's 1993

Denmark	83
France	81
Germany	74
United Kingdom	71
Japan	51

Source: *Yearbook of Labour Statistics*, 1994

This gender pay differential is narrow for young people. School leavers earn the same amount when they are first recruited into the labour force regardless of whether they are male or female, but the gender pay gap widens over time. Table 8.1 shows women's average earnings as a percentage of men's in a variety of developed countries. Although there is considerable variation between the more egalitarian Denmark where women earn 83 per cent of male rates and Japan where their rewards only approach 50 per cent of the man's equivalent, everywhere the disparity lies in the same direction. Women earn less than men throughout the developed countries of the world.

Wages and Prices in a Market Economy

All societies face the same problem; they need to allocate their resources between competing uses. In a market economy wages and prices have an important role to play in this process. Wages and prices function as an allocative mechanism signalling gluts and indicating shortages. If labour is scarce in one industry, then higher wages will be offered to attract labour to move from other sectors of the economy. Low wages, on the other hand, signal workers to seek better opportunities elsewhere. According to this view, the wage differential between men and women reflects differences in the underlying market conditions. The relationship between the supply and demand for women's and men's labour is different and this is reflected in the equilibrium wage rate at which these labour markets clear.

Neo-classical economics suggests that the operation of free market forces will result in an efficient allocation of scarce resources to provide the highest possible standard of living. Perfectly competitive markets, it is argued, will provide the best possible outcome. Both households and firms have a series of decisions to take in a market economy. These choices will be influenced by wage rates and prices. Households must decide upon which goods and services to spend their limited income and the terms on which their members wish to participate in labour markets. Firms take decisions concerning the production of goods and services and the employment of factors of production. Households and firms, it is assumed, will be trying to pursue their own self-interest; they will be trying to maximize their well-being subject to certain constraints. Since the days of Adam Smith, economists have believed that the outcome of these self-interested market choices would be of maximum benefit to society too. The 'Invisible Hand' of perfectly competitive markets would guide producers and consumers to an efficient outcome.

The fundamental principle underlying the household's market behaviour is its desire to maximize utility, or satisfaction. Utility is obtained from purchasing goods and services and from leisure activities. Work, on the other hand, is considered to be an unpleasant activity bringing disutility to the worker and only undertaken to earn an income, the spending of which brings satisfaction. The amount of time which a man or woman chooses to devote to paid employment will be guided by the utility maximizing principle and will be affected by the wage rate. Higher wages will thus encourage workers to spend more time in paid employment, whilst lower wages will shift the balance towards leisure and other activities. Women's real wages have been rising in Britain in the postwar period and this has been one factor influencing the increase in women's participation in labour markets. In this way wages help to influence the decisions which a utility maximizing worker will take.

The other decision for households concerns their consumption expenditure. Here too, the guiding principle is supposed to be the maximization of utility subject to a given set of relative prices. Consumers will carefully adjust their expenditure pattern to ensure that the particular combination of goods and services which they buy yields them the maximum possible satisfaction. Their market demands for goods and services will, in turn, affect the price of the commodities. Those items in high demand will rise in price whilst those for which the demand is falling will have their prices reduced in order to clear stocks.

The prices, in turn, affect the profitability of the products and hence the producers' decisions. As firms are assumed to be in business to maximize their profits, they will choose to expand the production of the more profitable products and reduce that of the less profitable ones. In this way consumer choices will influence the pattern of production and ensure that the goods and services produced reflect the strength of consumer demand. As producers expand profitable lines of production this will affect their demand for factors of production, including labour. In expanding industries there will be more job opportunities signalled by rising wages; workers in contracting industries will experience falling relative wages providing the incentive for them to seek alternative employment. In this way wages will allocate labour towards profitable uses.

Profit-maximizing producers will have to ensure that they employ the lowest cost methods of production. Inefficiency will be reflected in higher costs and lower profits so that profit maximization will not be achieved. Firms must decide on their production methods with profits in mind. They must strive to combine land, labour and capital in the most efficient way possible choosing whether to employ labour intensive or capital intensive production methods by considering the impact of these decisions on their costs of production. Cheap types of labour will be in high demand whilst, other things being equal, those workers who require higher wages will experience a reduction in the demand for their labour services. If men's and women's labour were perfect substitutes for each other but women earned less than men, then profit-maximizing employers would prefer to use cheaper women's labour since it would reduce their costs of production.

In the neo-classical model, wage differentials are important in achieving an efficient allocation of scarce resources. Wages should reflect the underlying forces of supply and demand. If one group of workers earn high wages, that should either be because they are in high demand or in short supply. Low wages will either be due to low demand or abundant supply. To explain why women earn less than men the factors affecting the supply and demand for labour must be examined. The factors which influence the employer's demand for labour will indicate whether there are any valid economic reasons for paying men more than women. The supply of labour originates in the household and is affected by the domestic division of labour. The need to accommodate unequal levels of domestic commitments will affect the supply of labour by men and women.

The Demand for Labour: the Market and the Firm

The market for a particular type of labour will include all firms wishing to employ that sort of labour and all workers seeking a job in that occupation. The market demand for labour reflects the total number of workers which all firms in the market wish to employ at a given wage rate. The market represents the total picture – that is the sum of the demand for labour by the individual firms.

The demand for labour by each one of these firms arises because they wish to supply goods and services to the product markets. The demand for labour reflects the value of that type of labour to the employer. It is linked to the demand for the final product and will vary with that demand. As incomes rise, the pattern of demand changes and those products with a high income elasticity of demand will find their market growing. The insurance industry and the catering trade, for example, have both benefited from such changes in the past decade and accordingly employment has increased in these sectors of the economy. Other industries, however, have been adversely affected. As incomes rise, families install central heating in their homes and the demand for domestic coal falls. Consequently miners' jobs suffer.

The conditions in the market for a certain type of labour will determine the wage rate. One individual firm in a perfectly competitive market has to take its employment decisions on the basis of this market wage rate. It has to decide how many men and women it wants to employ at the going wage rate. The firm alone cannot influence the wage rate; it merely accepts the market rate as given and hires or fires workers accordingly.

The neo-classical theory of the firm rests on the assumption that a firm's business objective is to maximize its profits. A firm will take employment decisions with this principle in mind. Extra workers employed will add to the firm's costs through their wage payment but they will also serve to increase the firm's revenue by the extra output which they produce. As long as the extra cost is more than offset by the increase in revenue, the firm will benefit from their employment. The marginal benefit will exceed the marginal cost. That man's or woman's employment will increase the firm's total profits; his or her employment will prove worthwhile for the firm.

But extra workers will only generate a rise in profits up to a point. When the last employee engaged only brings in sufficient extra revenue to cover their own wage, the firm is only just getting its money's worth. It will break even on that worker's employment but its profits will no longer be rising since total profits will have stabilized at a maximum level. A profit maximizing firm will seek to equate the marginal cost of engaging an additional employee with the marginal revenue which it might expect to gain from the worker's employment. The worker must justify the wage. It is only worthwhile for the firm to employ men and women as long as they bring in sufficient extra revenue to cover their wage. Workers produce output and so the extra benefit which a firm receives from employing additional workers will comprise the market value of this extra output. Highly productive workers add more to the firm's total output than the less productive and the productivity of the employees should be reflected in their wage rate. Profit-maximizing firms are prepared to pay workers what they are worth. If women earn less than men, this can only be justified on economic grounds if men are worth more to the firm than women.

Marginal Product and Diminishing Returns

As a firm employs extra workers, even assuming that all men and women are identical in skill, commitment, ability, training and so on, the firm will find that output does not vary proportionately with employment. These differences in output arise because the firm is employing labour in conjunction with other factors of production, namely capital and land. If the other factors of production are in fixed supply then engaging more men and women will not produce a steady increase in output due to the changing relationship between the fixed and the variable factors of production. In simple terms, some workers find plenty of machinery to work with whilst other employees find their work areas crowded. These differences in factor proportions give rise to variations in the output produced by the additional employees.

In the early stages of expansion, there will not be enough of the variable factor to make full use of the fixed factor. It is like employing only one worker to operate all the equipment in a brewery. There are so many operations to superintend that much time is wasted and production is rather slow. The brewery will be operating below full capacity because it has insufficient labour to make full use of its capital. Eventually as more men and women are employed, there will come a stage where there are enough employees to make full use of the machines. In this stage of production the relationship between fixed and variable factors of production will be satisfactory, in the sense that the firm will be employing sufficient labour to operate the machinery. Efficient production has become possible. During this stage of production the firm will find that as additional men or women are employed, total production will go on rising, but at a slower rate than before. Every extra employee taken on in the factory, for example, will help the firm to produce more jars of coffee. But each extra worker employed adds less to total output than previous employees. Coffee production is rising but at a decreasing rate; even though total product is increasing, marginal product is falling. The firm is now experiencing diminishing returns to labour as shown in Table 8.2. The sixth worker employed in instant coffee production increases the firm's weekly output by 80 jars, the seventh workers adds a further 65 jars, the eighth 50 jars and so on. Marginal product is falling.

Table 8.2: The Marginal Revenue Product

Number of workers	Jars of coffee per week	Marginal product (jars)	Marginal revenue product (£)
5	2220	–	–
6	2300	80	160
7	2365	65	130
8	2415	50	100
9	2450	35	70

Marginal product is a physical concept; it is measured in terms of the jars of coffee or the barrels of beer produced. To evaluate the benefits of employing one more worker, the market value of the additional worker's contribution to production must be considered. This will be a monetary concept, calculated in Britain in pounds and pence. The value of the worker's contribution to the firm's revenue, the marginal revenue product, will be the market value of that worker's marginal product. This can be calculated by multiplying the worker's marginal product by the market price for the product. If this firm is selling its product in perfectly competitive product markets, then it can sell as much or as little as it chooses to produce without any effect upon the price of the product. The perfectly competitive firm is a price taker in product markets too. The price of the product will remain fixed regardless of the firm's level of output. If the firm is producing jars of instant coffee which sell for £2 per jar, then this price will remain fixed whether the firm's weekly output is 25 jars, 250 jars or 2500 jars.

As the firm in Table 8.2 is experiencing diminishing returns to labour, the marginal revenue product falls as more workers are employed. If the seventh worker enables this firm to increase its output of jars of coffee by 65 jars per week and if coffee sells for £2 per jar, then the seventh worker's marginal revenue product will be £130 whilst the marginal revenue product of the ninth worker will only be £70. A profit-maximizing firm will employ more workers only as long as they earn their keep – that is until the marginal cost equals the marginal benefit. The wage is the marginal cost the firm incurs whilst the marginal revenue product represents the marginal benefit. A profit-maximizing firm will equate the wage with the marginal revenue product of the factor and decide how many workers to employ on this basis.

The Firm's Demand for Labour

If this firm is operating in a perfectly competitive labour market, then once again it is a price taker. It has to accept the wage rate as given and decide accordingly how many workers it wishes to employ. In Table 8.2, should the wage rate be £160 per week, then six workers will be employed, whilst if wages fall to £130 the firm will find it worthwhile to take on another employee. Wages must go right down to £70 a week, however, for the ninth worker to get a job. In other words the quantity of labour which a firm will employ at various alternative wage rates is determined by its marginal revenue product.

Thus the marginal revenue product of a factor represents the firm's demand for that factor. This demand curve is downward sloping due to the principle of diminishing returns. Figure 8.1 illustrates the downward sloping demand curve for labour.In this model a perfectly competitive firm decides how many men or women to employ purely and simply on the basis of that worker's value to production. Wages are determined by market forces and an individual firm then decides how many men and women it wants to employ at that going wage rate. If men and women are both equally productive and producing identical units of a product which sells in a perfectly competitive market, then the firm will have an identical demand curve for male and female workers. According to this theory, the age, race or gender of workers is immaterial to their employment. The labour demand is determined solely by factors such as the skill and productivity of workers and the market conditions for the product they produce. Neo-classical economics regards these factors as neutral; it is simply a question of productivity. The wage rate is thus a crucial indicator helping the firm to assess whether or not it is worthwhile employing an extra man or woman. High wages can only be justified by productive workers whilst lower productivity should be reflected in lower wage rates.

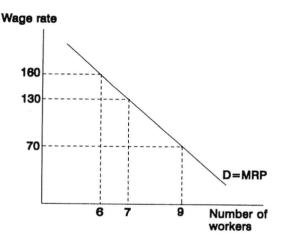

Figure 8.1: The Marginal Revenue Product for Labour

Shifts in the Demand Curve

Wage differentials between men and women will arise if the market conditions for male and female labour vary. On the supply side an abundance of female labour can drive women's wages down whilst a shortage of male labour will raise men's hourly wage rate. Demand factors too can prove significant. If women are less productive than men, or if they specialize in producing commodities whose demand is falling, then they will earn lower wages in competitive labour markets. Since a firm's demand for labour will reflect the worker's value to an employer, a more productive worker will justify a higher wage payment. Similarly workers, with the skills necessary to produce goods which are in high demand, will command high wages. The output of these workers is more valuable to the firm and the employee will be rewarded accordingly.

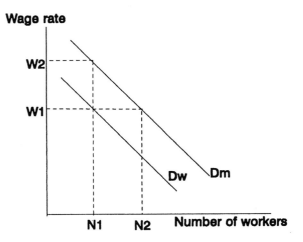

Figure 8.2: Men's and Women's Labour

The productivity of the worker will affect the demand for labour and hence will influence the wage rate. Whilst innate characteristics like talent and ability will influence a man's or a woman's productivity, there are many ways in which the worker's value to the employer can be enhanced. Education, training and on-the-job experience all represent human capital which can increase productivity. If workers possess, or are deemed to possess, human capital this will shift the demand curve for their labour outwards and employers will be prepared to pay higher wages for better skilled workers.

If men spend longer than women acquiring educational qualifications, if they get better access to training facilities, if they acquire more on-the-job experience, then these factors will render them more skilled and valuable to their employer. The possession of skill, however, can be subjective and socially constructed. Women's labour is sometimes perceived as being less skilled and hence less productive than male labour. One study, for example, in the footwear industry found female machinists operating machines which were more complicated than those worked by some of the men employed in the same firm. Nevertheless the women's work was regarded as unskilled (Armstrong 1982). Skill is not an objectively determined factor. Whether or not a worker is deemed as skilled can reflect the social position of the workers and indeed trade union pressure.

If women are deemed to be less skilled than men then they will be assigned to lower status jobs to which a lower wage is attached. The marginal revenue product from employing a male worker will, in this case, be, or be deemed to be, higher than that for a woman and employers will tend to favour male labour. The demand curve for male labour will be further to the right than that for women's labour and so a profit-maximizing firm will be prepared to pay a higher wage rate to a man. In Figure 8.2, D_m represents the demand for male labour whilst D_w shows the demand for women workers. If the firm wants to employ N_1 women and men, then it would be prepared to pay men a wage rate of W_2 whilst women only earn W_1.

Since women earn less than men, this diagram represents one possible explanation of the labour market conditions in the developed countries. Women's lower earnings might arise because their labour is simply less valuable to the employer than that of a man. If women were to achieve a lower level of educational qualifications, to receive less training and to acquire less experience, then their productivity would on average be less than that of a man. A comparison of the educational qualifications of women and men in Britain today will help to provide some evidence to support or refute this explanation of the gender wage gap.

The Skills and Qualifications of Men and Women

Certainly in the past women achieved a lower level of educational attainment than men. In 1970/71, 274 000 men, but only 182 000 women, were enrolled on full-time courses in universities in the United Kingdom (CSO 1995). Men accounted for 61 per cent of those in higher education. This pattern was replicated 20 years ago all the way down the educational spectrum; only 2 per cent of women of working age, but 6 per cent of men, had attained A levels in 1975; 65 per cent of women had left school with no educational qualifications at all whilst this applied to only 51 per cent of men. In the 1970s women did achieve lower educational qualifications than men. Many of these women are still in the labour force in the mid 1990s and this affects their productivity, their value to an employer, the jobs to which they are assigned and hence their wage rate.

Over the last 20 years though the picture has changed. Women have become more concerned to obtain educational and professional qualifications which increase their ability to support themselves from paid employment. Qualifications can indeed enhance a woman's economic independence. By 1992/93 the gap between the number of women and men in higher education had narrowed considerably; there were 496 000 men and 460 000 women enrolled in higher education. This represents a far more equal picture; 51 per cent of the students were men and 49 per cent were women (CSO 1995).

In the professions, too, women are now far more ready to acquire professional qualifications than ever they were in the past. In all the professional accounting bodies women are coming to represent an increasing proportion of new members. Women represented only 1 per cent of the total membership of the Institute of Chartered Accountants in England and Wales (ICAEW) in 1960 but by 1986 this proportion had risen to 8 per cent. Since women are relatively new recruits to the accounting profession they are concentrated amongst the newest members and 39 per cent of members aged between 23 and 26 are female (Crompton and Sanderson 1990). The Law Society reflects a similar trend; only 19 per cent of their successful candidates were women in 1975 but this had risen to 47 per cent by 1984 (Crompton and Sanderson 1986). Women are certainly beginning to acquire more educational and professional qualifications. So, the argument goes, it is only a matter of time before women will be as productive as men, equally valuable to an employer and hence will earn as much as men; wage equality is thought to follow automatically from educational qualifications.

Unfortunately the process is not as simple and straightforward as is suggested. Evidence shows that the returns which a woman receives from an investment in education are lower than those which a man can expect. This earnings gap is apparent at all levels of educational achievement. Women with degrees earn only 80 per cent of a male graduate's earnings whilst those women with no educational qualifications at all earn only 66 per cent of the equivalent male earnings. Women with higher education below degree level are the least disadvantaged group since their earnings will be 90 per cent of the equivalent man's earnings (OPCS 1994). In every case women earn less than their similarly qualified male counterparts.

Trade Unions and Skill

Educational achievement is not sufficient, in itself, to close the gender earnings gap. Market imperfections often intervene and influence the returns which women and men get from their training and education. If workers acquire skills or qualifications which enhance their productivity, they will be worth more to the employer. In Figure 8.3, D_1 represents the initial demand for labour and the labour market is in equilibrium at a wage of W_1. These workers then acquire additional skills which enhance their productivity and hence their value to their employer; the demand curve moves outwards to D_2. In a perfect market employers will be instantly aware of the extra skills which their workers have acquired and will increase the wage rate to W_2 accordingly. Employers who fail to remunerate workers for their extra skills will experience difficulty in retaining their skilled labour.

However, in practice many labour markets are imperfect. Employers might lack information about their workers' new skill levels. Unaware of the benefits they can obtain from increased productivity, firms might all be reluctant to reward their employees' skills through wage increases. Lack of information can impede the workings of the market. As long as a worker's skill remains unrecognized, wage rates will remain at W_1. In a perfect market the competitive process will ensure that workers are rewarded for their skills. If all employers remain ignorant of the value of their workers' skills, the lack of competition amongst employers will prevent workers from gaining suitable rewards for their skills.

Trade unions have been influential in helping to overcome this market imperfection. They have negotiated with employers for the recognition of skills and for the appropriate level of remuneration for their skilled members. Craft unions representing the interests of skilled manufacturing labour have been a significant influence upon wage differentials. If negotiation alone proves insufficient, trade unions can threaten collective action to persuade employers to reward the workers for their increase in productivity. If unions threaten to withdraw their members' labour at any wage below W_2 then the supply curve of labour becomes perfectly elastic at a wage of W_2 until point B is reached. Workers will of course be prepared to work at higher wages which will attract more men and women into the occupation. The supply curve therefore becomes W_2BS as a result of union pressure. Under these circumstances the firm will have to pay a wage rate of W_2 for unionized labour. By using their power in the labour market the union can induce the employers to reward their workers' skills. Union members receive W_2 whilst non-unionized employees are paid unskilled wage rates at W_1.

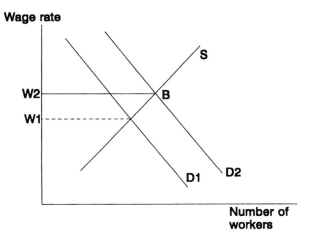

Figure 8.3: Trade Union Bargaining

Trade unions have in the past, and indeed still do, represent men's interests better than women's. The traditional stronghold for union membership in the United Kingdom has been amongst male employees in manufacturing industry. Trade unions are concerned to improve the terms and conditions of their members' employment. Whilst recent changes in the industrial structure have brought more women into the labour force affecting union membership, the union hierarchy remains predominantly male. The factors which impede women's promotion in an organization also limit their progress within the trade union movement. The extent of their domestic commitments, the discontinuity in employment, and their predominance in part-time work constrains women's active participation in union affairs. Even in unions like the Confederation of Health Service Employees (COHSE) and the National Union of Public Employees (NUPE) where women represent over 70 per cent of the membership, they hold a far smaller proportion of the key positions on the national executive or as delegates to the Trades Union Congress (Rees 1992). Unions have been instrumental in bargaining for the reward of members' skills whilst those of non-members go unrepresented and unrewarded. The workers whose union will negotiate for recognition of their skills and obtain a wage of W_2 in Figure 8.3 are more likely to be men, whilst those whose wage stays at W_1 through lack of union representation are likely to be women. The relative position of men's and women's wages can be affected by union negotiations.

Women's Employment, Skill and Experience

Social factors and expectations affect the career path which equally qualified men and women will pursue. A woman's pattern of paid work is likely to be different from that of a man. Even professional women are likely to look for career openings which enable them to combine domestic commitments with paid work. The concentration of women in part-time work prevents them from progressing up the hierarchy to the higher rungs of the career ladder. So even when the qualifications of men and women are identical there will be differences in rates of pay as women are more heavily concentrated at the lower levels of the hierarchy.

If mothers take career breaks and work on a part-time basis during the years when their children are small, this, in turn, will affect the on-the-job experience which they accumulate. Experience is often taken into account in pay scales and in promoting workers to higher levels of management. Career breaks and part-time working adversely affect the on-the-job experience which women accumulate. If mothers take career breaks when their children are small they lose some years' experience in the labour market. If women work part time then they lose hours of experience. Both these lost years and lost hours represent a depreciation of human capital in terms of lost experience. One study quantified the value of lost experience for a 'typical' woman with two children and GCSE education. It found that lost experience accounted for nearly 30 per cent of the lifetime earnings which such a woman might have expected to earn had she remained in full-time continuous employment (Joshi and Davies 1993).

An employer will make the assumption that a man or woman, who has been with the firm for a considerable period of time, will have acquired skills which will significantly enhance their value to the firm. Many occupations and organizations have pay structures by which employees are entitled to an annual increment until they reach the top of the scale. The economic rationale for this practice is that the worker is acquiring firm-specific skills and is thus becoming more productive and valuable to the employer. To achieve an efficient allocation of scarce resources these men and women should be rewarded accordingly. In some internal labour markets where promotions are internal to the firm, the criteria for promotion may include a specific reference to years of service.

These practices might appear to be gender neutral, as any man or woman who works continuously for the organization will be entitled to such increments, or in line for promotion. In Britain in the 1990s though it is still the norm for women, rather than men, to take a career break to raise a family. Women are more likely than men to take responsibility for arranging childcare and women are more likely than men to work part time to accommodate domestic commitments. Under these circumstances, pay by experience is far from gender neutral; it works in favour of men since they have a continuous work history.

A remuneration scale which rewards workers on the basis of their years of service can certainly be challenged on the grounds of equity; nevertheless such a system might promote efficiency. It might help to achieve the efficient allocation of resources, so the argument goes, by ensuring that a firm will reward its workers on the basis of their productivity. The assumption is that productivity depends upon the worker acquiring certain skills, which can only be obtained from continuous employment within the firm. Technology, however, is changing the work environment at a rapid pace. Banks are moving into new areas of financial services and spending far less time on routine tasks of cash dispensing; medical technology is bringing new practices into the health service and check-out technology in supermarkets is making retailing far more impersonal and capital intensive. In all these examples, the workers' old acquired skills are not particularly useful as the work environment changes. Under such circumstances higher rates of pay for those with the longest service might well not be the best route to efficiency.

The skills which a worker brings to an occupation are many and varied and can be acquired in a wide range of contexts. Education and work experience will certainly influence a worker's skill and productivity but other factors can also further this end as well. The role of the homemaker involves a wide range of skills. The job involves the use of technology, like the microwave oven or the washing machine. It requires the development of interpersonal skills such as negotiating between quarrelsome children and a parent must also have good time-management skills including the ability to prioritize tasks. These skills are also valuable in the work context. They enhance the worker's productivity and should accordingly be rewarded. A pay scale based upon seniority in the organization takes no account of skills acquired in the family context. If homemakers acquire and enhance their skills during their interlude from paid employment, then these skills will be increasing the worker's marginal revenue product and enhancing the value of the worker to the individual employer. These skills bring benefits to the firm and their value should be reflected in the wage rate in order to promote the efficient allocation of resources.

According to neo-classical economic theory the wage rate should accurately reflect the worker's contribution to output. It will then act as an incentive to both the worker and the employer. The wage rate will affect the worker's decision about the time allocated to paid employment. If women's wages do not reflect their productivity, then women will have less incentive to participate in paid employment. Low wage rates for women will affect the choices about the division of domestic labour; mothers will limit their involvement in paid work due to the low rewards which they are offered. A higher wage rate which reflected their contribution to the firm more accurately would encourage greater participation by women.

Employers, on the other hand, will not be encouraged by low wages to make full use of women's skills. They are paying them low wages and so they will be quite content with lower productivity than these workers are capable of achieving. There is no incentive to enhance their skills by training. Investment in British industry has indeed been inhibited by the low productivity of its low-wage workforce. The firm, and indeed the economy as a whole, experiences a lower level of output than it is possible to achieve since these women are not being deployed in their best possible use. The economy is not achieving an efficient use of its productive resources.

Women returners to the labour force seem particularly likely to make less than full use of their productive skills. Occupational downgrading has for many years been associated with career breaks for family formation. A study of British and American women between 1967 and 1980 found that in both countries there was a decline in the proportion of women employed in clerical occupations after a career break. This trend was particularly strong for British women. The proportion of women in the study employed in clerical work fell from 34 per cent before childbirth to only 19 per cent when these women returned to their first job after family formation. A similar, but less dramatic trend was apparent for semi-skilled factory work which attracted 21 per cent of the women workers before their break but only 18 per cent afterwards. Unskilled work and semi-skilled domestic work on the other hand attracted increasing proportions of women in the post-childbirth period (Dex and Shaw 1986).

If skilled or semi-skilled women work in unskilled occupations after they have children, then the economy is not making full use of their productive potential. These women are not making full use of their skills and training. The economy loses the output which they are capable of producing if their skills were fully deployed. The women lose by accepting lower wages but the whole economy loses since living standards are lower than they might have been. The efficient use of scarce resources is not being achieved.

Summary

Neo-classical economics suggests that labour markets should help to promote the efficient allocation of scarce resources between competing uses. Wages should assist this allocative process. The wage rate should provide workers with the incentive to move into occupations where rewards are highest and out of occupations which are relatively poorly paid. Such mobility can rarely be achieved by those with domestic commitments. Wage rates should encourage employers to employ men and women on the basis of their productivity. In this way the economy can achieve both productive and allocative efficiency.

In a neo-classical market system, the wage rates paid to men and women simply reflect their productivity, their value to the economic system. In practice though wage rates can be affected by power relationships. Trade unions represent the interests of their members and have been instrumental in obtaining recognition for men's skills and productivity. Women's interests have been less well represented by the union movement. The productive skills which homemakers practise in the domestic sphere are rarely reflected in the market wage rates. Employers are prepared to recognize labour market experience, but not experience gained in non-market roles. Consequently women's wages are less likely than men's to prove an accurate reflection of their productive value to the firm. If women are paid less than men, this has economic consequences since the economy is not putting their productive talents to the best possible use. The gender wage gap might not reflect the economic reality of productivity; it can be strongly influenced by institutional and social factors. The wage differentials between men and women could then serve to inhibit, rather than promote, the efficient allocation of resources.

9   Equal Pay?
Labour Markets in Practice

Introduction. Wage differentials and occupational mobility. Barriers to occupational mobility. Occupational segregation by gender. Segregation and wage rates. Discrimination in employment. Economic discrimination. Vertical segregation, discrimination and earnings. Statistical discrimination. Trade unions and earnings. Summary and conclusion.

Introduction

Wages and salaries provide one of the most important income sources for both men and women. In 1995 the average hourly earnings of a woman in Britain were nearly £2 lower than those of a man. If women earn less than men, they spend less than men; consequently they find it harder than men to achieve a satisfactory standard of living providing for their own support and that of their dependents. The gender earnings gap affects women's command over scarce resources and it constrains their ability to achieve economic autonomy. Women's lower earnings result from the interaction of several common features of labour markets. Workers in some occupations earn more than those in others and men predominate in the higher paying occupations. Those at the top of the hierarchy earn more than those further down the ladder and women tend to be concentrated at the lower end of organizational structures. Vertical and horizontal segregation interact to contribute to the differences in earnings between men and women.

Differences in average earnings are common to all industrialized countries and persist over time. Medical practitioners earn more than nurses, solicitors are better paid than secondary school teachers who are paid a higher rate than cleaners. Table 9.1 shows some of these variations in the average earnings, excluding overtime of full-time workers whose pay was not affected by absence in selected occupations in Great Britain in 1995. The occupation in which a worker is employed has an important influence on the rewards received for a week's work. Economic theory attempts to analyse why such differences in earnings arise between occupations and whether they are likely to persist in the long run.

Workers in different occupations receive different average earnings but Table 9.1 also illustrates another feature of wage differentials. There are substantial variations between the average earnings of men and women overall and within each occupational category. In each case men earn more than women. Since Equal Opportunities legislation has been on the Statute Book in Britain since 1970, these figures might seem surprising. If it is illegal to pay different rates for men and women in the same firm undertaking work of equal value, it seems anomalous to discover that there are such significant differences in pay between men and women within the same occupation. Yet clearly this is the case: the gender pay gap is all too evident in Table 9.1. The extent of the gap varies between occupations. On the basis of these figures it is most marked in the case of solicitors whilst in nursing the gender pay gap is less noticeable with women earning 92 per cent of the equivalent male rate.

Table 9.1: Hourly Earnings of Men and Women in Selected Occupations April 1995

Occupation	Men (£ per hour)	Women (£ per hour)	Women's earnings as % of men's
Medical Practitioners	19.11	16.61	87
Solicitors	17.74	13.61	77
Secondary school teachers	15.03	13.48	90
Nurses	9.37	8.61	92
Cleaners, domestics	4.47	3.99	89
All occupations	8.97	7.14	80

Source: *New Earnings Survey*, 1995

Economists attempt to explain the determination of wage rates through supply and demand in labour markets. The demand for labour will reflect the productivity of the workers and the strength of the demand for the final product, whilst the supply of labour is the outcome of the choices workers are making about the division of their time between paid employment, non-market work and leisure activities. The wage for a particular occupation will thus settle at the equilibrium rate, at which the number of workers the firm wishes to employ will exactly match the number of workers seeking jobs in that occupation. The labour market will clear at the equilibrium wage rate.

Neo-classical economics considers this market process to be gender neutral. If men and women are both equally productive and are willing to supply their labour in equal quantities to a particular occupation, then they should earn the same rate of pay. In practice this situation rarely occurs. Men and women often work in different occupations and men are more likely than women to progress to the upper rungs of the career ladder. Both horizontal and vertical segregation are common features of contemporary labour markets. The outcome of segregation in labour markets is that men earn more than women.

Wage Differentials and Occupational Mobility

Wage differentials between occupations are explained as the result of either temporary or permanent differences in the labour market conditions. Economists recognize two reasons for differences in wage rates: compensating differentials and non-compensating differentials. Compensating differentials are a permanent feature of labour markets arising to compensate workers for unpleasant features of their job. If an occupation involves working in dirty conditions or at unsocial times of the day, then it is argued that a wage premium should be offered in order to persuade workers to accept these terms and conditions of employment. Compensating differentials are needed to ensure that unpleasant occupations can attract sufficient labour to enable the final product to be supplied satisfactorily.

Compensating differentials can help to explain gender differences in earnings only if men work in less pleasant conditions and in less agreeable occupations than women. These occupations would then require higher wages to offset the inherent disadvantages of the job. If women work in pleasanter conditions then their wages will be lower than men's since their pay packet will not include any compensating differential. It is only under these circumstances that compensating differentials can be used to account for differences in earnings between men and women. Since many studies on compensating differentials have excluded women from the sample the available evidence fails to conclude whether this factor contributes to providing a satisfactory explanation of the gender earnings gap (Jacobsen 1994).

Non-compensating differentials are rather different; they serve to reflect the changing conditions in the economy. If labour is scarce in one particular occupation, this should be reflected in a high wage rate, whilst an abundance of labour will serve to drive wage rates down. In Britain in 1995, the average hourly earnings of a computer systems and data processing manager were £16.27 and this figure is substantially above the average hourly earnings of £8.97 (Department of Employment 1995). The computer industry has been expanding rapidly over the last decade and consequently there is a rising demand for computer managers. University degree programmes in computer skills are a very new area; thus the supply of skilled workers available to fill these positions is at present limited. In order to ration the supply of skilled computer managers between all those employers seeking to make use of their services, wage rates have risen above the average. The relatively high wage rates reflect the scarcity of this particular type of labour.

Bus or coach drivers, on the other hand, earn an hourly wage of £5.08 that is nearly £4.00 less than the average male hourly earnings (Department of

Employment 1995). The use of private cars has been reducing the demand for public transport. The demand for bus drivers has therefore been falling. The skills required for this occupation can be acquired quickly and easily; thus the supply of bus drivers is relatively plentiful. Low wages reflect the abundance of supply relative to demand in this particular occupation.

Differences in wage rates, like those between computer managers and bus drivers, serve a function. They promote flexibility and help the economy to adapt to a changing pattern of consumer demand. As bus drivers' wage rates fall, so some employees will be encouraged to seek better opportunities elsewhere and the supply of bus drivers will fall. The reduction in the number of bus drivers will eventually make their labour more scarce, increasing their wage rates. The economy will adapt to the changing pattern of consumer demand by reallocating labour away from declining sectors of the economy.

Computer managers are initially in a far more fortunate position since their wage rates are relatively high. Above average weekly earnings help their occupation to attract new entrants. Young people entering the labour market for the first time will seek employment in computer related occupations and the supply of labour to this occupation will expand. As the labour supply increases, computer managers are in more abundant supply. This will serve to moderate their wages.

Bus drivers' wages rise as workers look for other jobs; computer managers' wages fall as new entrants are attracted into this occupations. Thus the market mechanism will allocate labour between competing uses and in this process wage differentials will narrow.

Barriers to Occupational Mobility

Non-compensating wage differentials should therefore be eliminated if labour is sufficiently mobile between occupations. In practice though, occupational mobility of labour is often difficult to achieve. If all nurses could, in time, acquire the skills necessary to become solicitors then occupational mobility of labour will eliminate this non-compensating differential between the two occupations. Several issues can be identified in this respect. Firstly it takes time for new entrants to acquire the necessary skills and qualifications to practise law, secondly many professions limit entry and finally some workers might not possess the talents and ability necessary to acquire the qualifications needed for entry to the legal profession.

If the high earnings of solicitors provide an incentive, this will attract increasing numbers of new entrants to the profession. Law degree programmes will find their applications rising and post-graduate professional programmes will attract increasing numbers of students. If law degrees are able to expand their intake, it is only a matter of time before the supply of solicitors increases. But qualifications are not acquired instantaneously. It takes time for young men and women to acquire the necessary skills to enter professional occupations. It takes at least three years to graduate with a degree in law and then follows professional training and examinations. It will take many years before new entrants make any significant difference to the supply of fully qualified solicitors. Whilst this training takes place the market shortage will persist. Wage differentials between occupations reflect the time and speed with which the market can adjust to labour shortages. The more extensive the training period, the more inelastic the supply curve of labour will be and the longer the pay differential will persist.

In some cases, the market might never adjust fully. There might be barriers to entry which prevent the market supply of labour responding to the incentive offered by high wage rates. If law schools limit the number of students whom they admit for training, then the wage differential will be persistent. The shortage will not be overcome by market forces as the supply of solicitors will be unable to respond to the incentive provided by higher wages. Some potential lawyers will be refused entry to law school and so trained solicitors will remain in short supply.

Professional examinations and trainee/studentship requirements can also limit entry to a certain profession. These are very common in the professions such as accountancy and law. The failure rate in professional examinations is high and the number of trainees or pupillage places is limited, making for fierce competition between potential entrants to these lucrative careers. Once again the supply is unable to respond to the normal market incentives and the scarcity of qualified professional lawyers and accountants ensures the persistence of their high earnings.

Wage differentials also persist due to the uneven distribution of talent and ability. Some students are strong on quantitative skills, whilst others excel linguistically; some perform better in science subjects whilst others tend towards practical skills. These differences in ability will affect the worker's productivity in different occupations. Someone with little aptitude for numerical work will not prove to be a very efficient accountant. This unequal distribution of talents and ability will also impede occupational mobility. Young men and women will be influenced in their occupational choice by their assessment of their talents and abilities. However much veterinary surgeons earn, if a student has a strong fear of animals and no aptitude for scientific subjects, then the high rates of pay will not act as an incentive to encourage this student to enter the profession. Personal factors are restricting the mobility of labour.

The wage differential between some occupations therefore persists because the occupational mobility of labour is impeded. The adjustment process takes time and wage differentials will persist whilst adjustment is taking place. Furthermore some potential entrants to the more lucrative professions are prevented from increasing the labour supply since they are unable to gain the necessary qualifications. They are either denied entry because of the limited number of places on the requisite training programmes or they have talents and abilities which are inappropriate for this occupation. In this case it is unlikely that they will complete the necessary training. These occupations therefore remain a highly paid enclave.

Occupational Segregation by Gender

Table 9.1 showed that not only did solicitors earn more than nurses but also that the average hourly earnings of men, at £8.97, are almost £2 higher than those of women. There is both an occupational and a gender wage gap. Part of the explanation for the difference in average earnings between men and women lies in the fact that men and women are often employed in different occupations. In 1995 men represented 50 per cent of the employees in employment in Great Britain whilst women accounted for the remaining 50 per cent. There are however very few occupational categories in which the proportions of men and women employed come close to those overall averages. Men are heavily over-represented in some occupations like plant and machine operatives and craft and related occupations whilst women predominate in clerical and secretarial occupations and in personal services. The British Social Attitudes Survey reported that in 1987, 66 per cent of men worked only with other men whilst 49 per cent of women worked only with other women (Jowell et al. 1988).

If there are barriers impeding the movement of labour between men's and women's jobs, then the labour market is effectively divided into two sections. Wage differentials cannot perform their allocative function redistributing labour between occupations. Men's higher earnings will persist if their occupation is one into which women find it difficult to move. Occupational segregation can protect and perpetuate the gender wage gap. Occupational segregation is still very marked in Britain and in all other industrialized countries. It persists even in countries like Denmark where women participate in the working population to the same extent as men (Maruani 1992). Barriers to occupational mobility can arise either on the supply or the demand side of the labour market. On the supply side men and women might choose to enter different occupations. Human capital theory, differences in talents and abilities, entry barriers and social exclusion provide supply-side explanations of this occupational choice. Discrimination by employers who prefer to employ either men or women exclusively in an occupation is an attempt to explain segregation from the demand side of the labour market.

Human capital theory, which attempts to explain occupational choice in terms of men's and women's different expectations about their future labour force participation, was examined in Chapter 5. Women are represented as choosing to enter occupations requiring a lower investment in human capital or those in which human capital will not deteriorate during absences from the labour force. However, since the decline in earnings resulting from discontinuous employment is not significantly different in male and female occupations, yet the earnings are substantially higher in male occupations, rational choice hardly accounts for occupational segregation (England 1982).

Occupational segregation is sometimes explained in terms of differences in talent and ability between men and women. If men possess certain skills whilst women achieve better results in other areas, then it might be most efficient for firms to employ men and women in different occupations. Men might be better suited to operating machinery due to their superior physical strength whilst women might have greater manual dexterity, equipping them to be more efficient as typists. Occupational segregation would, according to this argument, have some economic rationale. Firms would achieve higher levels of productivity if they used men's and women's labour in its most productive use. With differences in talent and ability, occupational segregation improves efficiency. If, however, talent and ability are distributed more or less equally between men and women, with other factors like social class, educational opportunity and parental income proving more significant as determinants of educational achievement, then occupational segregation impedes the efficient operation of labour markets.

Segregation and Wage Rates

Whilst there are few occupations in which women and men are equally represented, occupational segregation is not simply a random process. Men do not just happen to be over-represented in some occupations whilst women predominate in others and then supply and demand determine the rewards accruing to these occupations. Occupational segregation helps to explain the differences in average earnings between men and women because men predominate in the highly paid occupations whilst women are clustered together in lower paid activities. Men earn more than women partly because the occupations in which men predominate are more lucrative than those that women enter. The Equal Opportunities Commission has noted that in five of the most highly paid professions women accounted for 10 per cent or less of total employment. Men represent 99 per cent of electrical engineers, 98 per cent of surgeons and 93 per cent of architects and in each of these occupations weekly earnings are substantially above the average in the economy as a whole. Women meanwhile constitute over 90 per cent of the employees in low paying occupations such as typists, nursing and telephone operators (EOC 1993). This high concentration of men in well paid occupations whilst women predominate in the less well remunerated sectors helps to explain why men on average earn more than women.

If there are barriers to entry then the labour supply curve for each occupation is specific. Wages cannot perform their allocative function since the movement of labour between men's jobs and women's jobs will be restricted. The wage rate in each of these occupations will then reflect the supply and demand conditions in these two different sections of the labour market. Women and men are often in non-competing groups within the labour market. Mothers with domestic commitments often seek part-time employment within their particular locality whilst men are more mobile geographically. Part-time jobs in Britain often provide little opportunity for promotion and thus limit women's mobility up the organizational hierarchy. Segregation in employment has restricted the supply of labour in male occupations and has served to keep wages high.

Even if the demand conditions for women's and men's labour are identical, supply factors will also be important in affecting the market determined wage rates. An abundant supply of women competing for a narrow range of occupations will drive wage rates downwards. Evidence shows that women are indeed concentrated in a narrower range of occupational categories than men. The three most numerous women's occupations employ 73 per cent of all women employed whilst the three most significant men's occupations accounted for only 59 per cent of their employment. Women are 'crowded' into a narrow range of occupational categories and this creates supply-side pressure which drives their market wage rates down.

Any individual employer will therefore find that the market rate for women is lower than that for men. In paying lower wages for women's jobs the individual firm will merely be reflecting the conditions which prevail in the different sections of the labour market. The profit-maximizing firm is acting rationally to equate marginal revenue product with the market determined wage rate. Were free movement possible between occupations then these wage differences would serve to allocate labour between these occupations. Workers would have an incentive to move into the higher paying jobs and out of those paying lower wages. The supply of labour would reallocate itself between these two occupations until wage differentials disappeared. Such reallocation does not happen since social and institutional factors are significant in keeping the labour market segregated. The gender wage gap persists due partly to the immobility of the labour supply. Wages are unable to reallocate labour between men's and women's occupations.

Discrimination in Employment

The demand side of the market also contributes to occupational segregation. Many jobs are widely regarded by employers and employees alike as either men's jobs or women's jobs. Although discrimination in recruitment is illegal in Britain and in many other European countries, firms might be reluctant to hire a women in a traditionally male occupation. They might argue that the presence of a woman in such an occupation will impede the efficient working of their business. Even if employers are convinced that women have sufficient skills to perform the work as effectively as men, they might be concerned that workplace romances and consequent rivalries could disrupt good working relationships and thus impede production. Employers are often reluctant to employ women in men's jobs just as women are often disinclined to work where they might experience social discomfort. The same can also apply in reverse; employers might be reluctant to employ men on an exclusively female production line for fear that efficient and productive working relationships might thereby be impeded.

Social structures and institutional arrangements in Britain fail to deliver equal outcomes for men and women. Boys and girls leave secondary education with different qualifications. Option choices at 14 often result in boys favouring technical subjects, which have a higher market value, whilst girls choose humanities. At General Certificate of Secondary Education (GCSE) examinations in England in 1992/93 boys outnumbered girls amongst examination entries in Physics, Computer Studies and Craft, Design and Technology whilst girls were more heavily represented in Modern Languages, Home Economics and Social Studies (Department of Education 1995). The human capital which boys and girls acquire within compulsory education affect their market value to employers. Parents might hold stereotypical views of family and influence their daughters' educational choices and career expectations (Rees 1992). Finally the lack of good quality childcare facilities limits a mother's employment opportunities especially in occupations which demand a full-time commitment. Studies of British working women consistently report that informal care by partners, relatives or friends accounts for well over half of all care arrangements (Brannen et al. 1994). These social and institutional factors will affect the employment of men and women in our society.

Economic Discrimination

Economic discrimination though is rather more specific. Economic discrimination occurs when one group of workers is treated less favourably than another group due to characteristics other than those which affect their labour market performance. If employers pay black workers less than they pay white workers of identical skill and ability, then this is a case of economic discrimination. If employers are unwilling to employ workers of a particular social class regardless of their qualifications, then this too is economic discrimination. If employers will only consider women for certain types of occupation or if they pay them less than the equivalent male rate, then this is economic discrimination. Such discrimination is illegal in Britain and in most other countries in Europe.

Economic discrimination is reflected in the demand curve for labour. The employer's demand for men and women is·different. Firms are making a distinction between these two types of labour; their demand for women's labour is lower than their demand for men's labour. In Figure 9.1 the firm's demand for female labour differs from the demand for male labour. The curve D_1 represents the employer's demand for women whilst D_2 represents the demand for men's labour.

This situation has sometimes been explained in terms of a 'taste for discrimination' (Becker 1957). It is argued that the employers – or indeed the consumers or the other employees in some cases – simply prefer one type of worker. Their preference is to engage men only, for example, and they are prepared to pay in order to indulge this preference. So, for example, if the average wage for women is £250 per week, the discriminating employer will be prepared to pay a premium for men. They might be willing to pay an extra £100 per week for equally productive male workers. The men's average weekly wage would then be equivalent to the women's wage plus the premium – or £250 + £100 = £350.

In Figure 9.1 the women's weekly wage is represented by W_1. The discriminating employer is willing to pay a premium equivalent to the vertical distance between the two demand curves – or the distance AB – in order to engage male workers. The men's wage rate then becomes W_2. It is not that this employer will never under any circumstances employ women; it is rather that they prefer men and are prepared to pay a premium for their employment. Should the male wage rate rise above the female rate plus the premium – that is above £350 in our previous example – then some women will be recruited.

This difference in the demand curves will result in one of two outcomes: either the equilibrium wage rate for women will be lower than for men or

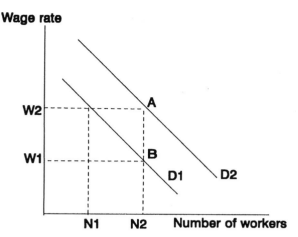

Figure 9.1: Economic Discrimination Between Men and Women

else fewer women than men will be employed in this occupation. Economists have often tried to test for discrimination and most studies of labour markets come up with a residual variable of difference in pay between men and women, part or all of which might be attributable to economic discrimination. A study of the British labour market based on the 1980 Women and Employment Survey estimated that women's pay would be 20 per cent higher than it actually is if discrimination were eliminated (Wright and Ermisch 1991). This finding suggests a much bigger discrimination co-efficient than had been estimated in previous studies.

Alternatively Figure 9.1 could represent a labour market in which discriminating employers have no option but to pay men and women the same wage rate. In this case their preference for male workers will result in rather a different outcome; employers will simply recruit fewer women. In Figure 9.1 if both women and men receive a wage rate of W_2, then the employer will want to engage N_2 men but only N_1 women. Men will therefore come to constitute the majority of the employees in this occupation and women will be in a distinct minority. Should this be a highly paid occupation, then the low proportion of women will help to account for women's lower average earnings. If women are poorly represented in highly paid occupations, then women as a group will earn less than men.

Some economists (Becker 1957) have argued that competitive market forces will make economic discrimination a self-defeating practice. If employers choose between workers on the basis of their non-market characteristics then these firms are denying themselves the opportunities which are available to their competitors. The discriminating employer who prefers to employ men and is prepared to pay higher wages to indulge this preference will experience higher costs than non-discriminating competitors. They are limiting their employment opportunities to only one type of worker – in this case men. The employer will be prepared to pay higher wages to indulge their preference for men as employees and their costs of production will reflect this decision.

Since women are assumed to be just as productive as men, the firm will be operating at a market disadvantage. It will experience higher unit costs of production than its non-discriminating competitors. Its prices will be higher than those of its close competitors and rational consumers will accordingly refrain from buying this firm's products, switching instead to the cheaper alternatives supplied by the non-discriminating firms. As this decline in market share takes place, the discriminating firm will eventually be competed out of the market. On this basis competitive markets make legislation against discrimination unnecessary. The discriminating firms will either see the error of their ways or will be forced into liquidation!

Whilst this scenario might be valid in a perfectly competitive market, very few markets in the real world conform to this textbook model. In practice firms often have a degree of market power. They therefore exercise some control over their price and can raise their price in order to cover their higher costs without losing all their market share. If the firm has a recognized position in the market and produces a product with a distinct brand image for which consumers are prepared to pay a premium, then the discriminating firm will not be competed out of existence. Its market power will protect it from extinction. Monopolies or oligopolies can therefore survive as discriminators.

Economic discrimination is reflected in differences in the demand curve for male and female labour but it can also interact with supply side factors to place women in a less favourable position than men. Discrimination by employers can result in women becoming segregated in just a limited range of occupations. Due to barriers to entry women might be unable to find jobs in the traditionally male areas of the economy and are forced to seek employment in traditionally female occupations. Actual or expected discrimination in labour markets can help to shape tastes and preferences which affect occupational choices (Ferber and Lowry 1976). Women's work is the only course open to them; this is not a free choice. As the women's labour force becomes concentrated in two or three major occupational categories, the supply of labour for these jobs is relatively abundant. Excess supply drives wage rates down and consequently women earn less than men. Discrimination interacts with occupational segregation to cause 'crowding' in women's occupations and thus their wages are lower than men's (Bergmann 1974).

Vertical Segregation, Discrimination and Earnings

Discrimination can work in other ways too; it can also affect women's promotion prospects within an occupation. If a firm's promotion criteria emphasize continuity of service or ability to work away from home, then these criteria indirectly discriminate against women. Their domestic commitments reduce their ability to meet such criteria. Women's participation in labour markets is on a different basis and the skills and experience which they bring to an occupation can differ substantially from those which a man offers. If a firm fails to take these factors into account in its recruitment and promotion criteria, then it will find that women will be, and will continue to be, under-represented, especially in the higher levels of the organization.

Men often occupy more senior positions whilst women are found in the lower levels of an organization. Even in traditionally female occupations men often occupy the most senior positions. In libraries women staff predominate but men are most likely to be senior librarians. A study of a university library in 1986 found that although men constituted only 5 per cent of the library's workforce, they occupied all the most senior positions (Luck 1991). Over 80 per cent of primary school teachers in England and Wales were women in 1992 but just over half of the headteachers of primary schools are men (Department of Education 1995). In building societies too, women outnumber men in the lower clerical grades whilst the majority of the managers are men (Crompton and Sanderson 1990). Such vertical segregation is an observed feature of men's and women's employment in Britain today. If British women return to work on a part-time basis then there is a strong possibility that this will involve some loss of occupational status.

Within an occupation or organization the salary scale will often be incremental. Senior management will earn more than middle-ranking employees, whilst they in their turn will receive more than juniors or trainees. If all senior executives and above are men whilst women are concentrated in the lower ranks then, within an organization, men will on average earn more than women. The average salary for a man will be pulled up by the inclusion of the high salaries of the executive rank whilst the average for a woman will be affected by a large number of women in junior posts. Vertical segregation is just as common as occupational segregation in Britain today. Women earn less than men in each occupational category partly because women are found at lower levels and do not progress to senior posts. Indirect discrimination undoubtedly contributes to vertical segregation.

Statistical Discrimination

Economic discrimination occurs when equally productive workers are treated differently but statistical discrimination occurs when employers base employment decisions upon group rather than individual performance. If one group of workers is found to be less suitable for a particular job, or less productive on average than another group, then employers might base their recruitment policies on these group averages. It becomes costly to assess each employee as an individual and so often firms will be guided by group averages. If most university graduates respond well to management training and perform satisfactorily in the job whilst most school leavers experience difficulty in coping with the work, then it seems sensible to recruit only graduates. The costs of recruitment are identical in each case but the benefits to the firm are substantially higher if graduates are recruited. The employer is using the degree qualification as a screening process to identify those groups of workers who are statistically most likely to respond to the training programme. Marriage and parenthood affects women's and men's employment prospects differently. If married men usually prove to be particularly dedicated and committed workers whilst married women often leave to have children, then firms will favour the recruitment of men. The costs of recruitment are identical but the benefits from hiring a man outweigh the gains from a woman's employment. Rational choice favours the recruitment of men.

In these cases, discrimination is occurring on the basis of statistical averages. The firm is basing its recruitment decisions upon the average performance of the group rather than on the individual's own performance. It judges that university graduates make better managers than school leavers, married men are more committed to their work than married women. Such procedures might well result in discrimination against particular individuals. A school leaver who has extraordinary ability might perform very well in the occupation but he or she will be denied the opportunity to prove themselves. They will be screened out by the statistical averages. Statistical discrimination is occurring.

A married woman who never intends to have children might suffer discrimination in employment because most women do have children. Employers might be reluctant to engage any young women as trainees. The costs of their training might never be recovered in future years of employment as firms fear that women will leave employment to have a baby and only return on a part-time basis. This is indeed a very typical pattern of employment for women in Britain in the 1990s and there is plenty of evidence to support these expectations. But for one particular woman, the employer's refusal to employ her might be discriminatory. She might have no intention of ever having children or she might have decided that children are not going to interfere with her career and she will combine motherhood with full-time employment. It would be beneficial to the firm to employ and train this particular woman. Her training would not be wasted as she intends to remain in the job. The problem, though, is that employers often have no means of separating these committed career women from those who conform more closely to the average. At the point of recruitment it would be either impossible or else prohibitively expensive to distinguish the few women who will, on their criteria, be worth training, from the rest. Consequently discrimination occurs against those who do not conform to the average pattern.

Statistical discrimination can contribute to wage differences between men and women. If men on average tend to be freer from domestic commitments, prepared to work late and to travel around the world if necessary on company business, then, on the basis of statistical averages, they will be judged most worthy of recruitment to senior posts. A woman candidate will start at a significant disadvantage. Consequently men are more likely than women to rise throughout the ranks and to be found at the higher levels within their chosen occupation. The average earnings of men will be higher than those of women due to the preponderance of men at the top of many occupational hierarchies. Statistical discrimination interacts with vertical segregation to help to account for the gender wage gap.

Trade Unions and Earnings

One final reason why some groups of workers earn more than others concerns membership of a trade union. A trade union replaces individual negotiation between the employer and the employee by collective bargaining whereby groups of workers negotiate with employers about wage rates and terms and conditions of employment. The market mechanism whereby individual men or women decide whether or not to accept work at a given wage rate is replaced by a collective decision concerning the acceptable level of remuneration for an occupation.

If the workers in a previously competitive market were to join a trade union whose objective was to increase workers' wages, then on the supply side of the market the situation would have changed. The workers would be acting together. They would be prepared to work for the wage the union demanded at the very least. If any wage below this level were offered then no labour would be supplied whilst at a higher wage market forces would again operate. If the union negotiates for a wage above the market rate, the market equilibrium wage will not be reached. The formation of a trade union will result in an increase in the wage rate for union members. The union secures a wage rise for its members who will now be earning more than non-unionized workers whose wage rates will still be determined by market forces. A wage differential comes into existence between unionized and non-unionized sections of the workforce.

In the United Kingdom union membership has traditionally been associated with manufacturing industry and male employees have predominated as union members. This pattern is changing today as women are now just as likely as men to become union members when they are full-time employees. Part-time employees though are only half as likely as full-timers to be union members. As women account for the majority of part-time workers this factor is decisive in accounting for the lower level of female membership in trade unions. Women's membership of trade unions has increased during the 1980s but it has not been accompanied by a corresponding rise in their participation in union decision making. Women's domestic responsibilities interfere with active participation in branch union meetings and women's discontinuous pattern of employment prevents them from acquiring the necessary experience and confidence to undertake union positions. Promotion at work and promotion within the union hierarchy often depend upon the same criteria – continuity in employment, experience, organizational know-how and so on – and consequently women are disadvantaged by their domestic commitments (Rees 1992). Trade unions have proved significant in gaining better terms and conditions of employment for those whose interests they represent. Under these circumstances union differentials serve to reinforce gender differential in earnings since men are more likely than women to see their interests represented by the union movement.

Summary and Conclusion

In Britain today, the rewards for a week's full-time work vary considerably between occupations. In April 1994 a man could earn nearly four times more as a medical practitioner than as a cleaner. These occupational differentials persist primarily because workers are imperfectly mobile between occupations and hence reallocation of labour cannot erode these differentials completely. Both compensating and non-compensating differentials will be apparent between occupations. Since men and women are not distributed equally throughout the occupational categories, these occupational differentials will affect the average earnings of men and women. Men tend to be over-represented in highly rewarded occupations whilst women form a large proportion of the workers in those occupations which command a lower wage rate. Occupational segregation therefore interacts with occupational wage differences to account for the difference in full-time average earnings between men and women.

Segregation in employment arises between occupations and between the different ranks of seniority within an occupation. Entry barriers impede the mobility of labour between predominantly male and predominantly female sectors of the economy. Vertical segregation by which men are found in more senior positions whilst women occupy the lower ranks helps to explain why men earn more than women even within a particular occupational group. Discrimination too affects the earnings of men and women. Factors both on the supply and demand side of the labour market account for vertical segregation.

Britain first enacted legislation against sex discrimination in employment and providing for equal pay for equal work, 20 years ago, yet substantial differentials still exist between both men's and women's average earnings and between the earnings of men and women employed in the same occupations. If women earn less than men this affects their economic autonomy and their standard of living. As a full-time worker a woman on average earns less than her male counterpart throughout the occupational categories. This affects her ability to support herself and maintain a reasonable standard of living. If she also supports dependents, then her economic situation becomes even more constrained.

Women and men are not treated equally in labour markets even when they are both working on a full-time basis. Part-time working, however, is becoming increasingly common and women are far more likely than men to be employed on this basis. Part-time work though brings in only part-time wages, thus undermining women's economic position still further.

The government could play a more active role in helping to ensure a woman-friendly work environment. The differences in the domestic responsibilities of men and women undoubtedly contribute to pay differentials. As long as childcare in Britain is regarded as a woman's issue rather than one which affects all parents and indeed the whole of society, it will be difficult for women to compete on equal terms with men in paid employment. Furthermore the government could introduce labour market policies to try and ensure greater equality for men and women in the workplace.

The determination of wage rates in labour markets is far from gender neutral. Discrimination affects the representation of women in certain occupations and in the higher levels of organizations. The supply of women's labour is crowded into a small range of occupations, driving their wage rate down. Equal pay might be enshrined in the Statute Book but it is far from being a reality for men and women in Britain today.

10 Labour Market Policies

Introduction. Equal pay legislation and economic discrimination. Equal pay legislation and productivity differences. Equal pay and single sex occupations. The consequences of the equal pay act. Maternity leave. The introduction of a minimum wage. A minimum wage in competitive labour markets. Monopsonistic labour markets and a minimum wage. Summary.

Introduction

Women and men often earn very similar rates of pay when they first enter the labour market but by their middle years there are considerable pay differentials between them (Maruani 1992). Labour market outcomes are the result of a complex conjunction of social, historical and economic factors arising out of men's and women's position in society which affects and constrains the terms on which they both participate in paid employment. The social position of women and men interacts with and affects their economic standing. Women are still expected, and still expect, to be the main care givers. This unpaid social role has an opportunity cost in terms of paid employment. A discontinuous career reduces the chances of promotion and adversely affects earnings. In a society where divorce is becoming increasingly common, men and women need to establish their own economic independence if they are to feel secure and free from poverty.

Economic factors too affect women's earnings. If women experience discrimination in employment and promotion, if they are confined to, or choose to enter, a narrow range of lowly paid occupations, if they earn less than men, then it becomes difficult for them to attain economic autonomy and security. Some of these issues can be addressed through labour market policies. A wide variety of government measures react upon and affect the labour market, the employment and the earnings of men and women. The floating exchange rate policy of the early 1980s resulted in a very high rate of exchange for sterling, damaging Britain's export position and aggravating the loss of jobs in manufacturing industry. Male unemployment, in particular, spiralled upwards. In this case the government's overall economic strategy had indirect implications for the labour market. In other instances the government has introduced legislation specifically designed to affect labour market outcomes.

Since 1970 a series of measures has been introduced in the United Kingdom with the specific objective of reducing gender inequalities in labour markets.

The Equal Pay Act, the Equal Pay Amendment, the Sex Discrimination Act and the Employment Protection Act provide examples of such measures. Yet, despite over 20 years of legislation, the gender wage gap remains one of the most glaring inequalities in labour markets today. Economic analysis can help to account for the limited success of these legislative measures. The introduction of a minimum wage provides another example of a policy aimed specifically at the labour market. A minimum wage would outlaw low wage rates and the likely consequences of this measure upon employment have become a fierce political issue. Economic analysis can help to identify the groups which will be affected, either directly or indirectly, by the introduction of a minimum wage.

Equal Pay Legislation and Economic Discrimination

Legislation on equal pay was first introduced in 1970 with the Equal Pay Act which made it illegal to pay different wage rates for men and women employed in the same firm and doing the same, or broadly similar, work. This Act came into force five years later in 1975 at the same time as the Sex Discrimination Act was introduced. The Sex Discrimination Act outlawed discrimination in employment, training and education. The Employment Protection Act of 1975 provided women with paid leave for childbirth and the right to maternity pay and protection from unfair dismissal.

The Equal Pay Act of 1970 was intended to promote wage equality between employed men and women. It established the principle of equal pay for equal work so that if a woman and a man were doing exactly the same job then it became illegal to offer them different rates of pay. The wage rate applied to the job regardless of the personal characteristics of those occupying the position. Since women earned less than men, it was assumed that their wage rate would increase to establish equality in those occupations which were performed by both men and women.

Legislation establishing equal pay inevitably interferes with the operation of market forces. Wage rates are no longer established only by the free interaction of supply and demand. The consequences of such legislation will depend upon the reasons why women and men initially earned different wage rates and on the assumptions one makes concerning the long- and short-run response of men and women to these changes in wage rates. Inequality in wage rates can result from economic discrimination which occurs when employers are less willing to employ women than men due to reasons unconnected with their ability to perform the job. Due to economic discrimination the demand for women's and men's labour will differ and it was this situation which the equal pay legislation was designed to remedy. Employers who discriminate against women will have a lower demand for women's labour than for men's labour. The discriminating employer will be prepared to employ men at a higher wage rate than they are prepared to offer an equally productive woman. In Figure 10.1 the demand for women's labour is represented by the demand curve D_1 whilst the employer is prepared to demand the labour of male workers on the basis of the demand curve D_2.

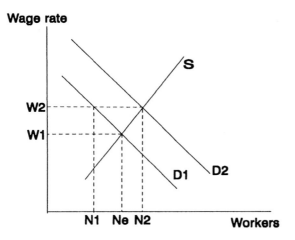

Figure 10.1: Equal Pay Legislation

Differences in the demand for labour result in different wage rates for men and women. Market forces would establish the equilibrium wage rates. The male wage rate would settle at W_2 whilst women would only be paid a rate of W_1. Economic discrimination would result in a lower market wage rate for women than for men. It was precisely this situation which the Equal Pay Act and the Sex Discrimination Act were designed to overcome. In effect the legislation made it illegal for employers to employ men and women on these different terms. All workers must be treated equally in labour markets and so the demand curve D_2 should come to represent the demand for both women's and men's labour. The legislation outlawed the different demand curve, D_1, for women's labour. Both men and women should be paid a wage of W_2 and N_2 women and men should be employed. It was hoped initially that by outlawing economic discrimination wage and employment equality would quickly be established.

Equal Pay Legislation and Productivity Differences

Wage equality in Britain is not simply the result of economic discrimination; other factors are also significant. If women are less productive than men this would provide an alternative reason why the demand curve for women's labour would be lower than that for male workers. On this basis employers would only be prepared to employ women at a lower rate of pay than men because women were less well trained, less qualified or less skilled than men. In Figure 10.1 the demand for women's labour is lower at D_1 due, in this case, to their lack of skill and training. Even without discrimination employers would then want to pay men a wage rate of W_2 whilst women receive a wage rate of W_1. These wage rates will enable the employer to equate the marginal revenue product of men's and women's labour with the marginal cost of labour, that is the wage rate.

If the government passes equal pay legislation then wage rates will be standardized. W_2 will be the wage rate at which both men and women will be employed. This represents no change in the initial position for men, but is an increase in wages for female employees. Equal wages for men and women would in this case impose a wage above the market equilibrium for women. Two outcomes are now possible: employers will either reduce the number of women in their labour force or else they will classify men's and women's jobs differently to avoid the legislation and maintain differentials.

Since the differences in the demand for men's and women's labour arises in this case from productivity differences, the legislation cannot simply outlaw the distinction. Profit-maximizing employers will want to pay workers according to the value of their marginal productivity. Men are worth more to the employer and on that basis male employment will be favoured. The legislation makes it illegal for an employer to pay men and women a different rate for 'equivalent jobs' and, faced with this situation, the employers might try to reclassify women's work as less skilled so that they can justify the payment of a lower wage rate. If women do not have, or are not deemed to have, the same skills and qualifications as men, then employers can argue that they are not doing the same job as men and are thus not entitled to an equivalent wage rate. In this case the introduction of equal pay legislation does not result in an equal wage for men and women. It leaves wage rates unchanged but reinforces gender segregation in employment.

The alternative outcome rests upon firms introducing wage equality but using the differences in productivity to justify reducing the number of women employed. In response to the legislation women's wages are increased to W_2 in Figure 10.1, yet the demand for women's labour is still represented by the demand curve D_1. The quantity of women's labour demanded will fall as employers move up along D_1. The increased cost of employing women will make the profit-maximizing firm re-evaluate its employment policies. As each extra woman employed now costs the firm W_2, the employers will want to ensure that they gain an equivalent increase in revenue resulting from that employment. They will want the marginal revenue product from the last woman employed to be equal in value to W_2. Since women are judged to have less training and skills than men, they are worth less to the employer who can only equate marginal revenue product with the wage rate of W_2 by reducing the number of women employed. When the higher wage rate of W_2 is imposed the firm will respond by moving up along the demand curve for women's labour, D_1, until only N_1 women are employed. The higher wage rate which employers are now obliged to pay to women will only be justified by employing a smaller proportion of women in their workforce. In the short run at least, one form of labour market inequality will have been replaced by another. Wages will be equal but labour market theory predicts that there might be a fall in the number of women employed in this occupation. In practice this reduction in women's employment has not occurred.

In the longer run the position might be different. Women might realize that they can indeed earn the same rates of pay as men if only they have equivalent qualifications and training. Equal pay legislation might provide the incentive for women to acquire the skills which justify the higher wages. There is indeed some evidence that this has been happening in Britain since the introduction of the Equal Pay Act in the 1970s. Women have increased their representation in higher education from 39 per cent of all undergraduates in 1970 to 49 per cent by 1992 (CSO 1995). Acquiring skills and qualifications shifts the demand curve for women's labour outwards towards D_2. The difference between the marginal revenue product of a woman and that of a man will narrow. Eventually when women have the same qualifications, skills and productivity as men, then there will be no economic justification for unequal treatment either in pay or employment. N_2 women and N_2 men will be employed at a wage rate of W_2 ending segregation in employment. Over a longer period of time equal pay legislation might therefore be more effective than it would appear to be in the short run.

Equal Pay and Single-Sex Occupations

During the 1970s equal pay did not apply in labour markets where women and men did different jobs. As the introduction of equal pay can cause a reduction in the number of women employed in mixed occupations, those women who lose their jobs in mixed sectors of the economy will seek work

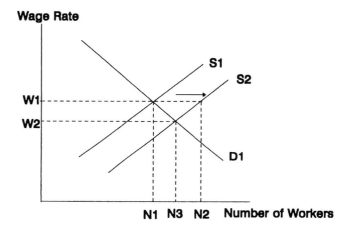

Figure 10.2: Increase in the Supply of Women's Labour

elsewhere. Labour will be displaced into exclusively female occupations. Those women made redundant as surveyors, for example, will seek jobs in predominantly female occupations, like school meals assistants.

As the redundant surveyors seek work as school meals supervisory assistants this will increase the supply of labour to this occupation. As the labour supply expands this creates an excess supply of labour at the going wage rate. In Figure 10.2 the effect of the increase in the labour supply of women is shown as a shift of the supply curve for women's labour from S_1 to S_2. At the initial equilibrium wage rate of W_1 there were N_1 women prepared to supply their labour to this occupation; but after female labour has been displaced from mixed occupations by the equal pay legislation, the supply of women prepared to work at a wage of W_1 increases to N_2. Employers will find that they have plenty of applicants for every vacancy which arises and workers will realize that there are many others who would be only too willing to take their job. This competition between workers will drive wage rates down to a new lower equilibrium level, W_2. In this exclusively female occupation, where there are no male workers with whom to compare wages, the equal pay legislation will not apply. Wages can fall and indeed the increased supply of labour provides one valid economic reason why such an outcome is likely. Paradoxically therefore the Equal Pay legislation might in fact serve to reduce the wage rates of those women who are employed in exclusively female occupations. In the final equilibrium in this market N_3 workers will be employed at a wage of W_2.

Consequences of the Equal Pay Act

The Equal Pay Act was amended in 1983 to bring the United Kingdom into line with the European Union. From 1984 onwards equal pay was introduced for work of equal value. Prior to this there was a strong possibility that on average the Equal Pay Act could have increased, rather than reduced, wage inequality between men and women by displacing labour from mixed into single-sex occupations.

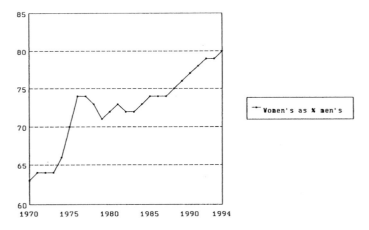

Figure 10.3: Women's Hourly Earnings as a Percentage of Men's (Great Britain).
Source: calculated from *New Earnings Survey*, various issues

The Equal Pay Amendment required employers to introduce equal pay for work of equal value; if men and women were doing different, but equivalent, jobs then they were entitled to the same rate of pay. This legislation enabled women to challenge the low wage rates paid to women in segregated occupations. It was no longer sufficient for an employer to justify low wage rates by claiming that there were no men in that occupation. If women could establish that their job required a similar level of skills, qualifications and responsibility as those demanded of male employees then they could demand wage equality. The first successful case under this amendment was a cook who claimed parity with male painters and welders working in a shipyard. In practice it has proved difficult and costly to establish comparability between jobs and between 1984 and 1993 there were only 23 successful claims under this legislation (the *Guardian* 20 June 1995). The Amendment has therefore only had a limited impact upon the gender pay gap. A comparison between men's and women's wages is provided in Figure 10.3. It shows that the gender wage gap is narrowing – but only slowly. In 1970 women's average earnings were 63 per cent of men's; by 1994 this proportion had risen to 80 per cent. Figure 10.3 shows that as the Equal Pay Act came into force in 1975 there was a significant narrowing of the gap between men's and women's earnings. Whilst this reduction in inequality can be partly attributed to the introduction of the legislation, the income policies of that time with their emphasis on flat rate wage increases were also influential. This trend was slightly reversed in the late 1970s but the gap has continued to decrease in recent years. Progress is being made, albeit very slowly. At the present rate it will take about 35 years – that is until the year 2030 – before women's and men's hourly average earnings are the same!

Maternity Leave

Labour markets do not exist in isolation from the rest of society. If women are treated differently from men in society then this will be reflected in labour market outcomes. Outlawing discrimination in pay, promotion and employment will not be sufficient to ensure wage equality in a society where women are expected, and indeed expect, to do the bulk of the caring. An alternative approach therefore would place the emphasis upon changing the factors which constrain women's position in society and thus affect their participation in labour markets. The domestic division of labour is particularly relevant since women's lower pay results in part from the childcare responsibilities which affect their employment. If mothers work part time, have limited opportunities in seeking employment and take career breaks during their children's pre-school years whilst men participate continuously in the working population on a full-time basis, these differences in labour market activity will result in lower earnings for women than for men. Differences in work experience would be reflected in a wage gap even if economic discrimination were non-existent.

The provision of maternity leave facilitates the combination of unpaid domestic responsibilities with paid employment. By protecting the employment rights of mothers the provision of maternity leave helps mothers to maintain a continuous attachment to the labour market whilst also fulfilling their parental role. Maternity leave refers to a woman's statutory right to stop work prior to the birth of her child and to be reinstated at some predetermined interval after the birth. It was first introduced in the United Kingdom in 1976. The United Kingdom, offering 40 weeks' statutory maternity leave, appears to be the most generous country within the European Union (Moss 1990); appearances however can be misleading! Of the 29 weeks' leave which British women are entitled to take after a birth, only 6 weeks are paid at 90 per cent of their earnings, a further 12 weeks are paid at a low flat rate and the remaining leave is unpaid. Not only is the provision of benefit somewhat limited but until recently large numbers of women were totally excluded from the scheme. Before a recent ruling in the European Court of Justice a British woman needed to have been working with her current employer for at least two years in order to be eligible for maternity leave. Such strict eligibility criteria effectively excluded 40 per cent of women from claiming maternity leave in 1988 (Brannen et al. 1994). The right to take maternity leave encourages continuity in women's employment. By ensuring that prospective mothers are not dismissed from employment women are encouraged to gain the qualifications, experience and seniority which enhance their salary prospects and help to close the gender wage gap.

Maternity leave has also been significant in enabling mothers to return to work. In the late 1970s only one mother in four returned to work within a year of childbirth but by 1988, 45 per cent of mothers were back at work eight to nine months after the birth of their first child (McRae 1991). If mothers are able to return to work this increases their labour market experience, enhances their human capital and should thus increase their earnings. Indeed maternity leave appears to have had a significant impact upon women's earnings with those mothers who returned to their original employer earning higher wages than other mothers (Waldfogel 1995). Continuous employment enhances earnings. The 1980s in Britain have seen the emergence of a significant minority of well-qualified women who continue to be employed even through the years of childbearing. Whilst 61 per cent of women with children under the age of four years old participate in paid employment, this percentage rises to 86 per cent for women with degrees (OPCS 1995). These women are able to overcome the pattern of disadvantage resulting from discontinuous employment.

For those women whose continuous employment has been facilitated by maternity leave, the advantages have already been considerable. Unfortunately though, very few British women have been in a position to benefit from the provision of maternity leave. Apart from ineligibility, financial reasons can prevent some women from taking maternity leave since the right to take leave is not accompanied by a corresponding right to receive benefit. The extent of maternity leave in the United Kingdom is indeed far more generous than the provision of benefit. Not surprisingly therefore most of those mothers resuming work do so well before the statutory period expires.

Furthermore, although mothers are entitled to return to work, the practicalities of so doing are complicated in a country where there is minimal public provision of childcare facilities. With relatively few publicly funded day care centres, private arrangements have to be made for the care of pre-school children. Nannies and childminders are expensive, amounting on average to 25 per cent of a mother's earnings. Since couples usually regard childcare costs as the mother's responsibility to be met out of her earnings (Brannen et al. 1994), nannies and childminders are used almost exclusively by those well-qualified mothers earning high salaries. For them their earnings both in the current and future are sufficient to offset the substantial costs incurred by working during their children's pre-school years.

Those whose earning potential is more limited usually rely on informal arrangements for childcare and this often limits their employment opportunities. These mothers are less likely to be able to return to full-time work since their earnings are rarely sufficient to cover payment for the continuous care of a pre-school child. Maternity leave is helping to narrow the gender pay gap amongst highly qualified professional men and women but it is of little benefit to those women with low earnings potential.

Women who use maternity leave benefit themselves from a rise in earnings over their whole life cycle, but their employers benefit too. Maternity leave provides employers with greater stability in their workforce. A mother's return to work enables her employers to capture any investment they might have made in her human capital and helps them to avoid frequent recruitment costs. Prior to the introduction of maternity leave, employers found it difficult to identify those women who would want to return to employment after childbirth. Since most women left employment at the time of the birth of their first child it was not considered worthwhile to continue to employ pregnant women; their skills were underutilized due to statistical discrimination. The introduction of maternity leave has helped to end this statistical discrimination. Employers can now make better use of the potential skills and talents of their female employees and this contributes to the more efficient use of resources.

The Introduction of a Minimum Wage

Since women form the majority of low paid workers a minimum wage would affect women to a greater extent than men. Establishing a minimum wage for all employees would render it illegal for employers to pay a lower wage rate. A minimum wage will prevent wages being driven down due to an increase in the supply of labour or for any other reason. The minimum wage would apply right across the economy to all industries and all occupations regardless of the personal characteristics of the employee. The impact of a

minimum wage upon pay and employment depends upon the level at which
it is introduced, the elasticity of demand for labour in affected occupations,
the degree of competition and the response of those workers earning above
the proposed minimum.

In 1994, 10 out of the 12 member states in the European Union had a
minimum wage. Only Britain and Ireland relied upon market forces in the
determination of wage rates. The introduction of a minimum wage would
establish a floor to wages. It would be perfectly legal to pay wage rates in
excess of this minimum wage but it would outlaw wage rates below this level.
Its immediate effects will therefore be asymmetrical, falling primarily upon
those earning less than the minimum. It is therefore important to establish
how many and which groups of workers are likely to be directly affected by
its introduction. Table 10.1 provides information on the percentage of full-
time workers whose hourly earnings excluding overtime fall below a stated
amount. As women earn less than men, a larger percentage of women than
men fall below any particular level of hourly earnings.

Table 10.1: Percentage with Hourly Earnings Below a Stated Amount
Great Britain

Hourly earnings below(£)	% of men below each level	% of women below each level
2.40	0.3	0.5
3.00	1.1	2.5
3.40	2.8	6.8
4.00	7.7	15.7
4.40	12.5	22.5

Source: *New Earnings Survey*, 1994

Since the *New Earnings Survey* excludes part-time workers and those
working in small firms yet these groups are likely to be amongst the lowest
paid in the economy, these figures understate the full extent of the problem.
The percentage of the workforce affected by the introduction of a minimum
wage will depend critically upon the level at which this measure is set, as
Table 10.1 shows. The higher the level of the minimum wage, the larger the
percentage of workers affected directly by its introduction and the greater
the impact upon the rate of inflation and the level of unemployment. If the
minimum wage were to be set at a relatively low level – for example an hourly
rate of £2.40 – then 0.3 per cent of male employees and 0.5 per cent of female
employees would be directly affected by its introduction. As these workers
represent such a small percentage of full-time employees such a measure would

have only a minimal effect upon inflation and unemployment. Were the minimum hourly wage to be fixed at £4.40 though, the results would be very different. Nearly one in four female employees and one in eight men would be affected by its introduction at this level; the impact upon wages, costs, inflation and unemployment would be far more significant.

The level at which a minimum wage might be established is a normative issue. It depends upon value judgements concerning the rate of pay which is deemed to be socially acceptable and there is no unanimity on this issue within the United Kingdom or in the European Union. Different groups are committed to different figures. The Labour Party has committed itself to introduce a minimum wage in the United Kingdom if it gains office at the next election but the level at which this will be established is not yet clear.

The Trades Union Congress has drawn attention to the three million workers who earn less than £3 per hour; two-thirds of these workers are women. Meanwhile the Low Pay Unit is committed to a 'decency threshold' of two-thirds of male median earnings (EOC 1993). In 1992 there were approximately 9.5 million workers earning below this level, concentrated in industries like retailing and catering which employ a predominantly female workforce. In 1994 women accounted for 63 per cent of all employees in the hotel and catering industry and 66 per cent of those in food retailing (Department of Employment 1994). It is these workers who would be affected immediately were a minimum wage to be introduced in the United Kingdom.

Many men who already earn more than the proposed minimum would not be directly affected by the introduction of minimum wage although they could still experience secondary or knock-on effects. Trade unions might make a case for maintaining the differentials between those workers whose pay has been increased to the minimum level and other groups of employees in the same industry. Chefs, for example, might argue that they should earn considerably more than bar staff. If bar staff are receiving a wage rise due to the introduction of a minimum wage, then chefs too might demand an increment to maintain the differentials. In this case the introduction of a minimum wage will have indirect effects upon those already earning above the minimum. Employers faced with rising costs might seek to reduce employment and unemployment would rise. The introduction of a minimum wage would in this case have far-reaching effects upon the wages bill, the rate of inflation and the level of employment.

A Minimum Wage in Competitive Labour Markets

Workers whose hourly rate falls below the minimum wage stand to gain from the introduction of such a measure since it would immediately raise their

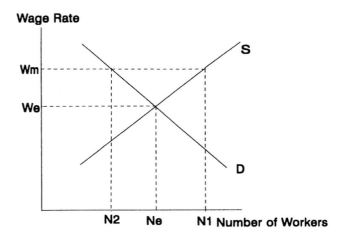

Figure 10.4: A Minimum Wage in Competitive Markets

rates of pay. In Figure 10.4 the introduction of a national minimum wage at W_m will immediately raise the rate of pay from the equilibrium level of W_e. This in turn will increase the incentive for workers to seek employment. It becomes more expensive not to work and the quantity of labour supplied will increase accordingly. This is represented in Figure 10.4 as a movement along the supply curve for labour from N_e to N_1. More workers will want jobs at the higher wage rate.

In competitive markets, however, the introduction of a minimum wage might not be an unambiguous gain since the higher wage rates might cause a loss of jobs. As wage rates rise above their equilibrium level, this will also cause a movement along the demand curve. In Figure 10.4 N_e workers were demanded at a wage rate of W_e. As wage rates are increased through the introduction of a minimum rate at W_m, this will reduce the number of workers demanded to N_2. Wage rates have risen and so employers will re-evaluate their production techniques and they might decide that as labour has become relatively more expensive they will switch to capital intensive production methods. Consequently there will be a reduction in the number of jobs on offer. Since more women than men earn less than any proposed minimum wage, many of the jobs lost will be women's jobs.

The extent of this job loss will depend upon the level at which the minimum wage is introduced and upon the price elasticity of demand for labour. The higher the level at which the minimum wage is introduced the greater the number of workers whose wages and employment will be affected. Furthermore a high minimum wage not only affects more workers but it also introduces a significant increase in the relative cost of labour in some occupations. In occupations which have been paying £2 per hour, the introduction of a minimum wage of £4 represents a doubling of their wage bill if employment levels remain unchanged. A minimum of £2.50 per hour only represents a 25 per cent increase in wages, which might be easier for the employers to absorb.

The price elasticity of demand for labour indicates the extent to which a wage increase will affect the firm's demand for labour; it shows the responsiveness of demand to a rise in the wage rate. If demand is elastic with respect to wages then the firm will cut back on its employment of labour by a greater percentage than the wage rise. For example a 25 per cent increase in wage rates might cause the firm to reduce its labour demand by 50 per cent. A high elasticity value indicates that the employer can easily substitute capital for labour and consequently will respond by cutting employment dramatically as wage rates rise. Should a national minimum wage affect sectors of the economy with high elasticities of demand for labour, then there will be a significant effect upon jobs.

If demand is inelastic with respect to wage rates, then this indicates that employment will fall less than proportionately to the wage increase. In this case a 25 per cent wage rise might only result in a 5 per cent reduction in the quantity of labour employed. In these cases it might be very difficult to replace labour with capital and consequently employment levels will be maintained even as wages rise. The extent of job loss depends crucially upon the price elasticity of demand for labour. The more elastic is the demand for labour the greater will be the loss of jobs. It is only in the unlikely situation that the demand for labour is totally inelastic that firms will continue to employ the same number of workers at the higher wage rate. In competitive labour markets the introduction of a minimum wage at a level above the market equilibrium rate will cause some loss of jobs.

Monopsonistic Labour Markets and a Minimum Wage

In practice though, competitive labour markets are rare. In many situations there is a divergence from the competitive conditions on either the employers' or the workers' side of the market. If there is only one employer of labour in a particular locality or if employers band together in employers' federations to agree the terms on which they are prepared to employ labour, then there is no longer competition in the demand for labour. The employers have gained undue market power in the buying of labour and the market has become a monopsony.

If a monopsonist is facing a competitive labour supply, then this will affect the determination of wage and employment levels. The monopsonist regards the supply of labour rather differently from the competitive employer. In perfect competition the individual employer of labour is a price taker; an individual firm's actions can have no effect upon the price of labour or the quantity which is supplied. For the monopsonist, the situation is different. The firm is the only employer of labour and since the supply curve of labour is upward sloping the monopsonist must recognize that more workers can only be employed if higher wage rates are offered to persuade workers to accept jobs. Table 10.2 shows that 300 workers can be employed at an hourly wage rate of £5 but if the firm wishes to increase its workforce to 400 workers then the hourly rate must be raised to £6.

The monopsonist therefore has to pay higher wages in order to increase the firm's workforce, and this higher wage rate will have to be paid to all employees, not just the last few who were employed. Employing a few extra workers will therefore make a considerable difference to the employer's total wage bill. In Table 10.2 increasing employment from 300 to 400 workers will raise the monopsonist's total wage bill from £1500 to £2400. The total wage bill rises by £900 when 100 additional workers are employed. In other words each extra worker employed is adding £9 to the firm's wage bill, £6 of which represents the worker's own wage and £3 will result from the extra £1 per hour which must now be paid to the 300 men and women who were already working for this employer. The marginal cost of labour, the cost of employing one additional worker, is £9 per hour. For a monopsonist the marginal cost of labour exceeds the average cost of labour, which is represented by the wage rate.

Table 10.2: The Supply of Labour to a Monopsonist

Number of workers (00s)	Hourly Wage (£) (average cost)	Total Wage Cost (£)	Marginal Cost of labour
2	4	800	–
3	5	1500	7
4	6	2400	9
5	7	3500	11

A profit-maximizing firm will seek to equate the marginal cost of labour with the marginal revenue product. The number of workers employed will be determined on this basis. In Figure 10.5 the marginal cost of labour, MC, is equal to the marginal revenue product when N_1 workers are employed. The profit-maximizing monopsonist will seek to employ N_1 workers and will pay them an hourly wage rate which is just sufficient to ensure that N_1 workers are prepared to supply their labour. In other words the wage rate will depend upon the average cost of labour. Table 10.2 showed that the average cost of labour will be lower than the marginal cost of labour and so the monopsonist need pay a wage of only W_1 in order to attract N_1 workers to work in the firm. The wage rate need only reflect the average cost of labour. The situation arises because the monopsonist as a large employer of labour has a significant degree of market power. The workers who are supplying labour on a competitive basis lack countervailing power in the labour market. This power imbalance results in the monopsonist paying the workers a wage rate below their marginal revenue product. The workers' wage is less than their value to the firm. The employer's wage offer need only reflect the average cost of labour which in a monopsonistic market is below the marginal revenue product at the equilibrium level of employment. The firm's market power results in the payment of a wage rate which is below the value of the workers' contribution to output.

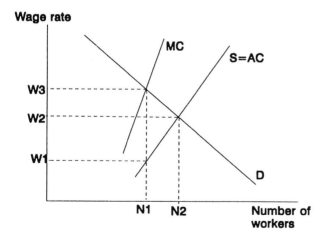

Figure 10.5: A Monopsonist Employer

In this market situation both the level of employment and the hourly wage rate have settled at a level below that which would have represented the competitive market equilibrium. Had this market been competitive then the forces of supply and demand would have determined the equilibrium wage rate at W_2 and the level of employment at N_2. The wage rate and the level of employment would both have been higher in the competitive situation.

In these circumstances the introduction of a minimum wage has interesting results. If the minimum wage is introduced at W_2 this represents a wage rate which is above the monopsonist's wage of W_1. The minimum wage will become the wage rate which must be paid to all workers. It becomes illegal to pay anyone an hourly rate of less than W_2. All men and women know that this is the lowest wage rate which they must accept and the horizontal line at W_2 therefore represents the supply curve of labour until N_2 workers are employed. The employers must now pay an hourly rate of W_2 to each man or woman until N_2 workers are employed. The firm's total wage bill rises by W_2 for each extra worker employed and so the minimum wage, W_2, represents the marginal cost of labour. Since W_2 is the wage rate it also represents the average cost of labour. Until N_2 workers are employed both the average and the marginal cost of labour are fixed at W_2, the minimum wage level.

A profit-maximizing employer is placed in a new situation by the introduction of a minimum wage at W_2. In Figure 10.5 the firm will equate marginal cost with marginal revenue by employing N_2 workers at the minimum wage rate of W_2. The introduction of a minimum wage increases wages from W_1 to W_2 whilst employment also rises from N_1 to N_2. In a monopsonistic market the introduction of a minimum wage can therefore increase both the wage rate and the level of employment. A wage of W_2 represents the greatest possible increase in jobs within this market but indeed a minimum wage could be introduced at any level between W_1 and W_3 and employment would also rise. At a wage of W_3, N_1 workers would be employed whilst at any wage rate between W_3 and W_1 employment levels would settle between N_1 and N_2 workers depending on the wage rate.

Several recent studies have suggested that in practice minimum wages rarely cost jobs. The Centre for Economic Performance has examined the impact of Wages Councils, which used to set minimum rates in certain industries and they have concluded that, if anything, there was a positive relationship between minimum wage levels and employment (Machin and Manning 1992). A controversial study in the United States has compared New Jersey, where minimum wages were increased, with Pennsylvania. In the fast food sector employment in New Jersey actually rose as minimum wages were increased (Card and Krueger 1992). So in some situations wage increases can be accompanied by an increase in employment levels. In this case the introduction of a minimum wage can only help to improve the position of those at present on very low rates of pay. Since women earn less than men, the majority of those whose wage rates would be affected by the introduction of a minimum wage are women.

Summary

Despite 25 years of legislation equal pay is still far from being a reality in Britain in the 1990s. Women on average earn £2 per hour less than men and there are considerable disparities in all occupations. The 1970 Equal Pay Act did not have the intended results partly because women and men rarely do exactly the same work. With widespread occupational segregation this legislation left a considerable loophole. It made no provision for lowly paid workers in single-sex occupations. Women in jobs employing only female labour had no redress under the 1970 Act, regardless of how low their wages might be. The 1984 Equal Pay amendment sought to address this issue since workers could claim equal pay if they were doing different but equally skilled jobs. The impact of this amendment has been limited due to the complexity and length of its procedures. A minimum wage would affect women to a greater extent than men and its impact will be felt by those workers currently earning very low wage rates. The consequences for employment are debatable, depending crucially upon the elasticity of demand for labour and upon the degree of competition in labour markets.

One significant factor contributing to gender inequalities in the workplace is the downward occupational mobility which many women in Britain experience on their return to work after childbirth. Maternity leave goes some way towards addressing this issue by facilitating continuous employment. But the take-up of maternity leave has been very uneven and the scarcity of childcare facilities in Britain encourages many women to return to work on a part-time basis only. Part-time jobs abound in the retail and catering sectors and they are often low paid, low skill positions offering little opportunity for training or promotion. To date maternity leave has helped to improve the position of well-qualified women, many of whom belong to dual income households. It has been less successful in helping the majority of British women who still experience considerable difficulty in combining full-time paid employment with childcare.

Labour market policies are designed to modify market outcomes. The measures introduced so far have attempted to reduce gender inequalities in wage rates by establishing the principle of equal pay. To the extent that wage inequalities result purely from economic discrimination the legislation has been relatively successful. However the gender wage gap arises from wider differences in the social position of men and women which labour market policies alone cannot eliminate.

11   Women in the European Union

The formation of the European Union. The political, social and economic dimensions of Europe. Equal pay, the single market and the Social Charter. Women's economic activity in the member states. Part-time employment in Europe. Women's pay, employment and unemployment. Women's employment and family friendly policies. Summary.

The Formation of the European Union

The European Union may prove to be one of the most powerful forces promoting equality for women. Since European Union law supersedes national law, initiatives in the field of social policy can have far-reaching implications for women and men in the member states. It was a European Court of Justice ruling which gave women in the United Kingdom the right to paid maternity leave even if they had not been in their current employment for the minimum of two years required by British law. Since 1957 the 6 founder members of the European Economic Community – France, Italy, the Federal Republic of Germany, Belgium, Luxemburg and the Netherlands – have been joined by 9 other countries to form a European Union of 15 member states. Many of the newly liberated countries of Central and Eastern Europe have declared their intention to seek membership of the Union. By the millennium the age-old dream of a united Europe could be close to realization.

The European Union has developed from the moves towards closer European integration in the years immediately following the Second World War. During the 1950s the Treaties of Rome and Paris established three communities: the European Coal and Steel Community, the European Economic Community and the European Atomic Community. Together these three came to be known as the European Community. With the signing of the Treaty of Maastricht in 1991 the European Union now has a more extensive brief encompassing the functions of the European Community. When the Treaty of Rome was signed in 1957 the economic advantages of closer co-operation were clearly apparent. The member states sought to enjoy the benefits of a larger market for their products, enabling producers to take advantage of economies of scale resulting in lower average costs of production. If costs fell, prices too could be reduced stimulating consumer demand and increasing production. If a Common Market could be realized then economic growth would follow.

Whilst the economic benefits were widely recognized, the move towards European integration in the 1950s was motivated primarily by non-economic factors. Twice during the first half of the twentieth century war had broken out within Europe and the formation of the European Community was prompted by a desire to avoid a third European war. Co-operation and integration offered peace by uniting the main countries of continental Europe. The formation of the European Economic Community diminished the internal threat to European security at the same time as the global situation was becoming more fragile. The outbreak of the Cold War made Western Europe particularly vulnerable. With the Soviet bloc on its eastern boundary and the United States of America to the west it was located geographically between the two superpowers. United, rather than divided, the nations of Western Europe might stand more chance of maintaining their independence in such a precarious world situation. On the political front the Community was formed to promote European security.

Economic integration cannot be achieved without political co-operation. The extent of this political co-operation and the forms it takes affect the speed at which a Common Market can be created. Membership of the European Community provided the opportunity for a more efficient use of productive resources creating the potential for a rise in living standards. Ensuring that these potential benefits were realized and were evenly distributed involved a social dimension to the Community. The wider market offered opportunities for gains to be made but those benefits might go to certain regions and groups within the Community unless a social policy were introduced. Social protection, necessary to ensure that vulnerable groups were not disadvantaged in the more competitive environment of an integrated Europe, was not a high priority in the early years of the Community's operation. Establishing economic integration seemed more important at first. Nearly 40 years after the signing of the Treaty of Rome the European Union is still trying to establish a balance between the economic, political and social dimensions.

The Political, Social and Economic Dimensions of Europe

During the 1960s progress towards economic integration was rapid. Tariffs and physical restrictions to trade were removed by 1968 and yet a truly common market proved elusive. Health and safety regulations, government procurement policies and administrative restrictions still impeded the free movement of goods and services. The recession of the mid 1970s made member states wary of further integration. With rising unemployment each country wished to protect its own industries and jobs and non-tariff barriers proliferated. During the 1970s and the early 1980s low and negative growth rates, rising unemployment and rapid inflation impeded any new initiatives on the Common Market. It was not until the European economy enjoyed a sustained period of economic growth in the mid 1980s that further progress could be achieved.

The Single European Act of 1986 aimed to create a unified market with free movement of goods, services, labour and capital by the end of 1992. This economic objective could only be achieved if there were the political will to enable the Community's institutions to enact the programme. Trading standards cannot be harmonized, passport controls cannot be removed, competition policy cannot be implemented without political co-operation. To build an economic Europe, political co-operation is necessary.

A unified market provides the potential for living standards to increase. If European producers can market their products throughout the 15 member states of the Union, free from tariffs, physical restrictions or different standards, then output can increase. Firms can take advantage of bulk buying discounts, the use of specialized machinery and rationalization of plant and equipment. The removal of tariffs and other restrictions on trade enables specialization to take place in Europe on the basis of comparative advantage. The larger European market opens the prospect of increased production, better employment opportunities and higher living standards. The potential is certainly there for European citizens to be better off but the way to translate this potential into actual benefits is rather more debatable.

Supporters of the free market philosophy, like Mrs Thatcher, believe in an absence of government interference. Market deregulation and liberalization provides the best way of encouraging firms to respond to the challenge of the Single Market. If tariffs, quotas and other barriers to trade are dismantled, then greater competition from other European producers should act as a spur to efficiency. Firms, free to respond to price and profit incentives, will invest to ensure that economies of scale are realized and the potential benefits of the wider market are transformed into higher living standards in Europe. Social policy imposes obligations on firms which raise their costs of production and interfere with the operation of market forces. The United Kingdom was so firmly committed to market forces that they – and they alone amongst the 12 member states – refused to adopt the Social Charter in 1989. Their refusal was extended to the Social Chapter appended to the Treaty of Maastricht in 1991. They believed that interference with the market process could only handicap Europe's economic growth and reduce the living standards of its citizens.

Not everyone accepts this viewpoint. Markets create winners and losers and if some groups fear they might lose from economic change then the potential gains of the wider market might not be realized. Jacques Delors, the President of the European Commission from 1985 until 1994, believed that the Single Market should be accompanied by strong social policies. For Delors, building a social consensus in which all workers felt that their rights were respected offered the best chance of introducing new technology, rationalizing production and making the changes necessary to ensure that European firms and workers responded to the challenge presented by the Single Market. A Single Market can bring benefits but market forces do not ensure that these benefits are evenly distributed. A market system provides advantages for those who can adapt quickly to new opportunities but penalizes those whose position as producers or consumers is constrained. The industrially developed countries might benefit more than the agricultural economies; producers might benefit as profits rise whilst workers' wages show little increase; the geographically mobile workers might gain from seeking employment on a Europe-wide basis whilst those whose horizons are limited by domestic responsibilities might find their job opportunities diminishing. The more marginal and vulnerable groups within the Community could find themselves disadvantaged as a result.

Some European countries have been concerned that the Single Market will result in social dumping. Countries which show social concern for the less advantaged groups within their midst fear that they might suffer in the more competitive environment of the Single Market. Firms, seeking to cut costs, might locate production in countries providing the lowest social benefits for workers. A reduction in holiday entitlement, the absence of a minimum wage and no benefit for maternity leave can all reduce employers' costs of production. Since firms are free to move products throughout the market without restraint, production will be located in the region which minimizes the firm's own costs of production. The lower the level of social provision, the lower those costs will be. The internal costs of production are reduced by locating in an area of low social protection but the external costs to workers could be considerable. Countries which have tried to raise the standard of social provision fear that jobs might be lost as production moves to lower cost locations where workers' rights are not so high on the agenda. The Single Market might offer the opportunity for higher living standards but the workers in some countries could find themselves without jobs unless a minimum level of social protection is enforced throughout the European Union.

The political process can provide a check on unfettered market forces. Strengthening social policies at the European level can help to ensure fair treatment for disadvantaged groups. Since women constitute one of the more vulnerable and marginal groups within the workforce, social policy can prove particularly significant in protecting and promoting their economic status. If men and women throughout the member states are confident that the Single Market will bring benefits to them, then they will be prepared to accept the changes in their work environment which its introduction involves. From this point of view the creation of an 'economic space' entails the need for a 'social space'.

Equal Pay, the Single Market and the Social Charter

The European Union became involved in equal opportunities policies from the very beginning. During the formation of the European Economic Community the French were concerned that their laws on equal pay for men and women might prove disadvantageous to French producers in a competitive European market. Since no other country had a similar requirement, the French feared that they would be at a disadvantage unless other countries also adopted their position. Consequently Article 119 of the Treaty of Rome called for equal pay for men and women. This was subsequently interpreted as equal pay for men and women doing work of equal value to ensure equality even when segregation in employment was widespread.

In practice since French producers proved perfectly able to compete in the wider market, enforcement of Article 119 was not seen as a high priority. Little was done to ensure compliance with this measure whilst trade barriers were being dismantled in the 1960s. The commitment to equal pay, however, was enshrined in the Treaty of Rome and it was the responsibility of the Commission as 'guardian of the treaties' to ensure that this requirement was ultimately enforced in the member states.

Some progress was made during the 1970s. Once tariffs and physical barriers to trade had been removed the Commission turned its attention to other areas of policy, including social policy. Measures began to develop to ensure compliance with Article 119. The European Court of Justice clarified the Article and established its applicability in the member states in 1974. Then in 1975 a directive was passed on equal pay. Directives, unlike resolutions and recommendations, are binding upon member states which are left with discretion concerning how to implement the measures – but not about whether to implement them.

Member states began to introduce their own legislation to implement the measure but progress was slow. In 1979 the Commission initiated infringement proceedings against seven out of the nine member states. Most countries then amended their legislation in line with the directive but Germany and the United Kingdom had to be taken to the European Court of Justice to ensure compliance. In the case of the United Kingdom, the government believed that the 1970 Equal Pay Act was sufficient to meet the requirements of the directive but the European Court of Justice thought otherwise. The United Kingdom's legislation had to be amended to encompass equal pay for work of equal value.

Legislation on equal pay alone, however, is insufficient to promote economic equality between women and men. It focuses entirely upon the labour market ignoring the deeper structural issues which affect women's position in society and are thus reflected in their labour market status. The European Community was slowly becoming aware that access to education, training, childcare facilities and indeed the division of domestic labour were all important issues if women's labour market disadvantage was to be removed.

The passing of the Single European Act in 1986 brought with it a concern for a social Europe to accompany the economic opportunities offered by the Single Market. To address these concerns the Social Charter of the fundamental social rights of workers was developed and adopted by 11 out of the 12 member states in 1989. This was then appended to the Maastricht Treaty in 1991 as the Social Chapter. Only the United Kingdom refused to sign. Article 16 of the Social Charter deals directly with women's issues. It calls for equal treatment and equal opportunities for men and women. It identifies the areas where it considers there is still considerable work to be done in some member states and ends with a statement asking for measures to enable men and women to reconcile their occupational and family obligations. This statement is a more far-reaching declaration than the Community had previously provided, demonstrating a greater awareness of women's position in the workplace and society at large. At present occupational and family responsibilities conflict, but to a different degree in the various member states and in distinctive ways for men and women. Men remain participant in the working population but spend less time with their families especially whilst their children are young. Their employment restricts their family life. Women in many member countries find it hard to maintain continuous employment whilst fulfilling their domestic role as mothers. The extent to which motherhood and paid employment conflict varies considerably throughout the European Union.

As the provisions of the Social Chapter are enacted in the European Union this will help to provide minimum standards of entitlement for both men and women. The Chapter also attempts to improve conditions for vulnerable workers in European labour markets. It thus refers to part-time working, temporary contracts, unemployment compensation and pension rights. In many of these areas women constitute the majority of those workers who are disadvantaged by the present arrangements. In this way the general provisions of the Social Chapter contribute to improving the position of those women who are citizens of the European Community.

Women's Economic Activity in the Member States

Throughout the 15 member states of the European Union more women are moving into the labour force. This trend has continued throughout the boom years of the mid 1980s and the recessions of the early 1990s and women's employment and unemployment has increased as a result. Demographic factors alone cannot account for this increase. Not only have there been increasing numbers of women seeking paid work but also a rising proportion of women of working age have been economically active. By 1989 in the European Union 64 per cent of women between the ages of 25 and 49 were economically active. The activity rate shows considerable variation between member states. In Denmark participation for women was almost universal, with an activity rate of 88 per cent, whilst in Ireland only 45 per cent of women of working age were participating in the labour force (Maruani 1992). Women do not enter employment on the same terms as men. They constitute the majority of part-time workers, experience higher rates of unemployment, receive lower wages and still remain responsible for the majority of domestic work. In all these ways women's position in labour markets is different from that of men.

One role of social policy is to ensure fair treatment for all workers despite differences in their labour market situation. The differences between men and women in labour markets are apparent in all European Union countries but the extent of the disparity varies considerably. In some member states young children severely limit their mothers' employment opportunities; in others part-time employment can be combined with domestic responsibilities whilst mothers in a few member states find that children make little or no difference to their workforce participation. The Social Chapter will be enacted against this diverse background. In some member states its provisions will make little or no difference to the economic position of women and men whilst in others its effects will prove significant.

The lifetime pattern of participation in the workforce still differs between women and men in the majority of member states. Whilst for men the pattern of continuous participation is standard throughout the European Union, varying very little between fathers and single men, for women the pattern is far more diverse. There are considerable differences throughout the member states in the extent to which women participate in the working population during their working life as well as variations in the degree to which motherhood affects and constrains labour market participation.

Participation rate

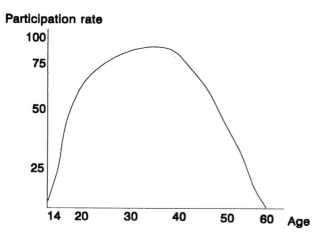

Figure 11.1: Continuous Participation in the Working Population

For men labour market participation is continuous and uninterrupted by the advent of their children. Their pattern of participation is bell-shaped, or resembles an inverted U as shown in Figure 11.1.

In France and Denmark family responsibilities act as little or no constraint upon women's workforce participation. Women, like men, show a high overall rate of participation which continues throughout their working life. Yet both Denmark and France have high fertility rates as well; French and Danish women are having children and also remaining in paid employment. In Denmark a woman with a child under the age of ten is just as likely to participate in the workforce as a woman without children (Moss 1992). The pattern of participation is continuous. In France, too, participation is scarcely affected by the birth of the first two children at least (Maruani 1992). One factor facilitating the employment of French and Danish mothers is the availability of publicly funded childcare services. Denmark provides places in publicly funded childcare services for a larger proportion of its pre-school children than any other European country and the provision in France is extremely comprehensive, covering 95 per cent of children between the ages of three and six years of age (Moss 1992). In France the taxation system and other structural factors encourage the employment of women on a full-time basis (Lane 1993). In both these countries women, like men, display bell-shaped patterns of participation as shown in Figure 11.1.

Whilst continuous participation predominates for men in all member states, for women – and especially for mothers – the pattern of participation varies considerably. Career breaks for mothers followed by a return to work, or non-participation after children are born, still represent the standard patterns of workforce participation for women in some member states. The bi-modal pattern of participation for women which has become familiar in the United Kingdom in postwar years is found in West Germany and the Netherlands too (Maruani 1992). Women participate in the labour force when they leave education, take a break for family formation and return to employment, first on a part-time and then a full-time basis, once the children are settled in school. This M-shaped pattern of participation indicates that motherhood constrains but does not prevent labour force participation. Figure 11.2 shows this pattern of discontinuous economic activity depicting the career break.

Evidence suggests that career breaks are getting shorter and more and more women are beginning to remain economically active even through the period of family formation. The dip in the M is becoming less marked than it was when the European Community was formed in the 1950s since the bi-modal pattern of participation seems to be evolving into a bell shape! As social constraints ease women are beginning to adopt patterns of labour market participation which are common amongst men.

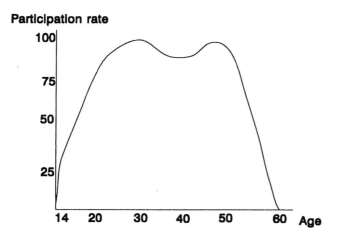

Figure 11.2: Bi-modal Pattern of Participation

In some countries a woman's participation in paid employment is still discontinued permanently when she becomes a mother. Women's participation rates will be high when they first leave full-time education but will fall as children are born. Economic inactivity will often predominate throughout the remainder of their working years. In these countries paid employment proves incompatible with family responsibilities and workforce participation is essentially for childless women. The pattern of participation over the life cycle will resemble a lone peak as shown in Figure 11.3. In this case women are working in paid employment until their mid twenties when children are born but after this point unpaid household work replaces paid employment. In Britain during the 1930s women's participation in the workforce followed the lone peak pattern.

This pattern is still displayed in Ireland, which has the highest fertility rate in the European Union and in Belgium, Luxemburg and the countries of Southern Europe. In Ireland where the influence of the Roman Catholic church is strong the 1937 Constitution explicitly prevents the state from taking any actions which might facilitate the paid employment of women at the expense of their duties in the home. The presence of children significantly reduces the participation rate for women in Ireland. For women without children 67 per cent of those between the ages of 20 and 39 were in paid employment in 1988 whilst this proportion fell to 23 per cent for women with a child under the age of ten years (Moss 1992).

Participation rate

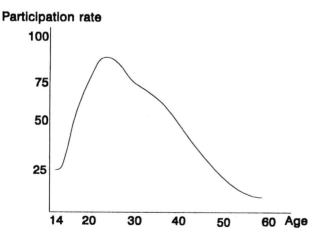

Figure 11.3: Inactivity After Childbirth

The countries in which women's participation rates fall dramatically after the birth of their children are those countries in which part-time job opportunities are scarce and there is little provision of publicly funded childcare for pre-school children. In Luxemburg, Ireland, Greece and Italy less than 5 per cent of the children under three years of age could find places in publicly funded childcare services (Moss 1992) and in all the countries of Southern Europe part-time jobs account for 12 per cent or less of total employment. The lack of part-time work, poor childcare provision, cultural factors and social constraints inhibit the workforce participation of women in these countries. These patterns of participation though are beginning to break down especially in Greece, Italy, Portugal and Spain as continuous activity, or at least a return to employment later in life, becomes more common (Maruani 1992). The lone peak is gradually being replaced by twin peaks as the bi-modal pattern emerges.

Throughout the European Union the patterns of participation displayed by women vary considerably between the countries. Mothers in some member states still find that children prevent or limit their economic activity and independence. Parenthood affects the labour force participation of men scarcely at all as European fathers experience no difficulty in continuing with paid employment. Since social policy can affect participation patterns and facilitate the extent to which mothers can participate in the working population, an effective social policy in Europe can help to provide equal opportunities for fathers, mothers and children.

Part-time Employment in Europe

In 9 of the 12 member states in the European Union during the 1980s part-time employment was increasing. In Greece and Portugal as well as in Denmark, a country with a particularly generous provision of publicly funded childcare, the share of part-time jobs in overall employment fell. Part-time jobs are concentrated predominantly in the service sector. By 1992 the service sector had come to account for 61 per cent of total civilian employment within the European Union whilst it had employed less than 40 per cent of the workforce in 1960 (EC 1994). The growth of the service sector and the increase in part-time jobs have occurred together.

During the boom of the mid 1980s the increase in employment opportunities was largely due to the creation of part-time jobs. These jobs have been concentrated in certain sectors and certain geographical areas of the European Union. Catering, cleaning and sales, which are all traditionally female sectors of employment, have seen a disproportionate increase in the number of part-time jobs available. The countries of northern Europe have experienced a considerable growth of part-time employment whilst this practice is still relatively uncommon in the countries of southern Europe. Part-time jobs are on the increase in the service sector of the countries of north-west Europe.

Part-time employment also accounts for a disproportionately large share of women's employment. Within the European Union countries in 1989, 13 per cent of overall employment, but 28 per cent of women's employment, was part time (Maruani 1992). Countries like Denmark, the United Kingdom and the Netherlands where the rate of participation for women was high all had a large proportion of their female workforce employed on a part-time basis. On the other hand the countries of southern Europe where women's participation in the labour force is far more uncommon had very few part-time job opportunities. Part-time work and women's work are often synonymous. For women the pay and employment conditions in part-time jobs are particularly important. Recent European Court of Justice decisions on these issues have included a ruling on the pension rights of part-time workers. Such decisions benefit a larger number of women than men.

Part-time working offers an intermediate position for parents with young children enabling them to retain some degree of economic independence whilst releasing time for parenting responsibilities. At present though only mothers restrict their hours of work to accommodate their parental responsibilities whilst fathers limit the time they spend with their family. Children have fathers as well as mothers and perhaps part-time employment for both men and women at the family formation stage would help to ensure a high quality of care for the young. Under present circumstances part-time employment for both partners would result in a lower level of income for the household since part-time jobs often command a lower rate of pay than the full-time equivalent. If part-time jobs offered opportunities for training and promotion, then they might be seen as an acceptable way for both men and women to combine parental responsibilities with paid employment. Without these safeguards though, part-time jobs merely lead to a waste of women's talents, to unequal opportunities for men and women and to the standard of living falling below its potential level.

Women's Pay, Employment and Unemployment

By 1992 there were over 56 million women in civilian employment in the European Union (European Commission 1994). The feminization of the European labour market brings with it the need for stronger policies to protect working women. Domestic responsibilities still impose a greater constraint upon women's employment than upon men's. Women receive lower pay than men, are vertically and horizontally segregated, are often in part-time or casualized employment and are less likely than men to receive compensation when unemployed. Women are in a more vulnerable position than men in labour markets.

As women have increased their participation in the working population, the European economy has coincidentally undergone a period of restructuring. As in Britain, manufacturing industry has declined in importance as an employer of labour whilst the service sector has expanded. Women have therefore found employment in traditionally female sectors of the economy and their move into paid employment has confirmed job segregation. Women accounted for between 53 and 73 per cent of employees in other services in the countries of the European Union in 1989 (Maruani 1992). They were also over-represented in banking, insurance and finance and in the distributive trades, hotels and catering.

With the advent of the Single Market this concentration of women's employment in certain specific sectors of the economy makes them particularly vulnerable. The performance of those sectors of industry in the more competitive environment of the internal market will have significant consequences for the welfare of working women in Europe. The textile industry is likely to face rationalization resulting from growing international competition and from the internal pressures of the Single Market. This industry is one of the most feminized sectors of manufacturing industry throughout the European Union and if it sheds labour this will undoubtedly be female labour. The public sector could also face considerable changes as national governments seek to meet the Maastricht criteria for public sector borrowing. In 1989 women accounted for 51 per cent of the employees in public administration in Denmark, 46 per cent in France and 41 per cent in the United Kingdom (Maruani 1992). Once again the consequences of job loss in this sector will be more significant for women than for men.

Despite the increase in women's employment levels, female unemployment has persisted. One of the most peculiar features of the boom of the mid 1980s was that the rise in employment which it generated was not matched by a corresponding fall in unemployment. With the exception of Luxemburg, the overall rate of unemployment in European Union countries remained above 5 per cent by the end of the decade. In every country except for the United Kingdom, the unemployment rate for women was higher than that for men. In 7 out of the 12 European Union countries female unemployment during the 1980s was double the rate for men. The rate of unemployment amongst women stood at 13 per cent at its peak in 1986, had fallen to 11 per cent by 1990 but rose again as the recession set in during the early 1990s (EC 1994). As unemployment is associated with a lower than average standard of living, women in Europe are worse off than men in this respect. Furthermore fewer women than men qualify to receive unemployment benefit or allowances. In 1989 34 per cent of unemployed men but only 27 per cent of unemployed women in the European Union were entitled to unemployment benefit (Maruani 1992). Not only does unemployment represent a waste of Europe's labour resources, it also contributes to poverty and inequality between men and women.

In employment too women are likely to be less well off than men. Despite the enactment of equal pay legislation, in all the member states women still earn less than men in full-time employment. Women earned between two-thirds and four-fifths of male earnings during the 1980s. A study of women's position on European labour markets during the 1980s found that there was no evidence to suggest that pay differentials were narrowing or were going to dwindle away during the forthcoming decade (Meulders et al. 1990).

The causes of the gender pay gap are familiar. Both horizontal and vertical segregation keep women in low paid, low status jobs. The responsibility for household tasks limits a woman's career prospects and sex discrimination contributes to pay differentials between men and women. These pay differentials affect a woman's economic independence but furthermore they can impede the efficient operation of the economy. Low-paid workers who are constrained to certain positions in the economic hierarchy will have little incentive to increase their productivity and make a full contribution to the economy. The economy will once again fail to achieve the level of output of which it is capable and living standards will be held down accordingly. Fair rewards for women are an equality issue but they are also an efficiency issue.

Women's Employment and Family Friendly Policies

As women's participation increases, the role which they play in the economy becomes more visible. For the European economy to achieve productive and allocative efficiency women and men must be fully employed in their most productive use either within the household or the labour market. Discrimination in employment, occupational segregation or the restriction of women to the domestic sphere whilst men play a minimal part in child rearing can all impede the achievement of this objective.

The Social Charter stated the intention of introducing measures to enable men and women to reconcile their occupational and parental obligations. If European social policy is to achieve this objective then those productive activities which take place within the household need to be recognized as equally valuable and important to the economy as those which take place in labour markets. An economy which uses its resources efficiently will not only produce motor vehicles and television sets, it will also ensure that its children and senior citizens are well cared for. At present men have little opportunity to play a full part in family life whilst women's employment is still restricted by domestic responsibilities. As women participate more fully in paid employment this helps to promote equal opportunities. Paid employment gives women greater economic autonomy and independence than unpaid household work can offer but as women seek paid employment domestic services must still be provided. Children need to be cared for, clothes need to be washed, beds need to be made regardless of whether or not women are in the working population. European countries need to consider how best to deliver the vital services which women used to provide unpaid for their families. Private provision of caring services, either by men or women, within the household might be desirable but it has an opportunity cost in terms of lost employment opportunities. In southern Europe much of women's working lives are spent in domestic work but increasingly women are disinclined to lose their economic independence for a domestic role. In Portugal 62 per cent of mothers with a child under the age of ten were in paid employment in 1988 (Moss 1992). Social policy can affect the ways in which childcare and other domestic services are delivered in Europe.

At present there is considerable variation in the method of delivering childcare services throughout the European Union. Private provision by women within the household predominates in Ireland, Greece and Luxemburg whilst public provision is the norm in France and Denmark. The cost and quality of these services varies too. The availability of nursery places affects a mother's access to paid employment as well as influencing her child's future opportunities. Nursery education improves the social skills and the educational development of pre-school children. When they enter compulsory education children who have attended nursery school are then better able to learn and their primary and secondary school performance is enhanced. The provision of nursery education is an investment in the human capital of future generations as well as benefiting their mothers whose employment is thereby facilitated. An investment in the human capital of the under fives can enable their mothers to make better use of their own human capital.

Caring for children is an activity of considerable importance for the future of the economy – and indeed of society. Children represent the future citizens and workers of the European Union and the care they receive during their early years amounts to an investment in the future. The quantity of care and the type of care which children require varies with their age. Very small babies need almost continuous care 24 hours a day. The provision of babycare is expensive indeed. Toddlers and pre-school children require the continuous presence of a responsible adult to provide for their personal care and to stimulate their development whilst school age children need an adult to whom they can relate after school hours and during holidays. For children of all ages it is not just their physical care which requires attention; their emotional development too is important. In this respect care giving is different from other forms of work in that the identity of the carer can be a crucial factor affecting the quality of the service provided (Himmelweit 1995). Sick children have different requirements from healthy children as they need nursing during the period of their illness and convalescence. Meeting these needs is very labour intensive. Childcare responsibilities conflict with paid employment, especially for women, since traditionally in Europe their unpaid labour has been used to provide this care. During the second half of the twentieth century women have been moving into the workforce and into paid employment. Under these circumstances social policy has an important role to play in helping to reconcile the dual responsibilities of working parents and in ensuring equal opportunities for men, women and children.

Not only does the provision of childcare differ throughout Europe, the policies on maternity, paternity and parental leave vary considerably too. Denmark provides one of the most family friendly models with 14 weeks of paid maternity leave, 2 weeks of paid paternity leave and 10 weeks of paid parental leave to be taken by either parent. Benefit is paid equivalent to 90 per cent of earnings up to a certain earnings limit. Sweden too offers a comprehensive package of leave and benefit to be taken by either parent. In Germany each parent is entitled to take paid leave to care for a sick child under the age of eight. In the 1980s half of the countries within the European Community provided such parental leave but this was only paid leave in Germany, Denmark and Portugal (Moss 1992). The United Kingdom has a particularly poor record on these issues. Although it provided for an apparently generous period of maternity leave – 40 weeks in total – in fact the strict eligibility criteria, requiring women to have been with their current employer for at least two years, excluded many women from claiming leave. The European Commission put forward a proposal in 1996 guaranteeing three months' unpaid leave for fathers following the birth of their child. If this proposal is accepted it will come into force in the 14 member states who signed the Social Chapter. Only in the United Kingdom will fathers have no right to leave when their children are born.

The entitlement to leave helps parents to reconcile employment with their parental responsibilities but not all parents make use of their leave entitlements. Take-up rates are high in Finland, Sweden, Denmark and Germany whereas less than 30 per cent of eligible women in the Netherlands make use of their leave entitlement (Coré and Koutsogeorgopoulou 1995). The take-up rate is affected by the provision of benefits, the relative earnings of men and women, the career potential of the parents and their access to childcare. Generous benefits enable even low income groups to use their leave entitlement and in the Scandinavian countries benefits certainly encourage the take up of leave. In Austria and Germany, on the other hand, the take up of leave is constrained by the limited availability of childcare. Well-qualified women might be reluctant to use their full leave entitlement since a break from work can adversely affect their career prospects. Since professional and managerial women often earn in excess of the benefit provision, they have a financial incentive to return early to work and can afford to do so as they earn sufficient to cover the high costs of care for a small baby.

Parental leave to care for a young child is often available for either fathers or mothers but very few fathers avail themselves of this opportunity. Since men earn more than women the loss of household income is minimized if women opt for parental leave. Under these circumstances the rational economic decision is to maximize the household's current income through the continued employment of the partner earning the higher income. Only in Sweden do men make any significant use of their right to parental leave (Coré and Koutsogeorgopoulou 1995).

Maternity leave, paternity leave and leave for family reasons all help working parents to reconcile their parental and employment obligations but it has implications for employers too. Once workers are entitled to leave, firms have to recognize that a proportion of their workforce might be absent at any one time. In 1992 those absent on family-related leave in the European Union accounted for just under 3 per cent of female employment in 1992 (Coré and Koutsogeorgopoulou 1995). This in itself represents a very small cost to the economy as a whole but for some employers the loss might be considerably heavier. Segregation in employment implies that the incidence of absence is likely to be concentrated in certain feminized sectors of the labour market like retailing and the textile industry. Employers, facing costs due to the output lost from these absent workers, must decide whether to recruit replacements. Whilst unskilled workers can be easily and cheaply recruited, highly qualified and skilled workers are hard to replace since the investment in new workers' human capital is unlikely to be recouped during the relatively short period of leave entitlement. The absence of skilled workers is unlikely to be covered by new recruits especially in large firms where adjustments in working practices are usually sufficient to provide cover for absent workers. Since maternity leave can be foreseen, firms have time to plan their adjustment strategies. Surveys indicate that it is unusual for maternity leave to create major difficulties for firms (Coré and Koutsogeorgopoulou 1995).

The Social Charter includes a call for measures to help men and women reconcile their occupational and domestic responsibilities. Establishing minimum levels of leave entitlement would help to achieve this objective.

Summary

Throughout the European Community differences between men and women in labour markets are widespread. Whilst men remain continuously participant in the labour force, women's patterns of participation are still likely to be disrupted by family formation and the resulting domestic responsibilities. The extent of this disruption varies considerably between member states. In the workforce women are less well rewarded for their work, are concentrated in certain industries thus increasing their vulnerability and stand a greater risk of being unemployed without the benefit of compensation. Not only is women's position in labour markets different from that occupied by men, it is also less favourable. The extent of the inequalities between men and women is far from uniform throughout the European Union.

As the Single Market reduces barriers to trade and mobility, the opportunity arises for the European economy to increase its level of output offering the potential for higher living standards for its citizens. These benefits will not automatically be evenly distributed through the free market mechanism and nor will they be fully realized unless the European Community makes full use of its resources. Women represent half of the adult population in the Community and they are moving into the labour force in ever greater numbers. The establishment of minimum social standards can help to prevent social dumping and to ensure that workers feel confident in accepting changes in their work environment as European firms seek to take advantage of the new opportunities afforded by the Single Market.

The role which women play in the economy is becoming increasingly visible but their unpaid work within the household should not be overlooked. These services are important and need to be provided both to ensure the maintenance of a healthy workforce at the present time and to produce the workers and citizens of the future. Women enter the working population on different terms from men and the role which women play in the economy needs to be carefully evaluated if the European Union is to make full and efficient use of all its labour resources. Measures to enhance women's rights and equal opportunities can therefore improve economic performance as well as creating a more just and equal society.

As European Union law overrides national law the decisions taken in Brussels can have a positive effect upon the position of women in member states. The United Kingdom in particular has proved laggard in complying with European directives and the European Court of Justice rulings have been significant in ensuring compliance. The Social Charter provides a statement of intent concerning the basic rights of European workers. It is being slowly implemented through the introduction of directives and other legislative measures and should improve the position of women in European labour markets.

12 Conclusion

Economic and social change. Economic change and government policy.
Men, women and care giving. Economics, statistics and policy.

Economic and Social Change

The last half of the twentieth century has brought some significant changes. Manufacturing industry which dominated the British economy in the 1950s has declined in importance as a producer, an exporter and an employer of labour. The elderly have come to represent a rising share of the population. Divorce has become more acceptable so that families headed by a lone parent have increased as a percentage of all families with children. Working conditions too have altered as some permanent full-time jobs have disappeared to be replaced by part-time or temporary employment. Men still earn more than women, form the majority of full-time workers and occupy more senior positions in the occupational hierarchy but, as de-industrialization takes place and labour markets are deregulated, unemployment is rising. Secure full-time employment becomes harder to find. The European Union, formed to enhance European security and economic co-operation, now has a wide agenda on social issues and as European Union law supersedes national law these social measures will influence the working environment in the member states. Many of these changes are mirrored in other European countries with profound implications for the lives of men and women. It is against this changing background that women have been moving into paid employment.

Women account for half of all employees in Britain in the mid 1990s but their position in labour markets is distinctive. Women work in different industries from men, earn less than men, form the majority of part-time workers and experience most difficulty combining parenthood with paid employment. The separate positions of men and women in labour markets result in varying degrees of exposure to changes in the economy and government policy measures. In the last two decades tax reductions, the deregulation of labour markets, and the high exchange rate policy of the early 1980s have not affected men and women to the same extent. Change brings benefits to some groups but disadvantages others. Whilst some men and some women are improving their economic position, for others changes in the economy and in economic policy have caused their position to decline both relatively and absolutely.

There are significant and growing differences in income between households in Britain in the 1990s. Changes in labour markets, in taxes and in benefits have widened the inequalities between households. Child free households are better off financially than those with children and the gap between these two groups actually widened between 1988 and 1991 (Goodman and Webb 1994). Families with two income earners are on the increase in Britain and are over £100 per week better off than those with only one employed partner. At the beginning of the 1980s dual earner households accounted for just 44 per cent of all households with two adults yet this share had risen to 57 per cent by the end of the decade (Brannen et al. 1994). The 1980s were characterized by the rise of the two earner household at the same time as no earner households were also on the increase. Women with an unemployed partner have been deterred by the benefits system from seeking paid employment. The rise in child poverty during the 1980s has been attributed to the high rate of unemployment in the United Kingdom, the increase in lowly paid workers and the growth of lone parent families (Brannen et al. 1994). These changes in the financial status of households are the result of changes in both the economy and economic policy.

Economic Change and Government Policy

The extent to which men and women are affected by economic change varies considerably. A rise in unemployment, for example, will not put all workers in danger of losing their jobs; those employed in some sectors of the economy will be more exposed to this risk than others. The high exchange rate policy which the British government pursued in the early 1980s contributed to the rundown of British manufacturing industry. With each cyclical downturn manufacturing industry sunk further into decline, shedding labour as a consequence. As over 70 per cent of manufacturing employees in the 1970s were men, male unemployment increased considerably. Men have undoubtedly been losers. Women, with their employment concentrated in the expanding service sector, have been relatively protected – but not totally unaffected – by these changes. Women were predominant in some manufacturing industries like textiles and tobacco and these women too experienced job loss. The female working population has also been rising steadily in recent decades as more women seek jobs. Women's unemployment has risen along with men's, but the extent of the increase has been less noticeable. Women are less likely than men to qualify for unemployment benefit when they are without work, hiding the full extent of female unemployment. Changes in the economy have brought rising unemployment for women as well but the extent of their job loss has been better concealed.

Fiscal policy too can affect men and women differently. The income tax reductions introduced by the Conservative government in the 1980s and 1990s have shifted the tax burden away from the income tax payer. The highest rate of tax has been reduced from 60 per cent to 40 per cent since 1980 whilst the standard rate of tax has fallen from 33 per cent to 25 per cent. Income tax changes do not affect those whose earnings fall below the tax threshold. Many women with part-time, low paid jobs will come into this category and their take home earnings have been unaffected by the tax reductions. They have received no incentive to vary their work patterns since their disposable income has remained constant. Mothers who remain out of employment whilst their children are young do not pay income tax and they too received no financial advantage from the tax changes. For those men and women on high earnings the tax policies have been far more significant and advantageous. Tax changes serve to increase the incomes of those earning the most whilst leaving low income earners or those dependent upon state benefits unaffected in absolute terms; the relative position of these low income groups therefore deteriorates.

Since 1979 the government has sought to limit the Public Sector Borrowing Requirement. The government's economic strategy was based on the premise that if government borrowing were restricted, then the money supply could be controlled, reducing the rate of inflation. Faced with falling tax receipts, this policy could only be implemented with cuts in the government expenditure programme. Benefits have come under close scrutiny and employment in the public sector has been threatened. Measures to restrict government spending have affected women adversely. Many women are dependent upon state benefit for their income, more women than men are senior citizens, and nine out of ten single parent households are headed by women whilst the public sector is a major employer of female labour. Each of these groups has suffered a decline in their relative and absolute position as a result of government policies. Many women have found themselves amongst the losers following changes in fiscal policy.

The deregulation of labour markets has also contributed to the decline in women's economic status. The abolition of the Wages Councils was intended to promote employment through allowing wages to fall to their equilibrium level. Lower wages, it was hoped, would increase the demand for labour, creating more jobs. Legal protection has thereby been dismantled for the sectors of the labour market which are not covered by unions. Such sectors employ a high proportion of female labour. The part-time, low-paid jobs created by these policies have been filled mainly by women. Whilst the wage gap between full-time male and female workers has been narrowing, the hourly pay rate for part-timers fell relative to full-time employees (Humphries and

Rubery 1992). Since women account for 86 per cent of part-time employees it is their wages which are undergoing this relative decline.

Deregulation is justified in the hope that it creates employment; wages might be low but at least workers can find jobs. In fact though, low-paid, low-skill jobs might impair the efficiency of British industry. Firms, deterred by the low productivity of their workforce, refrain from investing in the latest technology and without investment the quality of British products will decline, reducing competitiveness in world markets. If British goods are not in demand, then jobs will be lost in British industry. Low wages, low skill and low investment can in fact contribute to rising unemployment. The British government's refusal to sign the Social Charter could cost the British workers dearly.

Men, Women and Care Giving

Economic and social changes in recent decades have facilitated women's entry to paid employment. As family size has declined and technology has made housework less onerous, changes in labour markets have favoured women's employment. The working population has risen as women have increased their participation rate. As the working population increases, the output of goods and services in the marketed sector of economy grows. Gross Domestic Product rises as marketed output increases. If output rises, living standards should increase too. If more men move into the working population then this result undoubtedly occurs but the employment of women is subtly different. Both men and women work unpaid within the household; men clean the car, mow the lawn and repair electrical equipment whilst women cook the meals, fetch children from school and iron the clothes (CSO 1995). Although men undertake household tasks, they are less extensively involved than women in these unpaid household activities. Parenthood especially has different economic implications for men and women. It increases a mother's workload and interferes with her workforce participation whilst men, even when fathers, experience little difficulty in pursuing a continuous career.

As women move into the working population, the opportunity cost of their employment can be considerable. Care giving especially is affected by, and affects, women's employment. Organizing care for children and the elderly, taking responsibility for their general welfare and nursing them when they are sick imposes significant constraints upon the pursuit of a career for a woman. Caring labour, unlike housework, cannot be replaced by technology and the quality of the care can depend upon the identity of the care giver. A relative, due to their relationship with the dependent, might well provide a higher quality of care than the paid employee (Himmelweit 1995). As the population ages, more elderly people will need care and eldercare, unlike childcare, cannot be foreseen and is of indeterminable duration. Since employers expect workers to give a full-time and whole-hearted commitment to their job, care giving interferes with paid employment. The legitimate needs of dependents provide a competing claim upon time – especially for women. Motherhood interferes with a woman's employment with long-term implications for her earnings and her economic status.

Parenthood affects men differently; becoming a father does not have the same impact as motherhood upon employment status. Fathers in Britain are unlikely to take more than two weeks off work following the birth of their child; they are more likely to work full time than men in general and tend to increase their hours of paid work during their children's early years (Brannen et al. 1994). Full-time commitment to the job can even be enhanced and facilitated for the man who has a wife at home providing services from which he benefits. With his shirts washed, his meals cooked and his children cared for he can concentrate upon his career, gaining promotion and higher earnings. Men's economic status is actually enhanced by the prevailing division of domestic responsibilities.

Justifying the domestic division of labour by reference to men's superior earning power has a certain circularity. Women stay at home because they earn less than men yet discontinuous employment contributes to earnings differentials! A woman who withdraws completely from paid employment loses her current earnings and imperils her future earnings. Discontinuous work experience contributes to the deterioration of human capital and lack of on-the-job experience and training. These factors mar women's promotion prospects, contributing to their lower earnings.

Anticipated patterns of lifetime participation are different for men and women influencing their investment in human capital. Women are concentrated in the low-paid sectors of the economy, like catering, whilst men form the majority in better rewarded occupations. Trade unions have represented the interests of their predominantly male membership to ensure that their skills are recognized and rewarded in wage structures. Domestic responsibilities restrict women's active participation in the trade union movement and, lacking effective representation, women's interests have been less well served by trade unions. As a result of these factors women in Britain earn only 80 per cent of men's hourly rates of pay. Their economic status is impaired by care giving.

Neo-classical economics attempts to justify both the domestic division of labour and occupational segregation in the workplace in terms of free choice by rational economic agents. They argue that the efficient use of resources is furthered by the current situation with consequences for the standard of living. This position ignores the social constraints upon action and the differences in relative power between men and women.

Economics, Statistics and Policy

Care giving and housework are areas of economic activity which economists and statisticians have largely ignored. Housework and childcare are not marketed, not recognized as work, not included in statistics and not analysed within introductory economics textbooks (Palmer 1995). Washing shirts, cooking meals, bringing up children and caring for the elderly have been viewed as something that 'just happens' behind the scenes. Centre stage is market-based economic activity. The assumption is that the unpaid activity would continue to be provided as an add-on extra to the goods and services produced in the government and marketed sector of the economy.

This might have been a reasonable assumption 50 years ago. If married women were not expected to be – and indeed were not – in paid employment, then the services which they provided for their household remained constant, even if in the background. But in the mid 1990s this is no longer realistic. Women now are moving into the labour force in ever larger numbers and inevitably this will affect their productive role within the household. The economic services which women in Western Europe have traditionally provided unpaid for their partners, children and elderly parents must now be considered in order to evaluate the changes which are occurring in the economy of the 1990s. The household and the marketed sectors of the economy interact – especially for women. The focus upon unpaid activities within the household makes women's economic experience distinct and different from men's. As long as these peculiarly feminine activities are ignored or disregarded economists have an incomplete model of human experience. In Britain women are 52 per cent of the adult population, 50 per cent of all employees in employment and 44 per cent of the working population. They are too large a group to ignore.

Published statistics too focus upon marketed activity. The unemployment statistics include only those who are in the working population. Women as they move between employment and non-participation are under-represented in the unemployment statistics. National Income accounts too exclude non-marketed activity. Paid caring services provided in institutions are included in Gross Domestic Product whilst the same services provided within the household are omitted. Cleaning offices is recorded in Gross Domestic Product whilst cleaning one's own house is not. Including women's work in Gross Domestic Product accounts would increase their value by between 25 and 40 per cent (Waring 1988). Men's role in the economy is recorded fairly accurately by published data sets like the unemployment statistics and national income accounts. Since much of women's productive activity is located within the household it is omitted from the statistics.

The omission of women's productive and reproductive role not only distorts the data; it can also affect policy decisions. Information forms the basis for policy action and if the published statistics misrepresent women's experience, then policies too will be affected. If statistics suggest that male unemployment is higher than women's, it seems as if more men need jobs and the barriers affecting male employment will become the policy focus. If childcare within the family is excluded from the nation's accounts, it appears as if it is costless and the provision of care by the government or the market then appears expensive by comparison. Yet if women withdraw from paid employment to care for children or the elderly, their employer loses their labour services, the economy sacrifices their output and their family forgoes their earnings. Clearly there are substantial costs to all parties. Analysis, statistics and policy are interconnected. The omission of women from mainstream economic analysis therefore has serious implications for their well-being and that of their families.

Bibliography

Armstrong, P. (1982) 'If its's only women it doesn't matter so much' in *Work, Women and the Labour Market* West, J. (ed.) (London, Routledge and Kegan Paul)

Bacon, R. and Eltis, W. (1976) *Britain's Economic Problem – too few producers* (London, Macmillan)

Becker, G. (1965) 'A Theory of the Allocation of Time' in *Economic Journal* LXXV (299) (September) pp. 493–517

Becker, G. (1957) *The Economics of Discrimination* (Chicago, University of Chicago Press)

Beechey, V. and Perkins, T. (1987) *A Matter of Hours: Women, Part-time Work and the Labour Market* (Cambridge, Polity Press)

Bergmann, B. (1974) 'Occupational segregation, Wages and Profits when Employers Discriminate by Race or Sex' in *Eastern Economic Journal* Vol. 1 Nos. 2–3 pp. 103–10

Beveridge, W. (1942) *Social Insurance and Allied Services* Cmnd 6404 (London, HMSO)

Brannen, J. Mészáros, G. Moss, P. and Poland, G. (1994) *Employment and Family Life: A review of research in the UK (1980–1994)* Employment Department Research Series No. 41 (University of London, Institute of Education)

Bridgwood, A. and Savage, P. (1993) *General Household Survey 1991* (London, HMSO)

Bruegel, I. (1979) 'Women as a reserve army: a note on recent British experience' in *Feminist Review*, Vol. 3, pp. 12–23

Bruegel, I. and Perrons, D. (1995) 'Where do the Costs of Unequal Treatment for Women Fall? An analysis of the incidence of the costs of unequal pay and sex discrimination in the United Kingdom' in *Gender, Work and Organizations* Vol. 2 No. 3 (Blackwell) pp. 113–24

Card, D. and Krueger, A. (1992) *Minimum Wages and Employment; a case study of fast food in New Jersey and Pennsylvania* National Bureau of Economic Research Working Paper 4509

Central Statistical Office *Annual Abstract of Statistics* various issues (London, HMSO)

Central Statistical Office *Social Trends* various issues (London, HMSO)

Coré, F. (1994) 'Women and the Restructuring of Employment' in *OECD Observer*, No.186 (February/March) pp. 5–12

Coré, F. and Koutsogeorgopoulou, V. (1995) 'Parental Leave: What and Where?' in the *OECD Observer* No. 195 (Paris, OECD: August/September) pp. 15–20

Corti, L. and Dex, S. (1995) 'Informal Carers and Employment' in *Employment Gazette* Vol. 103 No. 3 (London, HMSO: March) pp. 101–7

Corti, L. and Laurie, H. (1993) *Caring and Employment* Unpublished report from ESRC Research Centre on Micro-Social Change (University of Essex)

Crompton, R. and Sanderson, K. (1986) 'Credentials and Careers: some implications of the increase in professional qualifications amongst women' in *Sociology*, Vol. 12, no. 1 pp. 25–42

Crompton, R. and Sanderson, K.(1990) *Gendered Jobs and Social Change* (London, Unwin Hyman)
Department of Education (1995) *Education Statistics for the UK 1994 edition* (London, HMSO)
Department of Employment *Employment Gazette* various issues (London, HMSO)
Department of Employment *New Earnings Survey* various issues (London, HMSO)
Dex, S. (1990) 'Women and Unemployment' *Economic Review* Vol. XX No. 1 (September) pp. 37–41
Dex, S. Clark, A. and Taylor, M. (1995) *Household Labour Supply* Employment Department No. 43 (University of Essex)
Dex, S. and Perry, S. (1984) 'Women's Employment Changes in the 1970s' in *Employment Gazette* Department of Employment (London, HMSO: April) pp. 151–62
Dex, S. and Shaw, L. (1986) *British and American Women at Work* (Basingstoke, Macmillan)
Dilnot, A. (1992) 'Social Security and Labour Market Policy' in *Understanding Unemployment* McLaughlin, E. (ed.) (London, Routledge)
Elias, P. (1988) 'Family Formation, Occupational Mobility and Part-time work' in Hunt A. (ed.) *Women and Paid Work* (London, Macmillan)
England, P. (1982) 'The Failure of human Capital Theory to explain Occupational Sex Segregation' in *The Journal of Human Resources* XVII.3 (Summer) pp. 358–70
Equal Opportunities Commission (1993) *Men and Women in Britain* (Manchester, EOC)
European Commission *Eurostat: The Basic Statistics of the Community* various issues (Luxemburg, EC)
Fallon, P. and Verry, D. (1988) *The Economics of Labour Markets* (London, Philip Allen)
Ferber, M. and Lowry, H. (1976) 'The Sex Differential in Earnings: A Reappraisal' in *Industrial and Labour Relations Review* No. 29 (April) pp. 377–87
Folbre, N. (1994) *Who Pays for the Kids?* (Routledge, London)
Gallie, D. Marsh, C. and Vogler, C. (ed.) (1993) *Social Change and Unemployment* (Oxford, Oxford University Press)
Game, A. and Pringle, R. (1983) *Gender at Work* (Pluto Press)
Goodman, A. and Webb, S. (1994) *For Richer, For Poorer: The Changing Distribution of Income in the United Kingdom, 1961–1991* (London, Institute of Fiscal Studies)
Gregson, M. and Lowe, N. (1994) *Servicing the Middle Classes* (London, Routledge)
Guardian (20 June 1995) 'Against a Glass Ceiling'
Hakim, C. (1993) 'The Myth of Rising Female Employment' in *Work, Employment and Society*, Vol. 7 No. 1 (March 1993) pp. 98–120
Harrop, A. and Moss, P. (1993) 'Trends in Parental Employment 1981–89' in *Social and Economic Circumstances of Families with Children Project* Working Paper No. 2 Thomas Coram Research Unit (University of London)
Hart, A.(1994) 'Women in HE still in lower grades' in *The Lecturer* (December)
Himmelweit, S. (1995) 'The Discovery of "Unpaid Work": the Social Consequences of the Expansion of "Work"' in *Feminist Economics* Vol. 1 No. 2 (London, Routledge) pp. 1–19
Holtermann, S. (1995) 'The Costs and Benefits to British Employers of Measures to Promote Equality of Opportunity' in *Gender, Work and Organization* Vol. 2 No. 3 (Blackwell: July) pp. 102–12

Humphries, J. and Rubery, J. (1992) 'The Legacy for Women's Employment' in *The Economic Legacy 1979–1992* Mitchie, J. (ed.) (London, Academic Press)

International Labour Office (1994) *Yearbook of Labour Statistics*

Jacobsen, J. (1994) *The Economics of Gender* (Oxford, Blackwell)

Joshi, H. and Davies, H. (1993) 'Mothers' Human Capital and Childcare in Britain' in *National Institute Economic Review* No. 146 pp. 50–63

Jowell, R. Witherspoon, S. and Brook, L. (1988) *British Social Attitudes Survey: the Fifth Report 1988–89* edn (Aldershot, Gower)

Jowell, R. Brook, L. Prior, G. and Taylor, B. (1992) *British Social Attitudes: the 9th edition* (Dartmouth Publishing Company Ltd, 1992/93)

Kanter, R.(1977) *Men and Women of the Corporation* (New York, Basic Books)

Lane, C. (1993) 'Gender and the Labour Market in Europe: Britain, Germany and France Compared' in *The Sociological Review* Vol. 41 No. 2 pp. 274–301

Luck, M. (1991) 'Gender and Library Work' in *Working Women* Redclift, N. and Sinclair, T. (eds) (London, Routledge)

Machin, S. and Manning, A. (1992) *Minimum Wages, Wage Dispersion and Employment: Evidence from the UK Wages Council* Centre for Economic Performance Paper 80

Maruani, M. (1992) *The Position of Women on the Labour Market* Women of Europe supplement No. 36 (Brussels, Commission of the EC)

McLaughlin, E. (ed.) (1992) *Understanding Unemployment* (London Routledge)

McRae, S. (1991) 'Occupational Change over Childbirth; Evidence from a national survey' in *Sociology* Vol. 25 No. 4 pp. 589–604

Meulders, D. Plasman, R. and Vander Stricht, V. (1990) *The Position of women on the labour market in the EEC – Development between 1983 and 1989–90* (Brussels, EC)

Moss, P. (ed.) (1990) *Childcare in the European Community 1985–1990* (Brussels, European Commission)

Naylor, K. (1994) 'Part-time Working – an historical analysis' in *Employment Gazette* (London, HMSO: December) pp. 473–84

Office of Population Censuses and Surveys *General Household Survey* various issues (London, HMSO)

Office of Population Censuses and Surveys *Labour Force Survey* various issues (London, HMSO)

Palmer, A. (1995) *The Gender of Economics and the Economics of Gender* Working Paper in Economics No. 15 (University of the West of England, Bristol)

Polachek, S. (1976) 'Occupational Segregation: An alternative hypothesis' in *Journal of Contemporary Business 5* pp. 1–12

Rees, T. (1992) *Women and the Labour Market* (London, Routledge)

Rubery, J. and Tarling, R.J. (1983) 'Women in the Recession', *Economic Reprint* No: 38 (Department of Applied Economics, University of Cambridge)

Walby, S. (1990) *Theorizing Patriarchy* (Oxford, Blackwell)

Waldfogel, J. (1995) Easing Labour Pains in *New Economy* (The Dryden Press)

Warde, A. and Hetherington, K. (1993) 'A Changing Domestic Division of Labour?' in *Work, Employment and Society* Vol. 7 No. 2 pp. 23–45

Waring, M. (1988) *If Women Counted: a New Feminist Economics* (Harper and Row, New York)

Wright, R. and Ermisch, J. (1991) 'Gender Discrimination in the British Labour Market: a Reassessment' in *Economic Journal* No. 101 (May) pp. 508–21

Index